SUCCESS AND HOW TO ATTAIN IT

ANDREW C. CARNEGIE & OTHERS

NEW YORK

Success and How to Attain It

© 2004 Cosimo, Inc.

Success and How to Attain It was originally published by F. Tennyson Neely in 1895.

Cover design by smythtype

ISBN: 1-59605-010-1

LECTURES.

FULL-PAGE PORTRAITS.

INTRODUCTION.

The eminent thinkers whose utterances are grouped in this volume have long occupied so prominent a place in public esteem as to make an introduction entirely unnecessary. What intelligent American is ignorant of the authority which attaches to the name of Michie, in education; of Seward and Bayard, in statesmanship; of Carnegie, in philanthropic enterprise; of Hammond, in physiology, to say nothing of the weighty remainder of this impressive list of lecturers?

A brief statement of the circumstances which have brought together these varied contributions under the common title of the Union College Practical Lecture Course may possibly be welcome.

They are the first fruits of a course instituted by Gen. Daniel Butterfield, LL.D., as a proof of his interest in his *Alma Mater*, in the young manhood of the present generation, and in the future which is to be of their making. In the Civil War he gave the strongest evidence of his attachment to the Union—time, energy, a remarkable talent for organization, and the hazard of his life; and became one of the forces that brought that struggle to a triumphant issue. In this educational enterprise he has given, in addition to liberal expenditures, time, energy, and executive talent to aid in developing a manhood worthy of a great Republic, and so declared his loyalty to another *Union*, from which he went forth as a forty-niner. His record as a soldier the whole country knows.

These lectures were delivered at varying intervals before an audience composed of faculty and students of the College and distinguished guests, as many, in fact, as the largest available room—the chapel—could hold, and it was with deep regret that the doors, for lack of space, had to be closed upon a great body of alumni and friends eager to hear.

When the first lecture had been given, by the able Dean of the Faculty of the *West Point Military Academy*, the present writer, in a review of that lecture, in the *Army and Navy Journal*, expressed the hope that this eminent educator's address might be given to the public as literature, and then, as lecture after lecture of high merit followed, he found himself steadily repeating the wish. To all denied the pleasure of hearing, the opportunity of reading these addresses offered by this publication will be particularly acceptable as the only possible gratification of their desire.

A special proof of interest already taken in this course of lectures is afforded by the fact that, for student-essays upon them, prizes amounting to more than twelve hundred dollars were offered by various gentlemen, contributing for this purpose with General Butterfield, who were convinced of the worth of his plan, and were anxious to secure a more than ordinarily attentive consideration of such ripe thought and valuable experience.

These prizes, with diplomas, were distributed by the founder at the Centennial Commencement of the venerable institution of which he had been himself an honorary Chancellor. Delivered in the presence of a great concourse of distinguished people, on a memorable occasion, they brought high honor and substantial aid to deserving young men whose merits had been determined by able and impartial juries of award.

As to the character of the lectures themselves, they were intended as a point of contact between scholastic and practical life; to emphasize the value of mental training by showing the fields of distinction for which it is a preparation; to put in brief space the views of competent authorities as to tendencies, values, and demands in various departments of the world's activities; to rouse worthy enthusiasm; to make dangers clearer and goals more definite. Varied, as beacons along maritime coasts, or signals of vessels passing on the high seas, each has its individual value as a message of guidance.

This value is accentuated by the consideration that these messages are, in the main, the words of those who have studied long and searchingly the problems of life, and that they were spoken with peculiar tenderness and solicitude to the young, the strong, the hopeful, who are to follow them. In one case they were a last message, delivered by one of Union's worthiest sons, and of Massachusetts' ablest statesmen—the late Hon. Alexander H. Rice—who, when he had reached years that would exempt him from the duties of the platform, yet came to speak in the room where he had once been taught, and with wisdom and feeling and humor gave utterance to his own passion for truth and duty and kindness to those who, as educated men, were, in an important sense, to become governors in a world which he was soon to leave.

He came once more, at the Centennial Jubilee. Too feeble then to take any part as speaker, he was an attentive auditor. On Commencement Day he stood up with those who sang the "Song to Old Union," looked lovingly over the great throng as it poured forth its feeling in the rich melodies of Ludlow's verse, and as one who, on that dividing line between the centuries, felt in the instant the pride and sadness of the vanished years and the hopes of the future and gave his parting benediction, he turned away to become so soon only a great and potent and cherished memory.

That these words of wisdom, and experience, and kindness may bring as much instruction and comfort to the boys of all ages who are outside college walls as they did to the boys who were undergraduates at Union during the years from 1892 to 1895, is the sincere wish of a friend of all boys.

JAMES R. TRUAX.

UNION COLLEGE, November, 1895.

PETER SMITH MICHIE.

Peter Smith Michie was born March 24, 1839, at Brechin, Forfarshire, Scotland. He emigrated in 1843, settling in Cincinnati, Ohio, where he attended its public schools and graduated from the Woodward High School in 1857. From that date until May, 1859, he was employed at Niles' Works in learning the manufacture of steam engines and machinery. In 1859 he was appointed by Hon. George H. Pendleton a cadet to the United States Military Academy, from the First Congressional District of Ohio, and was graduated second in his class from West Point in 1863, as first lieutenant, Corps of Engineers, United States Army.

During the Rebellion, from 1863 to 1865, he served as assistant engineer in the operations against Charleston, S. C.—June 29, 1863, to January 16, 1864—comprising the construction of batteries at the north end of Folly Island July 1 to 10, 1863—descent upon Morris Island, July 10, 1863, and building left breaching batteries against Fort Sumter, August 19 to 31, 1863. From September 1st to September 7th of that year he was in charge of siege operations against Fort Wagner, being the first officer to enter the fort and to send information of its evacuation to General Gillmore.

Later, in November, 1863, he erected the defences at Cole's Island, mouth of the Stono River; was chief engineer of the northern district, Department of the South, January 16 to February 6, 1864, and of the District of Florida, February 6, to April 13, 1864, being engaged in the Battle of Olustee February 20, 1864, and in fortifying Jacksonville, Palatka, and Yellow Bluff, St. John's River, February to April, 1864; as assistant engineer, Army of the James, May 1 to August 1, 1864, engaged in the skirmishes and combats near Drury's Bluff, May 14 to 16, 1864, and in constructing defensive works on the James River, May to September, 1864; entrusted with selecting the location and constructing the approaches of the pontoon bridge for crossing the Army of the Potomac over the James River, at Fort Powhatan, June 15 to 16, 1864; as chief engineer Army of the James and Department of Virginia and North Carolina, August 1 to December 2, 1864; in constructing bridges across the James River at Varina and Deep Bottom, September 29, 1864; assault and capture of Fort Harrison, September 29, 1864; constructing defensive lines for Army of James and Dutch Gap Canal, September 30 to December 2, 1864; as chief engineer of the Army of the James and Department of Virginia, December 2, 1864, to March 30, 1865; as assistant inspector general, 25 Army Corps, March 23 to July, 1865; and in charge of all engineer operations of the light marching column of 20,000 men under the command of Major-General Ord, on the left of the Army of the Potomac at Hatcher's Run, and in pursuit of the rebel army till the capitulation of General Lee at Appomattox Court House, March 30 to April 9, 1865. Was selected by General Grant to make the survey of the theatre of operations in the vicinity of Richmond, which was embodied in a series of maps published by the War Department. On leave of absence, April 20, 1866, to April 20, 1867. Ordered to duty at the United States Military Academy as assistant professor of civil and military engineering, and served as such until appointed professor of natural and experimental philosophy, February 14, 1871. He served also as instructor of practical military engineering, military signals, and telegraphy and as instructor of mineralogy and geology. He was appointed a member of a military commission to visit European countries to collect information on the fabrication of iron for defensive purposes in sea-coast fortifications, June 29 to November 22, 1870.

For services during the war he has received the following brevet commissions:

Brevet-Captain and Brevet-Major United States Army, October 28, 1864, for gallant and meritorious services during the campaign of 1864 against Richmond, Va.

Brevet Brigadier-General United States Volunteers, January 1, 1865, for meritorious services in 1864.

Brevet Lieutenant-Colonel United States Army, April 9, 1865, for gallant and meritorious services during the campaign terminating at Appomatox Court House, Virginia.

Promoted to Captain Corps of Engineers United States Army, November 23, 1865.

Civil History: Member of the Board of Overseers of the Thayer School of Civil Engineering, Dartmouth College, New Hampshire, since 1871. Degree of Ph.D. conferred by the College of New Jersey, July 10, 1871; of M.A. by Dartmouth College, June 27, 1873; and of LL.D. by Union College, June 28, 1893. Author of the "Elements of Wave Motion Relating to Sound and Light," 1882; of the "Life and Letters of General Upton," 1885; of the "Personnel of Sea-coast Defence," 1887; of the "Elements of Analytical Mechanics," 1886–87; of "Hydro-Mechanics," 1888; and of "Practical Astronomy" conjointly with Lieutenant Harlow, United States Army, in 1892.

WEST POINT: ITS PURPOSE, ITS TRAIN-ING, AND ITS RESULTS.

By Gen. P. S. Michie.

The people of this country are essentially a law-abiding people. They recognize the distinction between liberty and license. But while in the enjoyment of the one, they are scarcely conscious how dangerously near they are to the excesses of the other. The destructive tendencies of the evils that infest humanity are more active and aggressive than are the protective powers of its inherent good; and were it not for that Divine Providence that incessantly intervenes, to lead us, by reason and in freedom, from the greater to the lesser evil and thence to the good, we would revel in the complete destruction of all government. We have only to recall the railroad riots of Pennsylvania, and the court-house riots of Cincinnati, to realize the celerity with which the vicious and depraved snatch their opportunity, burst the bonds that usually restrain them, and, like long-famished beasts of prey, rejoice in anarchy and destruction. But, fortunately for humanity, the life of an organization depends on the truth that it carries in its bosom, and therefore gatherings of men actuated by the love of evil to overturn law and order soon cease to be, either by self-destruction or by being utterly dispersed by the repellent forces of their constituent elements.

In times of peace and plenty, an orderly procedure

marks the conduct of all classes of the community; civil processes suffice to correct all the minor infractions of the law on the part of those who need restraint, and the corrective punishments awarded by the minor law courts are necessary vents to relieve the pressure of the unlawful and disaffected. Modern civilization, however, is ever proposing new problems for solution, and in their progress toward a settlement the relations of one class of the people to another become strained almost to the point of rupture. Then it is that the evilly disposed seek their opportunity, relying on the fact that the executors of the law are not actively supported by the existing sentiment of the community. We have had some recent examples of such problems arising out of the new conditions of labor and capital, and it has been found necessary for the Executives of three States to call out their National Guards to enforce the execution of the law. Many people are beginning to learn, for the first time, that the last resort of law, even in our republican form of government, is the military force of the State. Similarly, by the provisions of the fourth article of the Constitution of the United States, the Regular Army is the last resort for the execution of the laws of the United States. Now, the army is but an insignificant force for such a country as this; but behind it, and giving it the grandest moral support, and, if need be, ready to give it the most efficient assistance, stand 65,000,000 of people. The mob in Pittsburgh in 1877 knew this when they heard the musket-butts of the regulars ring out on the cobble-stones of their streets, and the resistance to the law ended only at the command of the President of the United States. It is evident, then, even should there never be occasion to prepare for foreign war or to resist invasion, that there is always a necessity for a well-disciplined army of regular troops. It must be the standard for the drill, discipline, and organization of the National Guards of the several States, and of the volunteers and militia of the United States. The Military Academy, established for the fundamental education of the officers of the army, is the foundation on which our whole military system rests, and a knowledge of its history, character, purpose, and results will furnish a key to the sentiments by which the army is actuated and the manner in which it does its duty.

During the War of the Revolution, and for a long period thereafter, the country was dependent upon foreigners trained in the military schools and armies of Europe for that knowledge of the science and art of war necessary to the conduct of our military operations, whether offensive or defensive. In his last message, December, 1796, General Washington declared "that the desirableness of this institution (a military academy) had constantly increased with every new view he had taken of the subject." Further, "the institution of a military academy is also recommended by cogent reasons; however pacific the general policy of a nation may be, it ought never to be without an adequate stock of military knowledge for emergencies. . . . In proportion as the observance of pacific maxims might exempt a nation from the necessity of practising the rules of the military art ought to be its care in preserving and transmitting by proper establishments the knowledge of that art. Whatever argument may be drawn from particular examples, superficially viewed, a thorough examination of the subject will evince that the art of war is at once comprehensive and complicated, that it demands much previous study, and that the possession of it in its most improved and perfect state is always of great moment to the security of a nation.

This, therefore, ought to be a serious care of every government; and for this purpose an academy, where a regular course of instruction is given, is an obvious expedient which different nations have successfully employed." *

The earnest efforts of the patriot soldiers and states-men of the Revolution, animated by the words of the noble Washington, were finally successful, and the United States Military Academy was established by an act of Congress, March 16, 1802. Its early history is given in great fulness in the third volume of Cullum's " Biographical Register of the Graduates of the Military Academy," from which I have drawn the following particulars.

During the first period, from 1802 to 1812, the super-intendent was Colonel Jonathan Williams, a most for-tunate selection for the infant academy, for his judg-ment had been matured by an eventful experience during the Revolution, and his mind was stored with much scientific and general information. He was a polished gentleman and a brave and chivalric soldier; he possessed great decision of character, to which was added untiring zeal in the public service, industry, exactness, patience, and benevolence. Under his ad-ministration the Academy quickly received tone and character, steadily advanced in discipline and useful-ness, and brought forth golden fruit in its distinguished graduates, who did brilliant service in the war of 1812. Unfortunately for the Military Academy, Dr. William Eustis, who had been a hospital surgeon in the Conti-nental Army, was appointed Secretary of War March 7, 1809.   He began his administration by an effort to disperse the few cadets at the institution, degrade them

---

* Report of the Military Academy Commission, 1860, p. 22.

to common laborers, and deprive them of all educational advantages. By midsummer of 1810, he, by his failure to make new appointments, and by his constant detail of cadets for clerks and for subordinate company duties, had left so few at West Point that the Military Academy, except in name, had virtually ceased to exist; and discipline was so palsied by his constant intermeddling that only by the most summary measures could Colonel Williams preserve even its semblance. Eustis, though forced to resign his office January 13, 1813, had in the mean while succeeded in his treacherous design of destroying the academy for the time being, for he forced Williams to resign from the service, and had reduced the Academy, which by law should have consisted of 260 cadets, to but one poor "plebe" and the acting superintendent.

From this time on, for the next five years, the affairs of the institution were in a chaotic condition, being without system or regularity. The number of cadets was always much below the legal allowance, and even these had been admitted at all ages from twelve to thirty-four; some were maimed, and others married, and many were totally disqualified for the profession of arms. Preliminary examinations had been dispensed with; no classification by merit existed, and graduation depended more upon vacancies in the army, age, and growth of cadets, and fancied fitness to become officers, than upon any rigid test of attainments. Some became full-fledged officers in four months, and others again not till they had been pupils for nearly six years.

It now became painfully evident that a man of iron will, clear vision, and active brain was needed to revive and restore the institution. The Act of April 29, 1812, reorganizing the Academy, was all-sufficient when supplemented by suitable regulations for government and discipline, provided the proper administrator could be found. And most happily he was found in Brevet Major Sylvanus Thayer, of the corps of Engineers. This remarkable man, ever afterward known as "the Great Superintendent" and "Father of the Military Academy," was born at Braintree, Mass., June 9, 1785. Thrown upon his own resources when but nine years of age, he, nevertheless, overcame all obstacles, including poverty and adversity, in preparing for college, and was admitted to Dartmouth in 1803. Here he gained the highest honors of his class; afterward entered West Point and graduated, after less than a year's residence, in the Engineers in 1808. He greatly distinguished himself in the war of 1812, receiving his brevet of major; soon after he was sent abroad on professional duty, and only recalled to assume command of the Military Academy July 28, 1817, when he was but thirty-two years of age.

"Thayer fortunately entered upon his command almost simultaneously with Secretary Calhoun's succession to the War Department. Both were in the prime of vigorous manhood, and possessed many of the same strong salient points of mind and character, decision, firmness, analytical power, organizing capacity, knowledge of agents, skill to control, enlarged views, and towering ambition. They soon became fast friends, and entertained mutual respect for each other's character and motives. Under these fortuitous circumstances, Thayer, for the first eight years of his superintendency, had Calhoun's unswerving support and unbounded confidence in his appointed mission of leading the Academy from a dreary wilderness into a land of promise."

Now mark the sequence of the reforms instituted by Major Thayer, and you will have an epitome of the causes which has given West Point its magnificent success.

"Major Thayer's military experience in the field, his foreign travel and associations, his familiarity with the polite usages of society, his dignified bearing and refined mode of life, and, above all, his scientific acquirements, enlarged professional reading, and familiarity with the French and dead languages gave him immense vantage-ground for success. Almost by intuition he discovered the virulent ulcers destroying the vital parts of the Academy, and such as he could not cauterize into healing action, like a bold surgeon he promptly amputated. Examinations were at once held, the incompetent and vicious dismissed, and the indolent, who had lingered for many years without progress, quickly discovered that a like fate awaited a continuance of their dereliction. He promptly organized the cadets into a battalion of two companies, officered by members of their own body, with a colonel at its head and an adjutant and sergeant-major for his staff; appointed an officer of the army as Commandant of Cadets, responsible for their tactical instruction and soldierly discipline; transacted business with members of his command only at stated office hours; classified all cadets according to their proficiency in studies; divided classes into small sections for more thorough instruction by the teachers in charge; required weekly class reports, showing the daily progress of students according to a scale of marks; directed more thorough recitations and a freer use of the blackboard; greatly improved the curriculum of studies, according to a well-digested programme; reorganized a proper Academic Board, with the Superintendent at its head; introduced the check-book system, to curtail the prevailing extravagance of cadets, then deeply in debt; reduced the expenses of educating pupils to less than one-half the cost at the Woolwich Military Academy in England; had the officer of the day daily to dine with him, enabling himself thereby to learn all that was transpiring in camp or barracks; required cadets to obtain a permit from him for almost everything, even to a letter from the post-office, thus maintaining such constant intercourse as enabled him to call all by name, and understand their characters and habits; and made many other salutary provisions to secure thorough discipline, a high standard of honor, complete physical and mental development, and a generous rivalry for conspicuous soldiership and eminent class rank. . . .

"In the sixteen years of his successful administration, Thayer had gathered around him an able body of skilled officers, who materially aided him in his herculean task: Professors Douglass, Davies, and Courtenay, who had developed the analytical sciences, the true groundwork of military education; Torrey, Hopkins, and Mather, who had made the course of chemistry, mineralogy, and geology; Crozet and Mahan, who had skilfully applied all these branches to military and civil engineering and the science of war; McIlvaine and Warner, who had given their culture and eminent abilities to the teaching of ethics and law; the haughty Worth and the scholarly Hitchcock, who had impressed discipline and tone in their daily control of cadets; an able body of assistant professors, selected from the fittest of their classes, who efficiently aided their chiefs, and the soldierly members of his military staff, who had essentially lessened his burden of endless details. But the directing mind was the great Superintendent himself, a ripe scholar, acquainted with every science taught, passionately fond of military literature, and singularly gifted for his elevated command. To the discharge of his important functions he brought eminent personal qualifications, uniting decision with courtesy, authority with kindness, knowledge with consideration for ignorance, strict discipline with paternal admonition, unfaltering integrity to unflinching firmness, fidelity to his trust, and loyalty to his country, and with a restless energy and an untiring industry that never left anything unfinished or to chance. With such qualities and accomplishments it is not surprising that the Academy, which he found weak, imperfectly organized, low in prerequisites, and inferior in its course of training, should be raised by his knowledge of its wants and devotion to its interests to be the paragon of educational institutions in this country, and, judged by its fruits, not surpassed in the nations of the Old World." *

Grand as is this encomium, it is not undeserved. For we, who are charged to-day with the administration of the affairs of the Academy, heartily acknowledge that its past successful career and its present honorable reputation among men are legitimately the fruits of those principles of devotion to duty, honor, integrity, patriotism, and eminent fitness for the work in hand, which were so prominently characteristic of this great man.

The Academy of to-day is merely the development of that of 1833, when Thayer resigned the superintendency. Nothing has been added to the requirements for admission, save geography and United States history, and which, together with reading, writing, spelling, arithmetic, and grammar, now complete the list. These requirements are so simple that hundreds of boys all over the country, who would never dream of being able

---

* Cullum's Biographical Register, vol. iii.

to enter college, accept appointments to the Academy. At the knuckle-joint age very many boys are affected with heroic ambitions, while but few of them have had the requisite mental training to be able to master the exacting course of West Point. The following letter, received only last year, in reply to the usual circular sent to every applicant, will illustrate this point:

De Kalb Co. Tenn. Jan. 17, 1891.

"West Point Military Ac.

"Mr. Secretary, Hon. Sir:

"I received your terms some time since. I was not 17 yrs. of age when I heard from you. I can't come under any such terms. I will give you the terms that I will come under. I want only to study Military-tac-tics. I want to stay 3 yrs. I want $40.00 per month. At the end of the term I want a position over some army of the U. S. I want you to send me a round ticket there and back. I think I am both physically & mentally qualified to fill the position. I will not be out anything, but I want the position. Please answer this."

I once inquired of a young fellow why he came to the Academy. "Well," said he, "I made up my mind that the people of this country were going to be divided into two classes: the oppressed and the oppressors; and I wanted to be one of the oppressors." The cause of the widespread ignorance about West Point is that we are a peaceful people, rather averse to the profession of arms, and therefore the choice of a military career is, in general, an accident and not a purpose. It ought not then to be a matter of surprise that with the very liberal allowance of sixty-seven per cent of thorough, as a passing mark, one-third of the candidates fail of admission, and of those who are admitted only one-half succeed in graduating. Let us see what is done for these fortunate young fellows.

When the results of the entrance examination are announced, the successful candidates are drawn up into line to receive their first instruction. It is a pathetic sight to look upon their earnest faces and one well calculated to arouse our deepest emotions. In dress, appearance, culture, and material condition they are representative types of every section of the country and of every class of our people. But from this moment the cherished associations of birthplace and home pass little by little into that inner sanctuary where the love of mother abides, and the newer affections of service and country are gradually implanted. When he takes and subscribes the oath: " I —— do solemnly swear that I will support the Constitution of the United States, and bear true allegiance to the National Government; that I will maintain and defend the sovereignty of the United States paramount to any and all allegiance, sovereignty, or fealty I may owe to any state or country whatsoever; and that I will at all times obey the legal orders of my superior officers, and the rules and articles governing the armies of the United States"—he renounces of his own volition certain of his civil rights for the time being, and subordinates his will to his military superiors in certain well-defined particulars. It now becomes the duty of the Academy to thoroughly develop his physical, intellectual, and moral character so as to make him a fit and suitable person to be promoted to be an officer of the United States Army.

The first, or physical development, is a task simple enough with the very healthy boys that pass the severe scrutiny of the medical board of army surgeons. With simple but well-cooked food, ample outdoor exercise, and sufficient sleep and recreation, the bodily organs soon adjust themselves to their appropriate functions and give an elastic tone and a youthful vigor to the whole system. The erect carriage and graceful bearing of these young soldiers of the Republic always elicit the spontaneous admiration of strangers, and is certainly a handsome tribute for the trifling exactions of system and regularity. Very nearly all the out-door exercises pertain to the military drills of infantry, cavalry, artillery, and practical engineering, continued through the whole four years' course. So that, in addition to the healthy, vigorous exercise attendant thereon, a proficiency in the practical part of his profession is acquired at a time when it makes the deepest impression, and is, therefore, the more retentive and valuable.

The body, however, being the mere temporary dwelling-place of the man himself, its culture is relatively much less important than the mind in its intellectual and moral development, and it is for these ends that institutions of learning are established. We will therefore consider these in their order so far as the Academy is concerned.

From a superficial examination of the course of studies, it might appear that it is hardly extensive enough to accomplish its purpose. For it aims at what no military institution of Europe has accomplished, namely, to furnish our whole army with a body of well-educated military men, by instructing every pupil of the Academy in all branches of scientific and military knowledge regardless of the corps or arm to which he may be assigned. And it does this by exacting a very thorough study of the foundation of each branch rather than attempting an imperfect acquaintance of a much larger field of knowledge. A closer investigation will show that the subdivisions of the course number at least forty-five distinct subjects, and that nothing essential has been omitted.

The present course of instruction may rightly be considered to be the outcome of the matured judgment of the Academic Board (which, under the law, is made responsible for it) under the influence of the constant criticism and suggestions of more than a thousand officers of the army, and of the yearly investigation and reports of the official Boards of Visitors. "To learn a few things and to learn them well" is the rule of the Academy, and it is a good rule in the instruction of youth. Any attempt to combine an elementary school, a scientific academy, a high university, and a school of application for all branches of service would result in a failure of each of these projects. In order to produce an accomplished scholar in science, as in literature, much must be left to the individual exertions of the student, after his mind has received a proper direction from his early studies.

With these general principles in mind, it is provided that no cadet shall have, as a general rule, more than two distinct studies per day in which he shall have to prepare himself for recitation. These will require at least six hours of severe mental application for preparation and two and a half hours in the recitation-room to exhibit his proficiency thereon. Of the remainder of the sixteen hours, which constitute the official day, three hours are allotted to meals and recreation, and four and a half to drills, parade, and guard duty; in the winter months, however, when the drills are suspended, two hours are available for either additional study, exercise in the gymnasium, or recreation. The task assigned for each lesson is of sufficient difficulty to require the full employment of all the time at the disposal of the cadet for its thorough mastery. He is allowed no cuts or other like indulgence. A steady pace is kept up, and woe betide the unfortunate one that lingers by the way. Justice and judgment are served out impartially at the coming examination. The steady-goer, the patient plodder, the indefatigable student, is certain of success, but the fitful worker, the careless trifler, or the indifferent scholar soon finds that his military career is ended. With the present excellent discipline of the institution, and the great improvement in the methods of instruction, there are relatively but few failures after the first year. Whether some of these unfortunates might be saved to the service by the exercise of a greater liberality is, of course, an open question. Doubtless there are some that pass that are not any better than others that fail, for in education the line of demarcation is not always well defined. In a public institution of this kind the balance of judgment should incline toward public interest rather than individual benefit.

The immediate instructors of the cadets are army officers, temporarily detached from their regiments or corps, for a service of four years at the Academy. They are selected from among those on the active list who, when cadets, gave promise of ability in this particular direction, and afterward confirmed this hope during their active service in the army. They bring with them the existing sentiment of the army, which is not always in accord with the conservatism of the Academy; but after their tour of duty is completed their iconoclastic opinions are very considerably modified, and they return to the army much better satisfied with the administration of the affairs of the Academy than when they first joined. By this constant current of officers from the army to the Academy, and back again, both are mutually benefited, and both are kept in close touch with each other.

Good instruction is an expensive process, never fully appreciated by those who receive its benefits; but like all other things of value, it yields a satisfactory return on the investment. If we observe the loving mother teaching her tender child, we will note that she constantly employs forbearance and gentleness, together with wonderful patience, in her efforts to implant the germs of knowledge in its infantile mind. Every mind approaching a new branch of learning partakes of the same nature and needs the exercise of the same qualities in its teacher; but to secure the best intellectual advancement, it is essential that haste shall at first give way to thoroughness in learning the alphabet of the subject, for when the fundamentals are thoroughly well mastered they are like fat seeds in the mind, sending down strong roots by which to supply plenty of sap for a vigorous growth.

For the purpose of giving more thorough instruction, every class at the Academy is divided into sections of not more than twelve men in each, in the order of their ability as determined at the previous examination. As the course progresses, those who display the greater aptitude are transferred to higher sections, replacing others of less ability or industry. The marks given for recitations are posted every Saturday afternoon for the inspection of cadets, so that they may be informed of their relative progress and be incited to greater efforts. This publicity has also the advantage of causing the instructor to exercise greater care and impartiality in assigning marks, for in case of a just grievance the cadet has the right of appeal to higher authority for investigation and final judgment. Before beginning the recitation the opportunity is offered, and in the scientific departments freely taken advantage of by the cadets, of making known the difficulties that they have not been able to master in the lesson of the day. In such cases the instructor will show whether he is proficient in the application of his art. If he be an indifferent teacher, he will dilate upon the student's ignorance and make much of his own superior wisdom and ability. A good instructor, on the contrary, will suggest a question or offer such a judicious explanation that the intellectual step will be lessened, and thus enable the student to clear up the difficulty, as of himself, and wonder why he had not perceived it before. A true instructor, worthy of his high calling, must ever be capable of the greatest self-sacrifice in intellectual reputation, in order that the highest interests of his pupils may not suffer.

The Academy still holds to the text-book for use in instruction. I am aware that by some this is held to be antiquated; but in an academy or college, where elementary training is of more importance than the acquisition of knowledge, I doubt whether the close study of a suitable text can ever be displaced by the lecture system, which, however, may have a very appropriate field in a university. These text-books, especially in the sciences, have been compiled particularly for the use of the cadets and without regard to their availability elsewhere. They are constantly being made more concise and suitable for their purpose by means of the never-ending criticism to which they are daily subjected by the cadets, for the keen eyes of these earnest students often detect errors that would otherwise pass unnoticed.

Objections, too, have frequently been urged against the West Point course of instruction as being too mathematical and scientific. In answer to such criticisms, it may be said that war is essentially a science which can only be well learned by the same mental processes that apply to all sciences. My observation for the many years that I have been on duty at West Point confirms me in the belief that it would be detrimental to increase the humanities at the expense of the scientific studies. It would, of course, be very desirable to greatly enlarge the scope of the education given by the institution, but this would require many changes in the standards of admission, length of the course, and character of the subsequent service. These modifications are not, at present, in accord with public sentiment or policy, and can therefore be dismissed from immediate consideration. The average boy who is now sent to West Point to be educated may have had a good common-school training, but it is seldom the case that he has been taught how to study. Generally his masters have been content with a superficial knowledge of the tasks set for him, and in the learning of them his memory has played the more important part. The thing of most value that he acquires at West Point is a knowledge of the existence of his rational faculty and how to make use of it. He who learns this well will, in this present age, always be certain of success in the avocations of peace or the operations of war. Now in the mathematical studies and in all those which depend upon them, the student is first introduced to certain axioms, or self-evident truths, that he never questions, and then he is taught step by step the simple propositions, and gradually those of greater and greater complexity. When he has satisfactorily mastered the several branches of mathematics laid down in the course, he is ready to apply their principles to the acquisition of a knowledge of the various sciences that

are considered most essential for a preliminary education in the art of war.   Their value then is twofold:
First (and most important during the training period),
in giving strong discipline to the rational faculty of
the mind, and second (of increasing importance in after
years), in acquiring, classifying, and testing the facts
of knowledge that may be observed.   A brief exposition of the course in mechanics will serve to illustrate
the method of instruction in vogue at the Academy, as
well as the value of an analytical treatment of this subject in military education.

The time allotted to this subject is every week-day in
the first four months of the third year of the course.
Three and a half hours of study daily are required for
the preparation of each lesson, and one and a half hours
are devoted to the recitation.   The class have had a two
years' course of pure mathematics as a preparation and
their proficiency has been certified to by the Academic
Board after a rigid examination.   Now mechanics being
the doctrine of the action of force on matter, the first
object of instruction is to satisfactorily establish in the
mind of the pupil that there is a universal law governing all physical phenomena resulting from this action.
This is known as the "law of the conservation of
energy," and is thus stated: The total energy of any
conservative system is a quantity which cannot be increased or diminished by any mutual action of the
bodies of the system, and any change of either potential or kinetic energy must always be accompanied by
an equal but opposite change in the other.   The like
principle of the "conservation of matter" is readily
understood and of easy acceptance, and is used to assist
the mind in comprehending the meaning of its correlative.   In the beginning a great deal of careful instruction is necessary to explain that energy is quan-

tity, and that all the laws of quantity are applicable to it; that this principle has been formulated from a vast amount of scientific investigation, and at first must be held in the mind of the pupil as an assumption until he has reached that position of independent judgment where he can accept or reject it from sound reasons. Now it is found to be absolutely requisite to be very patient in dwelling upon the fundamental definitions, and at the same time very exacting and thorough, and generally it takes from two to three weeks of laborious teaching and explanation before the intellectual joints are limbered up and a satisfactory marching pace has been established. But when this condition has been reached, the only difficulty that is afterward met with is that due to imperfect mathematical knowledge, principally in the integral calculus.

By means of the symbolic language of mathematics this general law can easily be expressed in the form of an equation, which in all of its various transformations must embody the same fundamental truth, provided no errors have crept in from purely mathematical operations. No difficulty has been experienced at West Point in carrying each class through the successive steps of the application of this law to a free, rigid solid, and in deducing therefrom the general laws governing the motions of translation and rotation under the action of incessant forces, impulsions, and the two combined; and to show that these are in reality phenomena pertaining to the transformations of energy in the body; then successively a similar application to a body under constraint; to a group of bodies from which are deduced the laws of planetary motion; to fluids from which are deduced the laws of hydrostatics, hydraulics, the kinetic theory of gases and the mechanical theory of heat—all of which, with the assistance of numerous experiments illustrating each principle, intelligently prepares them to undertake, at the end of the four months, the study of the molecular sciences.

It will be seen from this exposition that this method of instruction in scientific studies, with faithful and competent instructors, combines the following advantages: First, the daily tasks require the full employment of all the study time apportioned to them, and thus is secured the invaluable mental effort and discipline due to a specified number of hours of hard study; second, the tasks are progressive and are based on fundamental principles, which require only the exercise of a rational faith, and develop a continual growth of confidence in the mind of the pupil, and a belief in his own ability to overcome each difficulty as it arises; third, there is given to the instructors the requisite authority to exact the full measure of intellectual endeavor from every pupil; and fourth, when the course is completed, the student finds himself equipped with a sound and satisfactory knowledge of the essential principles on which all physical science is based, to which he may add by further individual study, without the necessity of reconstructing his foundations.

Above all, the elements of character developed in the student—namely, confidence in his own powers, reliance on individual effort, and capacity to truly appreciate his sources of information—are of essential importance in a career where he may be called upon in emergencies to exercise self-control, and to meet manfully unforeseen difficulties; and are sufficient reasons for the adoption of this method at the Academy.

The third element in the training of cadets, that of their moral nature, is the most important of all; indeed, it is the all of any man. Without question, the religious faith implanted during the period of childhood, by parents and pastor, is the supreme source of all moral principles. These teachings abide with the internal man, the habitation of the Most High, and are "the remnant that saves." When the rational faculty is first being developed and running riot with its sensuous impressions, they may be for a time obscured, but they never can be dislodged from their strong fortress. So whatever knowledge, intelligence, or wisdom a man makes his own, these become merely the intellectual forms in which his interior affections reside and by which they are put into expression and use. Therefore the true end of education ought to be the suppression of the evil tendencies transmitted by heredity and the cultivation of the good affections, in order that the latter may be ultimated in use in every act of his life. The acquisition of knowledge and intellectual development, for purely personal ends, such as mere worldly success, professional advancement, literary fame, are evils to be deprecated. These may indeed be the first springs of action, but if the man becomes better, higher motives supplant them.

West Point has always enjoyed a high reputation for the inculcation of honor and integrity in its pupils and the manifestation of these virtues in its graduates; and it is a well-deserved one. Undoubtedly an important cause of this is the high character of the military profession in this country. For it is the service of the whole people and not that of any man, or dynasty, or party, or State, or section. It is too a service of self-sacrifice; its roll of honor bears the names of many heroes, and it has a glorious history behind it. Another cause is that these qualities, so eminently characteristic of Superintendent Thayer, enjoyed his sustaining care for so long a time that they became ingrained in the Academy, and have ever since been transmitted unsullied as a priceless legacy to his successors. And finally the *esprit de corps*, an ever-watchful sentinel of its honor, a jealous guardian of its integrity, and a powerful conserver of its reputation.

Subordination and personal responsibility form the basis of the military and academic discipline at West Point and are most important factors in the development of the moral character of cadets. The corps of cadets is organized into a battalion of four companies, its officers being selected from the three upper classes according to good conduct, military bearing, and class standing. The maintenance of good order is thus to a very great extent made dependent upon the cadets themselves, and as the enforcement of the regulations is made a military duty, which it is inconsistent with soldierly character to neglect, its performance does not expose the individual to the odium of his associates, but is with him a matter of professional pride. Hence there cannot be a distinct line of division between the governing and the governed, and to this may be attributed the existence of the honorable sentiment that pervades the cadets.

A very important consideration in this matter of responsibility is the variety of conditions which determine which cadet is in charge of the thing to be done. Of course the regulations are explicit and no dispute can arise in any case. Thus in all battalion formations precedence is according to military rank, and therefore sergeants and corporals may give orders to cadet privates of higher classes and longer service than themselves. In marching to recitations, class standing determines the relative rank, while at other times in class formations it may be according to alphabetical order or general class standing. Every subdivision in barracks has its cadet inspector, and every room its room orderly. Authority to order and power to execute are thus limited to specific duties, times, and places, each well defined by regulations. Under all other conditions cadets are comrades with each other, and are thus freed from that restraint that would otherwise be burdensome and that espionage that would fetter friendship.

As every one at the Academy, in the performance of a particular duty, is thus under the authority of some other one, so also is he clothed, for the time being, with the necessary power to exact obedience from his subordinates. The finger of authority can always be placed upon the individual who is responsible for the act done or not done, without regard to the actual violater of the regulation in question. It might at first be supposed that, in the application of such a system of discipline, many spiteful acts and mean revenges would be perpetrated by some cadets on others, under the cover of a high sense of duty in the execution of their office. But the system is found to carry its own correction along with it. There is an unwritten but well-recognized code of honor among the cadets which controls its administration; and besides there is the ever-watchful supervision of the army officers in command to prevent a too wide departure from right and justice. It has been repeatedly shown that where any attempt has been made to weaken the responsibility of the cadets by undue supervision, there has always been a serious falling off in discipline.

The first three months' service at the Academy are the most trying of all. The new life and surroundings, the severe physical exercise, the unwonted muscular soreness, the multitudinous duties, orders, and regulations that are to be learned and obeyed, do not make the life of the new cadet particularly enjoyable. The first lessons in military subordination are learned when one constrains himself to repress the stinging retort in response to the peremptory command, and obeys the order promptly and without question. We all know that the average American youth is rather more self-assertive than subordinate, and at West Point, as at college, it seems to devolve on the Sophomores to reverse the ratio. At the end of the summer encampment, at any rate, the Plebes have adjusted themselves to their environment, and have become a fine lot of active, alert, and graceful young fellows, marvellously improved in appearance, individually and collectively.

But the crowning glory of the Academy is the high sense of honor, the strict regard for the truth, and the manly integrity that pervades the whole corps of cadets. Every community among men has its unwritten standard of conduct. Within its boundaries much latitude is permitted, but beyond these limits there is ostracism on the one hand and voluntary separation on the other. The glorious history of our country is well calculated to inspire our American youth with the highest ideals of exalted patriotism, of integrity in positions of public trust, and of a self-sacrificing devotion to duty. The officers of the United States Army have ever cherished these ideals and have exemplified their teachings in their own conduct, even in times of extreme temptation. It is no wonder then that these same sentiments should be alive and active among the young men who are to succeed to these positions. These sentiments, however, cannot be called into being by the fiat of arbitrary power. They must spring from living seed and their surroundings be favorable to their healthy development; they must be watched with vigilant and anxious eyes lest noxious weeds spring up to diminish their vitality and threaten their life.

Every new class admitted to the Academy contains some men who have never been trained to a high sense of honor and a due regard for exactness of statement. They are soon instructed by the older cadets that their word must be held sacred; that they cannot lie nor prevaricate, nor in any way tamper with the truth; neither in studies nor in explanations of delinquencies submitted either in writing or by word of mouth to any official superior. The "honor of the corps" is jealously guarded by the upper classmen, and if no heed be paid to kindly admonition a trial by court-martial will follow the offense, to which publicity will then be given. So strong and active is this *esprit de corps* and so jealously is it guarded that I have known a time when it maintained the honor and discipline of the institution, even against the influence and example of some incapable officers, who were unfit for their administrative positions at the Academy. Under such conditions the general practice is never to question the word of a cadet. To doubt the truth of a statement, by word or manner, is an indignity arousing a sense of injury and wrong to the individual, which, if often repeated, might prove fatal to the practice of truth-telling.

As the members of the new class come to know each other better, those men who are found to be lacking in moral perception, or are weak in the power of resisting evil, are left on the outskirts of those intimacies that bring the finer men together. But evil tendencies are never content to be let alone; they desire to rule and to destroy. Soon happens the unpardonable act, and the class becomes purged one by one of its unworthy members.

The powerful influences that urge cadets to choose the right way are many; among these are a definite profession in full view from the very start of their educational career; an allowance made by the Government for their entire support while at the Academy; full employment of their time to remove the temptations of idleness; and almost a certainty that if successful they will be commissioned as second lieutenants of infantry in the U. S. Army on the day of graduation. These incentives are common to all, while for superior scholarship it is provided that the names of the five most distinguished cadets of each class shall be published in the *Army Register*, and at the end of their cadetship take precedence in the choice of corps or of favored regiments according to class rank.

If now the true object of education be the concurrent and co-ordinated development of the physical, the intellectual, and the moral natures of youth, how can we improve on the system here outlined? Under such training must not the principles of honor, rectitude, and charity which are cultivated during the formative period of life mainly control the conduct of the man whatever be his career? Let the record furnish the answer.

At the commencement of the war of 1812 there were but sixty-five graduates in service, and though their number was few and their preliminary preparation defective, due to criminal neglect and hostility of Secretary Eustis, yet they were among the very best officers of the army—their gallantry being attested by a loss of one-fourth of their number serving in the field in killed and wounded. On the breaking out of the Mexican War there were over 500 well-educated graduates in service. Of their value the veteran, General Scott, says: "I give it as my fixed opinion that, but for our graduated cadets, the war between the United States and Mexico might, and probably would, have lasted some four or five years with, in its first half, more defeats than victories falling to our share; whereas, in less than two campaigns we conquered a great country and a peace, without the loss of a single battle or skirmish."

The records of the Civil War sufficiently attest that the graduates of West Point, in loyalty, integrity, and ability, were equal to the vast responsibilities so suddenly thrust upon them by that great uprising. I say loyalty with deliberate purpose, for though the Southern-born graduates were cradled and reared in the belief of paramount allegiance to the State, yet 162, or nearly one-half of their number, remained true to the teachings of their Alma Mater, fighting against rebellion and resisting every temptation of family and friends to swerve them from their devotion to the Union. When the war was ended many of the graduates of West Point had won the highest military fame, all had gained honorable distinction, and none had lost his integrity.

Constant and unremitting savage warfare has been the lot of our little regular army in times of peace, from the Battle of Tippecanoe, November 7, 1811, to Wounded Knee Creek, December 29, 1891, and, in these more than 300 engagements the graduates have displayed their heroic qualities and grander self-sacrifice.

General George W. Cullum, of the class of 1833, bequeathed to his Alma Mater a quarter of a million of dollars to build a Memorial Hall, "which shall be a receptacle of statues, busts, mural tablets, and portraits of distinguished and deceased officers and graduates of the Military Academy, of paintings of battle scenes, trophies of war, and such objects as may tend to give

elevation to the military profession." But in his "Biographical Register of the Graduates of the Military
Academy," West Point has a yet grander memorial; for
it tells the story of every graduate from Joseph G.
Swift, class of 1802, graduate No. 1, to Horace G.
Hambright, class of 1892, graduate No. 3,511. It is the
completest justification of the wisdom of its organization, the thoroughness of its discipline, and the value
of its instruction. "Wherefore by their fruits shall ye
know them." This record shows that West Point "has
filled every arm of the military service with talent,
efficiency, and integrity; has materially aided in successfully conducting three great wars, extending our
national domain, and preserving the Union; has per-
petually pushed the wild savage from our borders, and
been the pioneer of advancing civilization; has constructed and armed our fortifications, improved our
harbors, lakes, and rivers, defined our boundaries, sur-
veyed and lighted our coasts, and explored the length
and breadth of our land; has given to our militia and
volunteers large numbers of valuable officers, and to
our colleges able presidents and professors; has furnished distinguished civil engineers, who have bound
our territory together with a network of railways and
canals; has supplied valuable city, state, and government functionaries; has improved our workshops and
the culture of the soil; has added its mite to the count-
ing house, the bar, and the pulpit; and, through the
contributions and text-books of its graduates, has
greatly elevated the scientific standard of most of the
educational institutions throughout our country, and
even extended its influence abroad."

Are there no black sheep in this flock? Unfortunately yes. Against the names of fifty-eight of the
graduates of West Point, or less than two per cent. of

the whole number, there is recorded "cashiered" or "dismissed the service of the United States," mainly, however, for dissipation and purely military offenses. The number of those who have been guilty of betrayal of trust, the loss of honor or integrity, is so few as to be expressed by a single significant figure. This is indeed a striking illustration of the truth of the saying, "that the exception proves the rule."

With such a record it is obvious that West Point has well fulfilled the purpose of its establishment. It cannot make great generals, but it can develop them. Education cannot create nor implant that which is originally lacking, but does bring to fruition the best that is in a man. But though genius be the intellectual inheritance of the very few, the moral sense is the common heritage of humanity. Therefore we who are charged with the instruction of youth are not responsible for the production of a definite number of intellectual geniuses per year, but we ought to be held to a strict accountability that every one of our pupils shall be an exemplar of the "honor of honesty."

Should war never again come to our beloved country the function of West Point as an institution for military instruction would in time fall into disuse; but as a seminary of sound learning and instruction in the physical, the intellectual, and the moral natures of youth, it will always deservedly occupy a high place in the educational system of the land. But when shall this time be? We read:

"And it shall come to pass in the last days that the mountain of the Lord's house shall be established on the top of the mountains and shall be exalted above the hills; and all nations shall flow unto it.

"And many people shall go and say, Come ye, and let us go up to the Mountain of the Lord, to the house

of the God of Jacob; and he will teach us his ways and
we will walk in his paths; for out of Zion shall go forth
the law and the word of the Lord from Jerusalem.

"And he shall judge among the nations and shall
rebuke many people; and they shall beat their swords
into ploughshares and their spears into pruning hooks;
nation shall not lift up sword against nation, neither
shall they learn war any more."

Now what is the law by which we shall be taught of
His ways and walk in His paths? Again we read:

"Then one of them, which was a lawyer, asked him
a question, tempting him, and saying,

"Master, which is the great commandment in the
law?

"Jesus said unto him, Thou shalt love the Lord thy
God with all thy heart, and with all thy soul, and with
all thy mind.

"This is the first and great commandment.

"And the second is like unto it, Thou shalt love thy
neighbor as thyself.

"On these two commandments hang all the law and
the prophets."

Alexander H. Rice

ALEXANDER H. RICE.

ALEXANDER H. RICE was born at Newton Lower Falls, Massachusetts, August 30th, 1818, a son of Thomas and Lydia Smith Rice. His father was a paper manufacturer, a native of Brighton (now a part of Boston), and his mother belonged to an old Puritan family. The subject of this sketch was educated at the public school in Newton, always among the best in New England, and at neighboring academies, and also when a boy had large intercourse with cultivated people who abounded in that part of Massachusetts. He entered Union College with the class of 1840, and therefore had his collegiate training under Dr. Nott, the rare and renowned educator. He had held a clerkship for a term of three years in a mercantile house in Boston before going to college, and his intention upon graduating was to become a lawyer. He had the valedictory oration of his class. The failure of his health, the result of a serious fall from a horse, changed his purpose in 1844, and being offered a partnership in the paper warehouse where he had previously served as a clerk, he embarked in that business, which he has ever since continued. But he soon gave his attention to public affairs and became a member of the Board of Government of Public Institutions in Boston and of the School Board. In 1853 he became a member of the Common Council of Boston, of which body he became president the following year, and was elected mayor of the city in the autumn of 1855, and was re-elected for a second term. His administration was successful, and was notable for the amicable settlement of many perplexing difficulties and for an aspiring advancement of the city without increase of the public burdens. One of his most accomplished oratorical efforts was his address at the dedication of the original Public Library in Boston. Union College conferred upon him the degree of A. M. in 1847, and Harvard College conferred the degree of LL. D. in 1876.

In 1859 he was elected to Congress from the then third district of Massachusetts, embracing six wards of Boston and the suburbs of Roxbury and Brookline ; he was three times re-elected, making a total service in Congress of eight years, covering one Congress before the war, the whole period of the war, and one Congress after the war During a portion of this important period he was chairman of the Committee on Naval Affairs of the National House of Representatives. Mr. Rice was a Republican in politics, though his district was Democratic.

In the autumn of 1875 he was elected Governor of Massachusetts and had two subsequent re-elections, when he declined further public service. At the time of his death he was still in active business, being president of the Rice Kendall Company in Boston, of the Keith Paper Company at Turner's Falls, and of the American Sulphite Pulp Company. He was also a director in the Montague Paper Company, was president of the National Sailors' Home, a director in the Massachusetts National Bank, a trustee of the American Loan and Trust Company of Boston, and of the Mutual Life Insurance Company of New York, and of many other business, educational, and philanthropic institutions.

On July 22d, 1895, ex-Governor Rice died, at Melrose, Mass.

SOME INSIDE VIEWS OF THE GUBER-NATORIAL OFFICE.

By Hon. Alexander H. Rice, Ex-Governor of Massachusetts.

Mr. President, Ladies and Gentlemen: Generosity is one of the noblest and most attractive attributes known among men; and had I been present at the gathering of the Alumni Association in the city of New York when General Butterfield proposed to establish, at his own cost, this course of lectures at his alma mater, I should have joined heartily in the rounds of applause which greeted that announcement; and if the echoes of that applause have in any degree died away upon the public ear, I am sure that the pulsations of gratitude toward him still throb vigorously in the heart of every Union man wherever he may be found. And while I praise his generosity, I think I may also compliment with a single exception his sagacity in the selection of the eminent men whom he has chosen to address you; but if the exception to which I allude shall prove less disappointing to you this afternoon than I have all along feared it might be, I shall be abundantly gratified. When General Butterfield asked me to participate in these lectures, owing to the then condition of my health he was kind enough to say that I need not prepare an elaborate address, but make a familiar talk, something after the manner of the late Dr. Nott. [Applause.] Fatal comparison! I well remember the eloquence and pathos with which the doctor was accustomed to address the students in my day, and I supposed his remarkable gifts passed out of the world when the doctor died, unless, perchance, they may have descended upon the present incumbent, his successor in office; in which case I heartily congratulate you. [Applause.] I see by your applause that you think they have so descended. [Applause and laughter.]

General Butterfield was good enough to supplement his first kindness by suggesting to me a topic upon which I should speak to you. It has already been gracefully announced by the genial President of our Alumni Association, viz., " Some Inside Views of the Gubernatorial Office." Thus, you will see that I am to speak not so much of the organic or constitutional characteristics of the office as of what may be termed the domestic view: as to what the governor thinks about, what he does, and of his environment generally. I suppose he selected this subject because of a little experience which I had in Massachusetts a while ago; or, more probably, because he expects each of you students to be governor of a State by and by, and thought a little anticipatory information might be acceptable to you. Governor of what? Governor of a " Commonwealth;" governor of a " State." Here curiosity arises and asks why those terms, " State" and " Commonwealth," are used. Is there any difference between them? If so, what is that difference? Why are some called Commonwealths? Why are some called States? We use the terms synonymously. There is *practically* no difference between them; theoretically and phraseologically there is a difference. " Commonwealth" seems to have a somewhat more ultimate meaning; touches more closely the individual; goes a little more into severalty, than the term " State." A

State is an aggregation of people living within certain territorial boundaries under one form of government; it may be a monarchy or otherwise. A State is an aggregation of the people of a territory. A "Commonwealth" is the aggregation not only of the people, but of the rights, privileges, and prerogatives of the people. We have come to use these terms synonymously, as I said, but still this is the distinction and about all the distinction there is; I think it worth while, however, when we call them "States," always to bear in mind the Commonwealth idea, because the last thing we can part with in this country is our personal liberty under the laws.

Well, one might suppose, at first glance, that the original thirteen States which had an original organic existence, or a previous colonial existence, might have been called "Commonwealths," and that the others that were formed· out of the public territory and admitted into the Union subsequently might have been called "States." We speak of the Commonwealth of Massachusetts, of the Commonwealth of Virginia, of the Commonwealth of Pennsylvania, and of the Commonwealth of Kentucky. Now, the first three of these belong to the original thirteen States, but Kentucky does not. Then, on the other hand, we speak of the State of New York, of the State of New Jersey, of the State of Rhode Island, etc., none of which were called "Commonwealths," and yet they all belong to the original thirteen States; therefore we see that this theory will not answer. How happened it then that some of the States were called Commonwealths? Let us look first to the Commonwealth of Massachusetts. John Adams was a native of Massachusetts and one of her foremost men. He was a great statesman; he was a builder of civil government; a natural organizer. John Adams wrote the constitution of Massachusetts, and although Massachusetts had already been called "a province," "a colony," and "a State," he inserted the word "Commonwealth" therein. John Adams was profoundly impressed with the ideals of the Commonwealth period in England, and especially with its ideas of personal independence in civil and religious affairs, as distinguished from the sovereignty of the crown. He desired beyond all else to establish by law like independence in this new country while its governments were in process of formation. Consequently he inserted the word "Commonwealth" in the Constitution, and hence we have the "Commonwealth of Massachusetts." Virginia had as her great statesman at that time Thomas Jefferson. Mr. Jefferson and Mr. Adams were personal friends and co-laborers. They built together with others the greater Commonwealth of the United States. Well, Mr. Jefferson and Mr. Adams, although they differed from each other on some points of party politics of a minor description, yet upon many broad questions of organic statesmanship they were very much in accord. Perhaps we shall find the origin of the "Commonwealth of Virginia" in the influence of Jefferson.

The "Commonwealth of Pennsylvania." Some people will tell us that the Commonwealth idea probably came from William Penn, to whom Pennsylvanians attribute almost every excellence; but we may remember that Benjamin Franklin lived in Pennsylvania. He was a Massachusetts man and a friend of Mr. Adams and of Mr. Jefferson, and he had to do with the framing of the Constitution of Pennsylvania. Perhaps we shall not go astray if we say that Pennsylvania got the title of "Commonwealth" through Benjamin Franklin, rather than through William Penn.

The "Commonwealth of Kentucky." Kentucky did

not belong to the original thirteen, but was formed afterward and admitted into the Union in 1792.

We have, as to their elements, three classes of States in this country, namely: States that had a previous colonial existence or an original formation; States that were formed by emigration from other States and from foreign countries; and there are States that were each formed bodily out of some other State. Kentucky was of this last description. The Alleghany Mountains separated one part of Virginia from the other. Virginia before the Revolutionary War was settled chiefly on the eastern side of the Alleghanies; but in process of time a goodly number of her people made their way into the territory west of the mountains, now called Kentucky; some also went from Southern Maryland, and some from Northern North Carolina, but the great bulk of the people of Kentucky was from Virginia. In fact, to all intents and purposes, up to the year 1792, when the section west of the mountains was separated from Virginia and admitted into the Union, Kentucky was part and parcel of Virginia; and when she separated she took the ideals and institutions of Virginia; and hence we have the "Commonwealth of Kentucky." Now, remember that, whether we call them "States" or "Commonwealths," we must be sure always to retain the Commonwealth idea, because of its great importance. The Government of the United States is only a larger Commonwealth. As Mr. Lincoln said in his immortal speech at Gettysburg: "It is a government of the people, by the people, and for the people." That is precisely what it is, and it is just that which constitutes it a great Commonwealth.

There is something analogous to, and illustrative of, the State idea and of the Commonwealth idea in the organization and constituency of the two Houses of

Congress. Thus, you will remember that every State, without regard to its territorial limits or to its population, is entitled to *two* senators in the Senate of the United States. *They* represent the State—the Statehood. The people are represented in the Senate of the United States by *States*. The United States House of Representatives is a more numerous body, and the number of its members varies according to the population of the several States. Thus Rhode Island, one of the *smallest* States in the Union, has *two* senators who represent the *State* of Rhode Island. The State of New York, one of the *largest* States in the Union, has but *two* senators who represent in the Senate of the United States the State of New York. Rhode Island has one or two representatives in the United States House of Representatives and New York has nearly forty. So you see that the United States Senate represents the *Statehood* of the States, and the other house, namely, the House of Representatives, represents, to a greater extent, the severalty of the *people*.

Now to the governor. The first thing that a governor does after his election is to prepare his inaugural address to the legislature. For that purpose he calls upon the heads of departments in the State to furnish him with the reports which they will later send to the legislature, or an abstract of these reports. He studies these reports, and embodies such portions of them as he pleases in his address, together with such recommendations, arguments, and suggestions as make up his policy for information to the legislature or to the people who may read his address. He will find very soon that his duties arrange themselves generally under two heads: a Department of Law, and a Department of Civics. Closer inspection will show him that there are two kinds of law, namely, constitutional law and statutory law. Under the heads of civics he may group such subjects as education, charity, crime or reform, sociology, etc. He will not have a great deal to do with constitutional law, except that he must study carefully the Constitution of the State in which he lives, and also the Constitution of the United States, because some of the statutes that will be proposed may contravene one or the other of these instruments. That is about all he will need to do with constitutional law. With statutory law he has more to do. He must see whether there be any statutes that may have become obsolete or unnecessary, in which case he will probably suggest their repeal. He will also see whether there are any statutes that are imperfect or inadequate for the purpose for which they were enacted, and if he finds such, will suggest that they be amended. He will prescribe the form of amendment or make a suggestion simply as the case may be. He will also see what subjects, if any there are, that in his opinion require regulation by statute, and will recommend that laws on these subjects for greater freedom, for limitation, or for punishment shall be enacted. Although the governor is not a member of either branch of the legislature, he is nevertheless a part of the lawmaking power; because no statute becomes valid until it has received his signature, unless he withholds his signature for a period beyond the constitutional limit, when the act will take effect because he has not signed it; but this is neither a very brave nor a very wise method of enacting laws. He had better always sign a bill, or else say that he declines to sign it, for that is the manly way to do.

While a governor always sits apart from the legislature in a room by himself and does not hear the arguments that are made in committee nor in either branch of the legislature, he knows only imperfectly what is going on in that body. Ordinarily he does not see a bill until it is presented to him for his signature. He would only be a rash and unsafe man who would voluntarily and without cause place himself in opposition to the two houses of the legislature. He does not wish to imply that, in his opinion, his judgment is superior to that of the legislators, neither does he wish to discredit their sagacity, their industry, or the soundness of their decisions. On the other hand, he would be, in my opinion, a man totally unfit for his place if he hesitated a single moment to veto a bill that seemed to him to be of a pernicious character. [Applause.]

I once knew a governor who sent during his term seven vetoes to the legislature, and they were every one of them approved, although some of the members may have voted otherwise on the original passage of the bills. Of course, a governor does not present his veto in person. He does it by message. That message is read in his absence; therefore it behooves him to make it as convincing as possible, because some of the members whose votes he now requires may have voted for the bill, and he is asking them to change their vote and he must give them good and sufficient reasons for doing so.

We now come to the Department of Civics. Almost every State has a Board of Education—I do not know but every one—and the governor is usually a member of the Board, generally its head. Consequently he is brought into immediate contact both with the *system* of education in the State, and with the *methods* of education. He may not feel it his duty to visit the primary and grammar schools, and the high schools in cities and in towns of a certain population; for these are more especially under the administration and direction of those cities and towns themselves; but through the agents of the Board of Education and otherwise he will become acquainted with the details of those schools. He will visit the normal schools, some of the training schools, the scientific and the technological schools, the colleges and universities, whether they be State institutions or whether he goes by invitation. Harvard College was originally a State institution.   It ceased to be so a number of years ago; but in olden times the college commencements at Harvard were great features in social life in eastern Massachusetts. To a certain extent they are so still. The governor was an important personage also in Massachusetts at this college, and the custom was for him to visit the college in *state*, that is, in his official capacity, on commencement day; and this custom, although dropped for one year, was almost immediately revived, so that now the Governor of Massachusetts attends in state the commencements of Harvard University. He goes from Boston to Cambridge with an escort of cavalry, accompanied by his civil and military staff, and is received at the University by the Sheriff of Middlesex (in which county the University is located), and by him passed over to the officers and faculty of the University, and with them he attends the commencement exercises and dinner of the alumni following. It is his custom to make a brief address there.

As to how far the State ought to go in the matter of free education of the higher sort, is a question still under discussion. Some are of the opinion that the State ought to provide educational facilities through all the grades of instruction from the lowest school up to and including the university. I think this is not the general idea; at any rate, it is not the plan adopted by the States generally, I believe. It is in a few of them. A reason given why it should be so adopted is that, inasmuch as the people are taxed for public instruction, the State ought to give to everybody the opportunity for full instruction, including a university training. On the other hand, it is said that if the State should make such provision, only a limited number can avail themselves of it after all; and that it is a waste of money and a waste of opportunities to make such provision. Others again think that a common-school education is sufficient provision for the State to make or to consider. However this may be, States sometimes grant scholarships in colleges and universities, and sometimes make special donations for such members of a community as desire to go to a college or university and yet are not able themselves to command the means. As a general rule, if a young man has made up his mind that he will have a college education he will get it in some honorable way. I have known young men who overcame great obstacles when in pursuit of that object, and I do not know that I ever knew a man of commendable ambition and determination of character who failed to achieve what he aimed at in that direction; therefore I do not think we need trouble ourselves very much upon that subject. But, as I said before, it is still an open question and one under discussion.

Another open question is whether or not we shall retain, to the present full extent, the study of the ancient languages, the classics, as they are termed. There is great pressure nowadays to throw out the classics and to take modern languages and scientific and industrial studies in their place. There is, no doubt, some weight in the argument for doing so. The remarkable discoveries of science in the last half or three-quarters of a century have stimulated the ambition as well as enlarged the knowledge of men universally, and the application of these discoveries to the industrial arts has kindled a fresh enthusiasm for scientific and technological instruction. The greater intercourse of people of different nations also necessitates a knowledge of modern languages. The claim for such instruction therefore goes to the front with a power that it did not have a few years ago, and I think it entitled to very great consideration, and that provision ought to be made in all colleges and in all high schools to give a pretty large place to the study of the modern languages and to scientific and technological education. At the same time, there will always be a certain number of people in every community who will aspire to high and elegant scholarship, and to the learned professions, as they are sometimes termed. Rome was the mistress of power, of organization, and of eloquence. Greece was the mistress of poetry and philosophy and of letters generally. And it may well be doubted whether this high and polished scholarship can be fully attained without an acquaintance with the language and the literature of both of these ancient nations. We sometimes hear it said that our public schools are our national defence. This is no rhetorical expression to be used only on occasions of high emotional or patriotic excitement. It is a solid fact. They are the bulwark of the nation and must be maintained by every effort and at every sacrifice necessary. The founders of this nation aspired to a higher example of civilization than had been yet attained by any people in the world. Among other things they made the suffrage universal. Our government, our liberties, our most precious interests of whatever description they may be, are involved in this matter of suffrage. These founders never dreamed that universal suffrage could stand on a basis of ignorance. They established a schoolhouse and a non-national Church; the first to train the intellect, and the second to train the heart. They intended that the schools should tell the voter, or give him the means of learning how to vote, to understand the government under which he lives, and when he went to the polls they expected him to vote as an intelligent man should vote. They established a Church as the minister of righteousness more than as the depository of theological dogmas. The basis of all true morality is religion. They aimed therefore at the intellect and at the heart, that with the cultivation of the two the man and the voter should be honest and that he should be intelligent. We cannot sacrifice to-day, with our great population and growing country and our rising influence among mankind, this great guardian of our liberties, this preserver of the government under which we live. We must maintain the public schools at every hazard.

Statistics show us that in every community there is a certain proportion of human infirmities. The measure of this proportion may be changed by various alleviating circumstances; but do what we will, there will be found in every community a certain ratio of infirmities according to the population. It will be found, for example, in the large cities, that about a given number of stores will be left unlocked during every night of the week, that an approximate number of houses will be left unprotected, that an estimated number of persons will nightly apply at the police stations for lodging; that there will be about so many cases of drunkenness, about so many cases of assault and battery, of larceny, and so on, in the enumeration. Now when these infirmities are unpremeditated, we call them misfortunes, and they come under the head of *charities*. When they are committed with premeditation, we call them *crimes*, and hence our prisons and systems of prison discipline. Under the head of charities, as of schools, the towns and cities have almshouses, and their local institutions of one kind or another, which they take care of and administer themselves; and the governor has only a general knowledge of them. But there are also other institutions—State almshouses, hospitals, infirmaries of various kinds and descriptions, houses for juvenile offenders, and all that. The governor is expected to visit them, and to know how they are administered, not merely in a general way as a stranger might go in and look them over, or merely to see such things as the superintendent points out to him; but the governor goes there with official authority, and the superintendent is for the time being in fact his subordinate, and is bound to extend to him every service desired. He is under the governor's authority. The governor does not look at what the superintendent chooses to show him, but takes precedence of him and directs the superintendent to show the whole place.

HOW WILL A GOVERNOR INSPECT AN INSTITUTION?

He probably will begin in the cellar and see if it is properly ventilated; that there are no substances producing impure odors or a malarious atmosphere. From the cellar he goes into the kitchen and makes himself acquainted with the kinds and the quantity of food served to the inmates. He will ask some questions about the cooking, though he is not supposed to know a great deal about that. [Applause.] He will inform himself, as far as it is possible for him to do so, about everything pertaining to the kitchen department. He

will go into the dining-room and examine the furniture,
look at the tables, the crockery, see if it is properly
washed and cleanly wiped and has no streaks upon it;
he will look through the glass and see if that is clean.
He will examine the cloths that are used for the wiping
towels. All these things may seem to be trivial, but
they are not. They are essential to the well-being of
the inmates in those institutions, and the governor is
their protector. It is secondarily a part of his business
to see that all necessary things are provided for them,
and that these things are properly used and kept. He
will go to the dormitories and will examine the clos-
ets, the furniture, and all utensils. He will examine
the beds, will strip off the coverlets, the blankets,
the sheets, tip the mattresses on the floor so that he
can examine the bedstead. [Laughter.] He will go
into the lavatories also; in fact, he will know all there
is to know in and about that establishment. If there
is anything out of order, he will impress his mind
with it, and feel it his duty to see that it is corrected.
He will do the same in hospitals. I do not know that
he will attempt to advise the physician as to the
administration of medicines or the diagnosis of diseases, etc. I think, however, he will know everything
that pertains to the ordinary administration of the hospital. He will especially regard all the children in
the charitable institutions, for they have generally
committed no offence, but are simply the children of
misfortune. They are sent to a public institution because they have no home, or because their homes are
worse than none,—because their parents have defaulted.
I knew once a governor who visited one of these
juvenile institutions where there were something like
twelve hundred children. He had never been there
before. The superintendent was a stalwart man, a

practical farmer, a man of intelligence, of sobriety, and of good character generally, but not possessing great knowledge as to how to conduct an institution such as he was at the head of. The first thing that attracted the governor's attention was, that the children were playing upon a gravel space outside of the building and exposed to the sun, on a very hot day in August, when the mercury was running up to nearly a hundred degrees. They were dressed after the style of the "Beggars' Brigade." They had a great variety of clothing; they had thin clothes and thick clothes; some had straw hats, some had woollen caps, and were about as uncomfortable-looking a set of juveniles as he had ever seen. He remained during dinner time, and it happened to be Friday, and he walked into the dining-room where the children were eating dinner. He observed that the tables had no covering upon them. They were mere boards, well scraped and cleaned to be sure. It was fish day, they had salt fish for dinner, and the little fellows—little children, because there were girls among them—were seated about these tables. There were brown pitchers of water but no tumblers or mugs for the table. The children seemed to enjoy good appetites, and were industriously engaged. After a time the governor passed from the dining-room into the kitchen, and in the course of the inspection lifted up a lid of one of the great boilers, and found it nearly full of drawn butter. I think the ladies call it a dressing for fish; and the governor asked the superintendent about that, why it was not served to the children? "Oh," he said, "that was surplus, the children were all supplied." It was found, however, upon the governor's return to the dining-room, that the children had no drawn butter upon their fish. He afterward examined the sleeping-rooms, the bathing

department, and the laundry, and all that. Then the
governor took his stand beside the superintendent in
the hall, as these children passed from their dinner,
and he observed that they all passed by the superintendent with downcast eyes, and that they had a sort of
huddled appearance, that is, they walked in the lock-
step as the prisoners do in the house of correction and
penitentiary. After they had all gone out, the governor
called the superintendent aside and said to him: The
State desires economy in the administration of her
charitable institutions, but not parsimony. I wish you
to build an awning under which these children may be
screened from the sun during their hours of amusement.
I wish you to buy suitable thin material to make two
suits of clothes for every one of these boys and girls,
that they may be dressed uniformly and comfortably,
and so that as fast as one suit gets soiled it may be
washed and cleansed, and that no one shall be able
to point to another as being more poorly dressed than
himself or herself. Then I wish you to buy some
tablecloths—they need not be expensive—to cover
every one of those tables, so that when the children
come to their meals there shall be something home-
like in the appearance of the room. Do not put the
potatoes on the tables with their jackets on, but have
them peeled and put into dishes, and be careful about
the fish sauce [laughter and applause] at their meals.
One thing more important than all that," said the
governor to him, "I do not want the children to be
taught the prison step here. They must not learn that
in any of our juvenile charitable institutions. We are
not training them here for maturer service in criminal
institutions; we hope they may never go there. Let
them go out in a more cheerful way, I do not care
even if it be a rampant way; that would be better than

this lock-step. I want to see them go out with more freedom and do not let too much discipline subordinate the childish instincts in them. Moreover, I observe," said the governor, "that these children look down as they pass by you, or if occasionally one raises his eyes to you, it is with a look of fear; there is no confidence in it; there is no affection in it. Each child looked at you as to a man from whom he expected to get a box on the ears or a reprimand. It was no familiar look; he did not expect an affectionate or sympathetic greeting from you, and that is an indication that he is not accustomed to getting it. I desire," he said, "that all this shall be changed and that you shall remember that, although you are at the head of an institution to govern these children, it must be a government so paternal that these children will look to you as their father, will expect paternal kindness, and will receive it."

Two or three months, more or less, rolled by, and the superintendent chanced one morning to put in an appearance at the State House, and the governor said to him: "I am glad to see you this morning. I was about to send you a note, but I had a great deal rather deliver in person the message that I have for you." "What is the message?" the superintendent asked. "Well," said the governor, "I was about to send you a message saying that I would accept your resignation whenever it would be convenient for you to tender it." Said the superintendent, "Are you dissatisfied with my work?" "Yes," said the governor, "I am." Said the superintendent, "I thought I had remedied the defects that you suggested to me when you visited the institution. I have provided clothing for the children, I have built the awning, I have covered the dinner-tables, and the fish sauce is all right." "Yes," said the governor, "I know that you are honest and faithful, and that you have done all these things, and I know that you are treating these children as kindly as your nature will permit; but you are not suited by nature to be the superintendent of an institution of that kind. If I wanted a warden for a State prison, if I wanted a master of a house of correction, or a first-class farmer, or an energetic, competent man to take charge of a gang of laborers, I would employ you. But I do not think that you are fit to take care of little children in an institution of that kind." "Perhaps you are right," said the superintendent, "I have some reason to think that my nature is too hard. Do you want my resignation to-day?" "No, certainly not," said the governor, "I do not wish to create a sensation about your removal, nor to do you any harm; but I shall be glad if you will look about and find some other employment, and if you want a recommendation from me I will give it you with great cheerfulness. When you have found such other employment, then send me your resignation." The resignation was received within a fortnight and his successor appointed. The superintendent had other employment, and there was no publicity given to the matter, and there was no cessation of the friendly relations that existed between the superintendent and the governor.

Offences that are committed with premeditation are called crimes. The governor must know all about them. He will know, whether he desires to or not. Still the administration of criminal law is a very great matter. The government of large cities and great communities is intricate, especially the criminal part of them. There are two systems of prison discipline in vogue in this country competing with each other for precedence. There is what we call the Pennsylvania system, or the solitary system, and the Auburn system,

or the congregate system.   The advocates of the Pennsylvania system, which is the solitary system, say in
favor of it that when a criminal enters a penitentiary
he goes into his cell and eats, sleeps, and works there,
and is seen by no person except his keeper during his
period of confinement; that he has no association whatever with his fellow-criminals, and learns no new
tricks, so that when he is discharged he goes into the
community comparatively a *fresh man.* [Applause.]
(Now I want to say to you Sophomores that there is no
pun intended.)   [Applause.]   That he cannot be recognized when he goes out into the community by anybody who has known him in prison; and, on the other
hand, that he has not mingled sufficiently with the
other criminals to have learned any new deviltry, so
as to be able to practise it on the resumption of his
liberty.   The advocates of the congregate system say
that the solitary system leads to a great amount of
insanity, and that it is cruel to shut a man out from all
human association; and they, therefore, think it better that the criminals shall have some association with
each other under proper restrictions, and that such
methods of discipline should be applied as will give
them as much reformation as is possible.

It is well enough to say right here that there are, as
a rule, two classes of criminals—criminals by nature, and criminals by association or by accident.
The one class may be reformed; the other cannot.   The
governor will make an inspection in course of the
prison similar to what I have described in the case
of the charitable institutions.   I once knew a governor
who visited the penitentiary of Massachusetts not very
long after he was inducted into office.   There were
about 750 criminals in the institution at that time.   He
went through the workshops and saw the criminals at

work, then he waited until after the working hours were over and the prisoners went to dinner. They repaired to their cells by way of the dining-room windows, and each took his pan of food into his cell. The governor took his seat in the centre of the place, and watched the criminals as they came out and returned to their work; and the first thing that struck his observation was the *apparent youthfulness* of these criminals. While the governor passed through the workshops and hospitals he had had pointed out to him old men between seventy and eighty years of age, and some octogenarians.

It occurred to him that if one hundred of the oldest of the prisoners were taken out, there would still remain 650, or thereabouts, criminals who must have committed their offences before they reached their majority. That to him was a most startling fact. He asked the warden if he could give him about the average age of the criminals, and the warden said the average was not far from twenty-four years; so that allowing for the time they had been in prison before and after sentence, and during their trial, they had probably committed their offences before they had reached their majority. That was, as has been already said, a very startling fact, and the governor inquired of the warden who these people were. Whence did they come? He had in view the finding out where such material was raised in the Commonwealth, and to see if that place was capable of producing anything better. The warden told him whence they came (I shall not tell you), and the governor set himself about investigating the matter. He went to the parties who were responsible and stated to them the startling fact. "Now," said the governor, "you are responsible for those criminal people, and it behooves you to make such appliances as shall stop the product of this number in future, and shall relieve the State from the ignominy of having within its borders and from the cost of maintaining so large a class of young criminals." These criminals were men who had not been overcome by misfortunes amid the temptations and trials of mature life, because they had committed their offences before they had reached practical manhood. "They must have been bad boys all their lives to become criminals of the highest class, save one, before they had reached their majority, and I must hold you responsible for them," said the governor.

I intended to say something about the pardoning power, and its exercise by the governor, about appointments to office, and about the militia, and such matters, but the time allotted me will not permit.

I will only say in general about pardons that no cases should be considered as subjects for exec tive clemency until *after trial* by the courts, and that the pardoning power should always remember that it is neither a legislature nor a court; it should therefore neither hear nor act upon any arguments upon the justice or expediency of the laws. It is the duty of the governor not to make but to execute the laws.

Neither should the pardoning power consider itself a *court* to try cases and determine the guilt or innocence of parties. But after the action of the courts the pardoning power may consider whether there are any mitigating circumstances which call for executive clemency—circumstances involving new mental or physical conditions of the criminal, new evidence, discovered since the trial, which had it been known would probably have influenced the verdict, or some like influential conditions.

If I were to attempt to describe to you events in detail under the head of sociology I should enter into a very broad field. The governor is invited everywhere, and is expected everywhere, and the people are dissatisfied if he does not go wherever he is invited. He must attend dinners, parties, receptions, social and patriotic occasions, commencements of colleges and universities, lyceums and associations. He must especially be present at the dedication of notable buildings and monuments; he must attend the centennial, the semi-centennial, bi-centennial anniversaries of the towns and cities. And they generally expect him to say something on these occasions. If the people are pleased with what he says, he is acquitted of any offence. [Laughter.] If they are not pleased, he is in danger of being sent to Coventry or somewhere else. It would be useless for me to attempt to describe to you a celebration or display or dedication of an important character in a city. Of course, everything that good taste can suggest, and that ample means can provide, is brought into requisition there. It will be intellectual, sumptuous, and otherwise a refined occasion. The best of everything and the best of everybody will be present.

In the rural district and country towns it is not always so, but the governor is expected to go to the rustic place as well as to the urban place; and I may as well say right here that one is just as genuine as the other. It would be unmanly to make any discrimination between places in this respect. The rustic citizen of a county town may have just as large, just as generous a heart as the most ostentatious citizen of a crowded city. Therefore the guests will find as much hospitality and as much genuine good feeling and respect in the one place as he will in the other, although the outward demonstration will be quite different. I have a mind to describe to you one of these celebrations in a rustic neighborhood.   If I do so, you must remember that all the incidents did not occur in a single place. Perhaps I may gather the incidents out of several places, combining them into one.   Possibly I may put in a little coloring from imagination. [Laughter.] But, after all, when you each become governor of a State, as General Butterfield evidently expects you will be, you will find that the picture that I shall paint will be substantially verified by your own experience. Well, let us suppose it is the centennial anniversary of Droll Town; we will call it that for the want of a better name.   [Laughter.]   The governor and his staff and other distinguished guests arrive in Droll Town in the early forenoon, and are met at headquarters by the town committee of arrangements, headed by a venerable octogenarian, a man who has held all the local offices in the town, has been justice of the peace, and is trustee for all the widows and half of the orphans in the neighborhood.   [Applause and laughter.]   The octogenarian gives the governor a homely but cordial welcome and describes to him the programme of the day.   He said: "We have borrowed two pieces of artillery for salutes, there is to be a trade procession, a dinner and speeches by illustrious persons. By the way," said he, "I suppose we ought to have fired a salute when you arrived, but the omission was not because we did not know we ought to do it, and we did not forget it either. But (rather confidentially) the fact is, that our folks are not much used to handling those big guns, and we killed our gunners firing the sunrise salute [applause and laughter], and inasmuch as we did not wish to depopulate the town, we thought we would not try any more experiments in artillery practice." The governor expressed his grateful appreciation of the intended honor, and, in consideration of his personal safety, said he would waive the firing of the salute. [Applause.] In due time the governor was escorted to join the procession. The roads were ground to powder by the practising of the procession during several of the preceding days, that they might all be in order.

The governor, his staff and others were, placed in open carriages, and in due time the procession was brought into line. There was the town militia company, and the town fire company with its engine was also there; and the tinsmith's cart, and whatever other resources and exponents of local industry they had were in the procession. It was intensely hot, as the rays of the sun poured down upon them. Just as the procession was about to start a cavalcade came into line directly in front of the governor's carriage. A cavalcade of 100 or more horses and riders. Such horses!— such riders!—[Laughter.] The dress of the riders was marvellous! it seemed as if the misfits had been gathered out of a carnival of tailors. [Laughter.] Some of the riders wore boots, some were barefooted! some rode saddleback, some bareback, and as they rode their trousers seemed to be ambitious to get above their necks. [Applause.] If it had not been for the peculiar shape of the human form divine, I think they would have gone over their heads. [Applause and laughter.] The horses—there is no knowing what half a peck of oats might have done for them. They were evidently straw-fed, each one hung his drowsy head with blinking eyes, while his tail hung behind like a plug of pig-iron. [Laughter.] Some were chafed and galled, and most of them uncurried. Each was a sort of dejected Bucephalus, which looked as if he were going into the galleys rather than to take part in a festive procession like this centennial. When the procession started, including the cavalcade, it was found that each of the horses had a back spring to his hind legs, similar to that of a cow running, as you have no doubt seen. Well, this motion stirred up the dust violently, and the procession had not gone far before the governor and the other guests looked as if they had served an apprenticeship in a flour-mill; and their faces were enamelled with dust held in place by the perspiration that oozed from every pore. The route of procession was laid around the town graveyard. I said that the roads had been well travelled during the preceding days. Around they went in the burning heat, and on the third or fourth time going around, the octogenarian pointed with his finger, directing the governor's attention, and said, "That is our town graveyard or cemetery." "Yes," said the governor, "I have seen that before," and he said to himself, "If you attempt to carry me around many times more, I shall certainly land inside of it." However, in due time the procession was dismissed and the announcement was made that dinner would be served in a neighboring grove in one hour from that time.

The governor seized the opportunity and went to a neighboring house, where he had an acquaintance, and ask for a bucket of water and a brush-broom and a hair-brush, and spent the next few moments endeavoring to rid himself of the dust that had accumulated upon his face and clothing. When he had accomplished that he returned to the grove, where there was a vast concourse of people gathered about the table, access to which was impossible to fresh comers. Finally the town constable appeared with his white staff, and the command was given to "Make room for the governor!" Room was soon made, a passage was opened, and he went to the table and took a seat beside the octogenarian, who was president of the day. The octogenarian apologized by saying: "Our folks got dreadfully uneasy and we did not know how to pacify them; so we had dinner a little ahead of time. But," said he, "we have saved yours." [Laughter.] The governor looked about but saw no crockery nor food upon the table. The octogenarian said, "You will find it in that paper box," which the governor uncovered and there he saw a doughnut and a piece of apple-pie. The chairman said, "I think if you dig down there you will find some meat or a piece of chicken."

The dinner being over, the literary exercises commenced. First there was a prayer, which was, of course, beyond comment; then there was an address of welcome by the chairman of the committee of arrangements, which was all very well. Then there was singing by the united choirs of Droll Town; and as they arose to perform this duty, one would have supposed they were a delegation from an old-folks' concert. Their harmony was as varied as their attire. Well, they gave us "America"—"My Country, 'Tis of Thee" —"Auld Lang Syne," and other patriotic and plaintive melodies. After that, the brass band gave us "Yankee Doodle," with an emphasis that thoroughly demonstrated the blatant powers of their trumpets and the strength of their drumheads. Then came an address by a young gentleman (I do not know that he was a graduate of any college, but he talked as if he might have been hopeful in that direction). Then came the oration of the day by the town cobbler, who had the reputation of being their *thinking man;* and as he *waxed* warm and long in his discourse the audience began to fear that they would be compelled to aid in finding his *waxed end.* [Laughter.]

The governor was at length called upon to say something, but fortunately for the multitude the train bell rang in the distance, the assemblage broke up, and the public exercises of the day were over. What the young men and maidens dreamed of the night following this most eventful day in their lives I cannot say, but the next days were solemnized by the funeral of the aspiring cannonaders who lost their lives in firing the sunrise salute; and then the centennial anniversary of Droll Town passed into history, the further details of which you will find in a volume when it shall be written.

Young gentlemen, I wish now that I could command some golden words, full of ennobling and inspiring thoughts, that should give you a higher appreciation than you ever had of the value and dignity of American citizenship. I believe it is the greatest worldly heritage ever vouchsafed to any people upon earth. I beg you to summon the heights and depths of your manhood, that you may enter into a just estimate of its value and a thorough perception of its great privileges and enjoyments. Sell your lives as American citizens for the most that you can get for them, and remember always that you owe your utmost and constant duty to God, to your country, and to mankind. [Applause.]

J. W. Clous.
Lt. Col., Deputy Judge Adv. Gen'l.
Professor of Law U.S.M.A.

JOHN W. CLOUS.

Lieutenant-Colonel John W. Clous, deputy judge-advocate general, professor of law of the United States Military Academy, was born in Germany in 1837. After completing his education he came to the United States and for a time followed mercantile pursuits. He entered the regular army as a private. In 1862, while serving as quartermaster-sergeant of the 6th U. S. Infantry, he was, in consequence of his "praiseworthy conduct during the movement of the Army of the Potomac from the Chickahominy to the James River, and his cool behavior at the battle of Malvern Hill in the performance of his duties"—appointed by President Lincoln to a second lieutenancy in that regiment. He remained on duty with the latter during its entire field service in the Army of the Potomac, participating in the battles, et cetera, in which his regiment took part. He was brevetted first lieutenant and captain for gallant and meritorious services in the battle of Gettysburg. He was regimental quarter-master from February 1st, 1864, to April 1st, 1865, and regimental adjutant from the latter date to March 28th, 1867. On March 28th, 1865, he was promoted first lieutenant in his regiment. After a short term of service at Savannah, Ga., and at Hilton Head, S. C., with his regiment, he took station at Charleston, S. C. While at this place, Lieutenant Clous, in addition to his duties as regimental adjutant, was in March, 1866, detailed as adjutant-general of the Department of South Carolina, continuing in that capacity upon the consolidation of the latter with the departments of the Carolinas and of the South, and subsequently into the Second Military District—of all of which Major-General Daniel E. Sickles was the permanent commander.

During his government and reconstruction of the States of North and South Carolina Lieutenant Clous rendered most valuable and efficient service. Having been appointed captain in the 38th Infantry, he was in September, 1867, at his own request, relieved from duty as adjutant-general.

Joining his company in March, 1868, in the Department of the

Missouri, Captain Clous took the field escorting the construction forces of the Union Pacific Railroad, E. D. (now Kansas Pacific). In October, 1868, he was detailed as an acting aide-de-camp on the staff of Major-General Sheridan during the latter's winter campaign against the hostile Indian tribes of the Southwest. Returning in March, 1869, he conducted an expeditionary force from Fort Hayes, Kans., through the Indian country to Fort Richardson, Tex. Having been, through consolidation, transferred to the 24th Infantry, Captain Clous served from 1869 to 1877 with his company on the frontier of Texas at Forts Griffin, McKavett, and Brown, taking part, in 1872, as acting engineer officer, in General Mackenzie's reconnaissance of, and expedition across, the Staked Plains, and in the Indian engagement of the latter's command on September 29th, 1872, at North Fork of the Red River, Texas. For gallant conduct in that engagement Captain Clous was specially mentioned by General Sherman in general orders published to the army.

Having begun the study of law before his entry into the army, Captain Clous continued the same during his military career and qualified himself for the bar. Beginning with his service as a commissioned officer of the army, he was frequently detailed as judge-advocate of general courts-martial and conducted many important trials. From January, 1881, to August, 1884, he served as judge advocate of the Department of Texas. In April, 1886, upon the recommendations of Major-General Hancock and other prominent officers of the army, as well as of the judges and lawyers of the bar of which he was a member, he was appointed major and judge-advocate. In May, 1887, upon motion of the Attorney-General of the United States, he was admitted as an attorney and counsellor of the Supreme Court of the United States. From May, 1886, to August, 1890, he served in Washington, as the assistant of the judge-advocate general of the army. On August 28th, 1890, he became, by assignment of the Secretary of War, professor of law of the United States Military Academy, West Point, N. Y., where he is now serving. On February 12th, 1892, he was promoted lieutenant-colonel and deputy judge-advocate general, United States Army.

MILITARY LAW, MARTIAL LAW,

AND THE

SUSPENSION OF THE WRIT OF HABEAS CORPUS.

By Lieut.-Colonel John W. Clous.

"The end of the law is peace. The means to that end is war."
—"The Struggle for Law," Von Ihering.

International law contemplates the world as divided into independent sovereign states, and regards these states as being either in a state of war or in a state of peace. It prescribes rules of conduct to be observed in the mutual dealings of nations which are at peace with each other, and of nations which are at war with each other; and it fixes the rights and duties of belligerents and neutral nations. The rules which govern nations in war are more voluminous and more certain than those which govern nations in time of peace.

The United States, upon ceasing to be a part of the British Empire and assuming the character of an independent nation, became subject to international law, and acquired thereby all the rights of a sovereign state admitted into the family of nations, and became charged with their corresponding duties and obligations. The most important of these is independence or, in other words, the right of a nation to a free and independent existence within its territorial limits, and to manage all its affairs, whether external or internal, without interference from other nations or states. This involves the corresponding obligation to abstain from interfering in the internal concerns of other sovereign states. This gives rise, first, To the right of self-preservation. This is called into being whenever the corporate existence of the state as a nation is menaced. It corresponds to the individual right of self-defence. The danger may be external or internal. A celebrated author said that "the right of self-preservation is the first law of nations as it is of individuals. A society which is not in a condition to repel aggressions from without is wanting in its principal duty to the members of which it is composed and to the chief end of its institution." Second, To the right of redress. As there is no authority to which a nation can appeal for redress when any of its sovereign rights have been trespassed upon, denied, or imperilled in their exercise, it is compelled, as a last resort, to redress its own injury or wrong. Again, in the performance of its duty of protecting its citizens and their property from acts of domestic violence, a government sometimes finds its ordinary legal machinery inadequate to the purpose, and is compelled to make use of the public armed force in order to compel obedience to the law, to quell insurrection and rebellion, or to enforce respect for its neutral obligations. In the exercise of both of these rights a nation organizes its land and naval forces in time of peace or war as it may deem them adequate to the national defence.

In recognition of these rights and duties as an independent nation the people of the United States, in the exercise of their sovereign power, have in their Constitution empowered Congress, as the legislative branch of the Government:

"To define and punish offences against the law of nations.

"To declare war, grant letters of marque and reprisal, and make rules concerning captures on land and water.

"To raise and support armies.

"To provide and maintain a navy.

"To make rules for the government and regulation of the land and naval forces.

"To provide for the calling forth the militia to execute the laws of the Union, suppress insurrection, and repel invasions.

"To provide for the organizing, arming, and disciplining the militia, and for governing such part of them as may be employed in the service of the United States," and further, generally, "To make all laws which shall be necessary and proper for carrying into execution the foregoing powers and all other powers vested by this Constitution in the Government of the United States or in any department or officer thereof."

To make these grants complete, the Constitution provides that "the President shall be Commander-in-Chief of the army and navy of the United States and of the militia of the several States when called into actual service of the United States," and further, that it shall be his duty to "take care that the laws be faithfully executed." And in the fifth amendment to the Constitution it is provided that "No person shall be held to answer for a capital or otherwise infamous crime unless on a presentment or indictment of a grand jury, except in cases arising in the land or naval forces, or in the militia when in actual service in time of war or public danger."

Under these powers Congress has from time to time authorized the raising and maintenance of an army, prescribed rules for its government, limited and defined the purposes for which it may be employed, and framed laws for the enrolling, organizing, governing, and calling forth of the militia. The Constitution and these enactments are the source and authority of our military law of to-day.

For a great number of years all military jurisdiction was generally termed "martial law," and it was not until about the commencement of the present century that a distinction between military and martial law was recognized.

The confusion in the application of these terms was due to the absence of investigation of the principles underlying each. Blackstone, in his Commentaries, says: "Martial law, which is built upon no settled principles, but is arbitrary in its decisions, is, as Sir Mathew Hale observes, in truth and reality no law, but something indulged in rather than allowed as law. The necessity of order and discipline in an army is the only thing which can give it countenance; and therefore it ought not to be permitted in time of peace, when the higher courts are open for all persons to receive justice according to the law of the land."

Sir Mathew Hale and Sir William Blackstone, men profoundly versed in the civil law of their country, which they have most ably explained and illustrated, have but incidentally touched on the subject of martial law, of which they had no call to propound the doctrines, and therefore were at no pains to investigate the principles. Had these great masters of civil jurisprudence bestowed the same attention on this subject that they have exercised on those which fell immediately within their own department, we should not have met with the rash and ill-founded positions just quoted.

While well-known commentators of our own time and our own country have copied and adhered to these erroneous views, other writers have made a distinction between military and martial law by defining the former to be the law which relates to the government and discipline of the military forces of a state, and the latter as consisting in the right to govern by military force the territory of the enemy, or to apply a like rule of government at home to cases of insurrection, rebellion, or domestic violence when the public danger requires its exercise. But it remained for the Chief Justice of the United States, when speaking for the minority of the Supreme Court, in the case of *Ex parte* Milligan, to analyze, define, and separate the different kinds of military jurisdiction. Omitting from this opinion such parts as are not in harmony with, nor opposed to, the decision of the court in this celebrated case we find the following: "There are . . . three kinds of military jurisdiction: one to be exercised both in peace and war: another to be exercised in time of foreign war without the boundaries of the United States, or in time of rebellion and civil war within the States or districts occupied by rebels treated as belligerents; and a third to be exercised in time of invasion or insurrection within the limits of the United States, or during rebellion within the limits of States maintaining adhesion to the National Government, when public danger requires its exercise. The first of these may be called jurisdiction under military law, and is found in Acts of Congress prescribing rules and articles of war, or otherwise providing for the government of the National forces. The second may be distinguished as military government, superseding, as far as may be deemed expedient, the local law, and exercised by the military commander under the direction of the President . . . ; while the third may be denominated martial law proper, and is called into action . . . in the case of justifying or excusing peril, by the President, in times of insurrection of invasion or of civil or foreign war, within districts or localities where ordinary law no longer adequately secures public safety and private right."

This modified definition of the subject is more nearly in accord with the history of the exercise of the various kinds of military jurisdiction since the formation of our Government. Similar distinctions had not only been made by the eminent jurist, the Honorable Caleb Cushing, while Attorney-General of the United States, but have also been followed by well-known publicists and law writers. They are to-day the foundation of text-books on military law.

For the purposes of this paper a similar division will be followed, and military law, or the law administered by the military power, will be divided into—I. Military Law Proper. II. The Law of War.

I. Military Law Proper.

This is defined to be the specific law which governs the army, as a separate community, alike in peace and in war. By entering into this community the citizen becomes a soldier. His relations to the state and to the public are changed. He acquires a new status with correlative rights and duties. He waives, in some particulars, his rights as a civilian, surrenders his personal liberty during the existence of his new status, and consents to come and go at the will of his superior officers. He agrees to relinquish his right to trial by jury, to become amenable to the military courts, and to be disciplined for offences unknown to the civil law. The very nature of this community makes it evident that it cannot be governed by the code of laws which applies to the great body of citizens. Military exigencies require, not individual liberty, but subordination, obedience. The very rules which are found to protect the individual rights of the people would destroy an army. But this subjection of the soldier to the military code does not place him beyond the jurisdiction of the civil law of the land. He is equally, with all other classes of citizens, bound to the same strict observance of the laws of the country, and is alike amenable to the ordinary civil and criminal courts of the country in any matter properly coming within their cognizance.

Our military law in its origin is considerably older than the Constitution.

A majority of our present Articles of War, which form the greatest part of our written military law, are derived from those adopted by the Continental Congress between 1775–1786, which were themselves taken from pre-existing British articles having their origin in remote antiquity.

From historical research, it seems that in England in former days every commander of an army, under the authority given him in his commission by the crown, enacted "ordinances" for the government of his forces, or the sovereign with the advice of the constable or the peers issued "Articles of War" for the same purpose.

Grosse, in his "Military Antiquities," gives the ordinances for those going by sea to the Holy Land in the time of Richard I. They state that a man drawing his knife on another was to have his hand cut off, that a murderer was to be tied to the dead body and cast into the sea, or if on shore, buried with it; that a thief was to have his head shaved, to be then tarred and feathered and put on shore. In the same work are also to be found the regulations for the government of the English armies during the Fifteenth, Sixteenth, and Seventeenth Centuries. The punishments mentioned in them are very severe. Just before the issuance by the Earl of Northumberland of the articles of 1639, under the authority of Charles I., there appeared in London a publication of the code of Gustavus Adolphus published to his army in 1621. This code left its impress upon the English codes of a later date, and even in our own Articles of War of to-day may be found quaint expressions traceable to this early code.

The prerogative to command and regulate the military force of the kingdom rested with the crown. This was acknowledged in Edward I.'s time, and a clause made that punishment should not extend to life and limb.

Up to 1689 the *personnel* of the army of England was regarded as so many personal retainers of the sovereign rather than the servants of the State, and mainly governed by the will of the sovereign, under the ordinances and articles described. But after the Revolution the relative positions of the army and the nation were considerably changed. A standing army became necessary for the defence of the country against anticipated invasion. The Bill of Rights had, in a great measure, tied the hands of King William III. as the commander-in-chief; the necessity for the better government of the standing army, although already manifest, became intensified when the king ordered the Royal Scots to be sent to Holland to replace some Dutch troops. Believing that the king could not send them out of the country, they seized four guns and the military chest and marched for Scotland. They were subdued, but the king knew not how to deal with the mutineers as such. This caused the passage by Parliament, April 3d, 1689, of the famous act known as the Mutiny Act, in which it was stated that the maintenance of standing armies and the holding of courts-martial in the kingdom, unless by consent of Parliament, was unlawful; but, in consideration of the perils of the time, no man mustered in the pay of the crown should desert or mutiny on pain of death. This act has been annually renewed with few exceptions, and was gradually enlarged from time to time. In consequence the British army was governed for years by a military code, partly found in an act of Parliament, and partly in articles of war promulgated by the sovereign. This led eventually to occasional variance between them. To remedy this, Parliament in 1879 consolidated the Mutiny Act and the articles in one statute, known as the Army Discipline and Regulation Act.

Let us now take a glance at the origin of the courts and instrumentalities by which these military codes were administered. English history tells us that in the early times military offences were punished under the direction of the lord high constable and the marshal or earl marshal; the former was originally the king's general and the latter usually the second in command. These two great officers together constituted the Court of Chivalry, and formed part of the *Aula Regia* established in England by William the Conqueror. In time of war this court followed the army, and punished summarily, according to the Articles of War or Ordinances for the time being in force. When military operations were carried on in different quarters, the crown, by special commission, created several constables and marshals, in order to provide for the administration of military law at different places. In time the Court of Chivalry began to encroach on the Courts of Common Law; acts were passed limiting its power, and it practically became extinct in the reign of Henry VIII. The jurisdiction to administer military law was then vested in the commanders-in-chief, who, in their commissions from the sovereign, were authorized to sit in judgment themselves, or to appoint deputies for that purpose. These deputies, so appointed, were army officers, and out of their sitting arose a new form of court, under the name of Council of War, and instead of a marshal we find an officer styled president of the High Court of War. In time these courts and councils became known as courts-marshal, and from them our present courts-martial have taken their present form.

Our military law proper, or, as we will now term it, in general, simply military law, in contradistinction to the law administered by the civil tribunals, consists, like the latter, in a written and an unwritten law. The written military law consists of the Articles of War, Army Regulations, and General and Special Orders.

The Articles of War, as has already been stated, are derived from those adopted by the Continental Congress, which were themselves taken from pre-existing British articles. The first code adopted was that of 1775—it was reported by a committee composed of George Washington, Philip Schuyler, Silas Deane, Thomas Cushing, and Joseph Hewitt, and consisted of the existing British code in force in the ministerial army. But it did not remain long in force, for in the following year, under the direction of Congress, a committee consisting of John Adams, Thomas Jefferson, John Rutledge, James Wilson, and R. R. Livingston prepared new articles of war, which were agreed to by Congress on September 20th, 1776. This code was an enlargement with modifications of that of 1775. It remained in force till after the date of the adoption of the Constitution, undergoing certain amendments, and was then expressly recognized and made to apply to the existing army. By the act of April 10th, 1806, a new code was inaugurated, which in turn was superseded by the revised code of 1874, which, together with certain amendments, is in force to-day. In all the amendments and changes made many of the articles remain the same as originally adopted from the British code.

Army Regulations are authoritative directions as to the details of military duty and discipline. The authority for them is found in the distinctive functions of the President as Commander-in-Chief and as Executive. The Supreme Court held that " The power of the Executive to establish rules and regulations for the government of the army is undoubted; and that the power to establish implies necessarily the power to modify or repeal or create anew." But to have legal effect regulations must not contravene existing law and must not legislate.

The remaining component part of written military law embraces the General and Special Orders emanating from the War Department or issued by Commanders of Departments. Special Orders relate to individuals, by which direction is given as to change of stations, details for special service, and the like. General Orders cover a great variety of particulars connected with the discipline, employment, pay, etc., of the army.

The unwritten military law consists of certain established principles and usages peculiar or pertaining to the military status and service, and which, though unenacted, are recognized in the 84th Article of War under the designation of " The Customs of War," as a means for the guiding of courts-martial in the administration of justice in doubtful cases. The same are also recognized by the courts and legal authorities as operative and conclusive as to questions in regard to which the written military law is silent.

Justice is administered in the army under the provisions of the Articles of War by courts-martial, and the jurisdiction over offences is, with some minor exceptions, principally divided between the General Court-Martial and the Inferior Courts-Martial. Only minor offences committed by enlisted men are tried before the latter, and their power of punishment is limited to a fine not exceeding one month's pay and confinement, or hard labor for one month. The former, however, has jurisdiction of all offences committed by commissioned officers and the more serious offences committed by soldiers.

Of the Inferior Courts-Martial the Summary Court is the principal one. It consists of the officer next in rank to the commanding officer and is in time of peace a permanent institution in every post or garrison. All minor offences committed by soldiers must be brought before it, within twenty-four hours from the time of the arrest of the offender. Its procedure is summary in character and not unlike that of the ordinary municipal police courts. No record is kept of the testimony. The offence committed, the plea, the findings, and sentence, if any, are entered in a docket. The judgment of the court is subject to the approval of the commanding officer, who may either approve the punishment awarded or remit or mitigate it, if in his judgment it should be necessary.

Any general officer commanding an army or territorial division or a department, a colonel commanding a separate department, may appoint General Courts-Martial whenever necessary. When, however, any such commander is the accuser or prosecutor of any officer under his command, the court must be appointed by the President. While there is no specific enactment authorizing the President to institute such courts, generally the power to do so is included in his constitutional functions of Commander-in-Chief. In time of war commanders of divisions and separate brigades are also empowered to convene General Courts Martial.

General Courts-Martial may consist of any number of officers from five to thirteen, and when it can be avoided, no officer is to be tried by officers inferior to him in rank. The senior officer on the detail presides, preserves order, and acts as the organ of the court. A judge-advocate is detailed for the court whose duty it is to prosecute in the name of the United States; but when the prisoner has made his plea, he must so far consider himself the counsel of the prisoner as to protect the essential rights of the prisoner. The judge-advocate is also the legal adviser of the court, and must act as recorder.

The procedure of General Courts-Martial is, as far as possible, assimilated to that of the civil courts of criminal jurisdiction. The accused may challenge any member of the court for cause. He is allowed counsel, and if he is a soldier and applies for counsel, the commanding officer is bound to detail a competent officer to assist him in his defence. The members of the court are sworn to truly try and determine, according to evidence before them, and administer justice without partiality, favor, or affection, according to the provisions of the Rules and Articles of War; and if any doubt should arise, not explained by the said articles, then according to their conscience, the best of their understanding, and the customs of war in like cases.

The court combines the functions of judge and jury,—judging of the facts as well as of the law. It determines the guilt or innocence of the accused, and, in case of conviction, pronounces sentence. While Congress has authorized courts-martial, established their composition, jurisdiction, and rules of procedure, it has never prescribed the rules of evidence which shall govern their proceedings. Being courts of criminal jurisdiction, courts-martial must therefore adhere to the rules of evidence of the United States criminal courts. These rules are the common-law rules of evidence in criminal cases except where Congress has prescribed otherwise. The only other exceptions which are permitted are those which are of necessity created by the nature of the service, and by the constitution of the court and its course of procedure. The testimony of the witnesses before General Courts-Martial and all material proceedings are reduced to writing; in important cases, however, a stenographer is appointed, and then the examination of witnesses is conducted orally by both sides and the same freedom of addressing the court, making objections, etc., is accorded counsel as in civil courts. The record of the court is upon the completion of the case submitted to the officer convening the court for his action. The sentence of a court-martial is interlocutory and inchoate till confirmed. It is not definitive, but merely in the nature of an inquest to inform the conscience of the commanding officer. He alone could not punish without the judgment of the court-martial, and it is clear that the court could not punish without his order of confirmation. The commanding officer may approve or disapprove the proceedings or any part thereof, and he may remit or mitigate any punishment awarded.

The offences brought to the cognizance of courts-martial are defined in the Articles of War, and may be divided into offences against authority, peace, and good order; execution of duty; persons under civil authority; involving cowardice or treachery, etc.

The punishments which may be awarded were, under the code, in a majority of cases for a number of years discretionary with courts-martial, but two years ago

Congress authorized the President to prescribe the limits
of such punishments, and he has consequently issued a
scale of punishments, which is rigidly adhered to.   Unusual or cruel punishments in the army are not permitted; and the infliction of arbitrary punishment is
of the rarest occurrence, and when brought to the attention of higher authority its author is promptly brought
to justice.

The officer and the soldier have also the protection of
the civil law. An inferior may sue a superior for an
alleged illegal or excessive punishment inflicted, unreasonable measure of discipline enforced, or unauthorized arrest imposed, and although the court-martial has
as such no judicial superior to which appeal can be
taken from its judgment, yet when its action has been
unauthorized and illegal and upon approval effectuated,
a person who has suffered therefrom may pursue his
remedy in the civil courts.

Analyzing this code we find that it exacts from all
officers and soldiers implicit obedience to all lawful orders of their superiors, faithful performance of every
military duty and orderly behavior, on or off duty, in
or out of the garrison. While it recognizes the exclusive jurisdiction of military authority in the lawful
administration of legal punishments for purely military
offences, it also asserts the principle of subordination of
the military authority to the civil, and of the consequent amenability of military persons in their civil
capacity to the civil jurisdiction for breaches of the
criminal law of the land. It decrees that an officer of
the army found guilty of conduct unbecoming an
officer and a gentleman shall be dismissed, and thus,
in the language of the Supreme Court of the United
States, in a leading case, extends the jurisdiction of
courts-martial to the trial and punishment of acts of

military officers which tend to bring disgrace and reproach upon the service of which they are members, whether those acts are done in the performance of military duties, or in a civil position, or in a social relation, or in private business.

It will thus be perceived that this code, with the agencies therein established for its execution, affords ample aid to the Executive in properly commanding the army and enforcing discipline therein under his orders or those of his authorized military representatives. In other words, it supplies that "authority from above," and requires that "obedience from below," which is necessary to "make up the soul of the army—in one word, discipline." A celebrated general of modern times has aptly remarked that an army without discipline is always costly, in war useless, and in peace dangerous.

Our present military code, which has practically been in force for more than a century, has governed our armies in peace and in war, at home and abroad, in the midst of civilization and on the frontier, in warfare with savages and in struggles with the trained soldiery of foreign nations. It has served its purposes in the greatest of modern civil wars, and formed the rule of conduct for the Union as well as for the rebel forces. Its efficacy must be judged by its results. It may contain some obsolete features and be antiquated in some of its language, but in the main it is simple and well adapted to the great body of citizen soldiery which in the past has been governed by it.

II. *The Law of War.*

In a general sense the law of war is that branch of international law which regulates the intercourse of belligerents during war—war being itself defined as

"an armed contest between states or parts of states,"
or as "that state in which a nation prosecutes its rights
by force." But jurists, publicists, and text-writers of
modern times have given the term "law of war" a
more definite and specific meaning. "By it," says Col.
Winthrop, in his treatise on military law, "is intended
those principles and usages which in time of war
define the rights and obligations, and regulate the relations, not only of enemies—whether or not in arms—
but also of persons under military government or martial law, and persons simply resident or being upon the
theatre of war, and which authorize their trial and
punishment when offenders."

"The law of war in this country is not a formal
written code, but consists mainly of general rules derived from the law of nations, supplemented by acts
and orders of the military power and a few legislative
provisions."

Laws for the amelioration of severity in wars are of
very ancient date in European history. These laws
are constantly changing to adapt them to the ever-
changing conditions of modern warfare and advancing
civilization. The tendency of these changes is, and
always has been, in the direction of greater humanity
and liberality. Harsh usages are modified, cruel practices become obsolete, or are abandoned by treaty or
general consent, and new methods are constantly suggested for diminishing the inevitable hardships of war.

The most important contribution in this direction
was furnished by the United States during our War of
the Rebellion. Recognizing the necessity of a positive
code of instructions to our armies, Mr. Lincoln requested Dr. Francis Lieber, an eminent jurist and
publicist, to prepare such instructions. He formulated
a set of comprehensive rules which, after approval by

a board of officers, were published to the armies of the United States in 1863 for their government and guidance. These rules are to-day the law for our army, they have furnished the basis for the works of modern text-writers upon the usages of war, and are accepted as a standard of authority, having been practically carried out during one of the greatest contests of modern times.

Sheldon Amos, an English writer of note, in speaking of Dr. Lieber's code, says: "This is a matter of some interest, because of the close relationship observable between these instructions and the regulations of the so-called Prussian Military Code, a code which has never been published, but the substance of which can be pretty accurately collected from the constant references made to it by Prussian commanders in the proclamations and manifestoes issued in the course of the late invasion of France. The instructions here referred to were, in fact, the first attempt to make a comprehensive survey of all the exigencies to which a war of invasion is likely to give rise, and it is said on good authority that, with one exception (that of concealing in an occupied district arms and provisions for the enemy), no case presented itself during the Franco-German War in 1870 which had not been provided for in the American instructions."

The work thus begun by President Lincoln for the alleviation of the miseries of war brought its fruits on the other side of the Atlantic.

In 1864 a convention was signed at Geneva, which has since been acceded to by the United States and by all the European Powers, laying down rules for the treatment of the sick and wounded, and those who tend them in time of war. Under it the neutralization of ambulances and military hospitals, and of all persons engaged in the medical service, or the transportation of the wounded, and also of Chaplains, has been effected, and a distinctive badge, a red cross on a white field, adopted.

Time and place forbid me to enter into an extended discussion of the law of war; a consideration of some of the general rules as evidenced by the practice of our wars will be sufficient to illustrate the subject.

While the law of war is, in general, quite independent of the ordinary law, yet where it affects the rights of our own people the commander and those acting under him are responsible to the courts of the land for any act not justified by the law of war. This is particularly illustrated in the taking or destruction of personal property. It is a rule that an army operating in time of war in our own territory can take or destroy private property by way of military necessity; the circumstances must be most urgent; the exigency immediate, not contingent or remote. This rule laid down by the Supreme Court of the United States has been observed in repeated subsequent adjudications.

The effect of a war duly declared, or officially recognized, is to place every individual of the one belligerent Power in legal hostility to every individual of which the other belligerent Power is composed, and these individuals retain the legal character of enemies, in whatever country they may be found. War effects an absolute interruption of all commercial intercourse and dealings between the subjects of the two countries. All the property of the one state and each of its citizens is deemed hostile with respect to the opposing belligerents.

It is a general rule that in carrying on war no greater harm shall be done the enemy than necessity requires for the purpose of bringing him to terms.

This principle concludes gratuitous barbarities and every description of cruelty and insult that serve only to exasperate the sufferings of the enemy without weakening his strength. To take the lives of, or commit violence against non-combatants and private individuals not in arms, including women and children and the sick, or also persons taken prisoners or surrendering, is strictly prohibited.

Under the humane maxims of modern international law private property of enemies is seized only by way of military necessity for the support or other benefit of the army. Public institutions of a civil character such as state houses, court houses, churches, asylums, colleges, museums and the like, are exempted from the operations of war, and works of art, libraries, scientific collections are protected by the enemy from destruction and all unavoidable injury.

Guerilla warfare, abuse of a flag of truce, improper treatment of prisoners of war, are offences against the law of war and severely punished by all civilized nations.

The law of occupation or rules relating to military government form an important branch of our law of war and require special mention. This sort of government is defined by Chief Justice Chase as a form of "military jurisdiction to be exercised under the discretion of the President, in time of foreign war without the boundaries of the United States, or in time of rebellion and civil war within States and districts occupied by rebels treated as belligerents."

Under the instructions laid down for the government of the army of the United States, military rule in a hostile country consists "in the suspension, by the occupying military authority, of the criminal and civil law, and of the domestic administration and government in the occupied place or territory, and in the substitution of military rule and force for the same, as well as in the dictation of general laws as far as military necessity requires this suspension, substitution, or dictation.

"The commander of the forces may proclaim that the administration of all civil and usual law shall continue, either wholly or in part, as in times of peace, unless otherwise ordered by the military authority."

The Supreme Court of the United States, in speaking of this power, said that the governing authority "may do anything necessary to strengthen itself and weaken the enemy. There is no limit to the powers that may be exerted in such cases save those which are found in the laws and usages of war. . . . In such cases the laws of war take the place of the Constitution and laws of the United States as applied in time of peace."

Under this power General Kearny organized a provisional civil government in taking possession of New Mexico in 1846 and in California in 1847; both of these governments were held to be legal by the Supreme Court.

During the War of the Rebellion, judges were appointed and courts created in many places in the Southern States by the military commanders. The courts exercised all the jurisdiction, criminal and civil, which belonged under ordinary circumstances to civil courts, and in the cases where their judgments came before the Supreme Court of the United States their jurisdiction was upheld.

In Mexico General Scott established a civil police to act in conjunction with the army. In the Southern States military commanders instituted quarantine regulations, regulated the employment of the freedmen, and provided for the education of their children.

As an aid for the exercise of military government,

and as an instrumentality for the more efficient execution of the law of war, military commissions are
created. These have in practice been constituted by
the same commanders as are empowered to order general courts-martial. They have been composed of
officers of the army, and commonly conducted according
to the rules and forms governing courts-martial.

The jurisdiction of military commissions is territorially restricted to the theatre of war, or to the place or
district under military government, and, in respect to
the character of offences, confined to violations of the
law of war, crimes and offences cognizable by the local
courts, but which cannot be tried by such courts because not open or in operation, and to breaches of military orders and regulations committed by persons not
triable by courts-martial under the Articles of War.
The persons amenable to this jurisdiction are individuals of the enemy's army, inhabitants of the enemy's
country, and officers and soldiers of our army, or persons
serving with it, who in time of war become charged
with offences and cognizable under the Articles of War.

In connection with the subject of the law of war may
be noticed the military government of the Southern
States during the period of reconstruction of 1867–70.

Some months after the cessation of hostilities in the
field between the contending forces and after the dis-
banding of the rebel army and the honorable discharge
of the volunteer forces of the Union army, President
Johnson issued a proclamation delaring the War of the
Rebellion to be at an end.

The constitutionality of this act was questioned by
Congress on the ground that the legislative branch of
the Government, being empowered by the Constitution
to declare war and suppress insurrection, was the only
authority to determine when the rebellion should be

considered as finally suppressed and the pre-existing normal condition restored.

The power to re-establish the broken relations of the rebel States with the Union was claimed to reside in Congress by reason of the provision in the Constitution that "the United States shall guarantee to every State in this Union a republican form of government."

This claim was subsequently supported by the Supreme Court in a decision in which it was held that "the power to carry into effect the clause of guaranty is primarily a legislative power and resides in Congress." Congress, by the acts of March 2d and 23d, 1867, and July 19th, 1867, placed the insurrectionary States under military government, in which they were to remain until they had under certain prescribed conditions formed new State constitutions, organized new State governments, adopted the then pending constitutional amendments, and had been restored to their constitutional relations.

An unwelcome task of great magnitude was thus imposed upon the army by the political power of the Government. The rebel States were divided into five military districts, and the officers entered upon their duties. While in general each branch of the existing civil authority was left to discharge its appropriate functions, yet the military exercised a general supervision, removing civil officers and making new appointments when occasion demanded. The legislative power was exercised in the interest of the people; for instance, in some districts the commanders abolished imprisonment for debt, suspended the sale of property on execution for one year where unreasonable sacrifice and oppression would result, made wages for labor a lien on the crop, and abolished the punishment of crimes by maiming and branding.

The police and constabulary of cities, towns, and counties were placed under the immediate direction of the military in the interest of law and order. In fine, all the phases of civil government were at one time or other administered by military officers during the critical years of reconstruction.

The manifestations of arbitrary power by individual officers were unfrequent. The officers of the army discharged their duties conscientiously to the best of their abilities, earning the respect and good-will of those whom they had formerly encountered on the field of battle, and the gratitude of those who had suffered from oppression.

We now come to consider "*Martial Law*"; and, as incident thereto, the *Suspension of the Writ of Habeas Corpus.*

Martial Law is military rule exercised by the United States, or a State, over its own citizens in an emergency justifying it—*i.e.*, when ordinary law no longer secures public safety and private rights.

The origin of "Martial Law" is to be found in English history. We have seen in the first part of this paper that in the early days of England the constable and the earl marshal administered justice in the army. This gave rise to the term "Law of the Marshal," in which was comprehended both the rule necessary for the government of the army, and also for the government of the occupied territory or district while the ordinary law was in abeyance. In course of time the "Law of the Marshal" came to be called "Martial Law," a term signifying both the rule or law which governed, during times of disturbance, the population generally, and also the law for the government of the forces.

When a standing army was established in England

this term continued to be applied to the rule by which the army was governed, both in war and peace, and at the same time retained its meaning as the special government established for disturbed districts during times of war and rebellion. This original double meaning of the term had led to misunderstanding as to its present meaning, and to the confusion by many writers of "Martial Law" and "Military Law." But whatever the original meaning of martial law may have been, it is now distinctly understood to be the term applied to describe the authorized use of military force and jurisdiction when ordinary law is in abeyance.

In the days of the Tudors and other English sovereigns of former days, the power to punish civilians in time of peace by martial law was often assumed. And the attempt by Charles I. to enforce this power was considered as an attempt to undermine the liberties of England, and as one of the causes of the great rebellion.

The subject of martial law has been much discussed in Great Britain and has been the subject of many treatises and some judicial decisions. Martial law as such has not been proclaimed in England since 1688. There is in that country a system of laws in existence relating to unlawful assemblies, riots, and insurrections under which the military acting in aid of civil authority may attack mobs not duly dispersing. These laws seem to have proved sufficient for the suppression of such disorders as have occurred. That martial law may be resorted to in the event of actual rebellion seems to be conceded. That it has been repeatedly resorted to outside of England—*i.e.*, in Ireland and in the British colonies—is a matter of history.

In the United States the question whether there is

any exigency under which the Government may suspend the guarantees of civil liberty as to persons not in the military service, and place them under military jurisdiction, or, in other words, initiate martial law, has received both a practical and a judicial answer, and the one contradicts in some respects the other.

In our history we find that martial law was proclaimed in 1775 in Boston by General Gage, and in Virginia by Governor Dunmore. General Wilkinson substantially exercised it in Louisiana during the Burr conspiracy in 1806. In 1814, when the British forces threatened the city of New Orleans, General Andrew Jackson placed that city and its environs under the strictest sort of military rule, which he maintained for some months.

The most marked illustrations of the assertion and exercise of this power are furnished in the period during and immediately succeeding the late War of the Rebellion. Martial law was introduced throughout the whole United States; both upon the immediate theatre of the conflict, and at points territorially far removed from it. The proclamation of the President of September 24th, 1862, made subject to martial law "not only insurgent enemies in the insurrectionary States, but also their aiders and abettors within the United States, and all persons discouraging volunteer enlistments, resisting militia drafts, or guilty of any disloyal practice affording aid and comfort to rebels against the authority of the United States."

On July 5th, 1864, the President established martial law in Kentucky, not because that State was then the immediate theatre of war, but for the reason that combinations had been formed within that State with the purpose of inciting the rebel forces to renew their previous operations of civil war and thereby embarrass the United States armies operating elsewhere. The civil government of the State was left in the discharge of all its functions, except on such matters as affected the military operations or the constituted authorities of the Government of the United States.

In 1861, General Fremont declared martial law in Missouri. In 1862 the State of Kansas was placed under military rule with a view of suppressing "jay-hawking," and many other instances occurring during the late war might be cited.

Of recent instances of the exercise of this power after the close of the War of the Rebellion may be cited the action of the commanding general at New Orleans when, on July 30th, 1866, he resorted to the declaration of martial law on the occasion of a serious riot.

Under the reconstruction acts of Congress of 1867 the Southern States that had taken part in the War of the Rebellion were practically placed under martial law, and in 1871, during the so-called "Ku-Klux" disturbances, the President in certain designated counties of South Carolina suspended the privilege of the writ of habeas corpus and thus initiated martial law.

While these instances occurred under the Government of the United States, history supplies us with cases in which this authority was invoked by States. On the occasion of the so-called Dorr rebellion in Rhode Island in 1842 the legislature placed the State under martial law. During the War of the Rebellion the legislatures and the governors of some of the States of the Southern Confederacy, as well as the executive of the Confederacy, did not hesitate to exercise similar authority in territory not the immediate theatre of war.

In the Territory of Washington during the Chinese riots of 1886 the governor proclaimed martial law, and was seconded in his efforts by the President of the

United States.   And the most recent successful application of this power is found in the action of the governor of Idaho in the case of the Cœur d'Alene mines. Although not strictly in the line of the precedents quoted, we ought not to omit to call attention to the array of militia in Tennessee, at the Homestead (Pennsylvania) Mills, and the extensive railroad depots at Buffalo, N. Y., as illustrations of the necessity of military force as an aid to the civil authority in securing the protection of life and property when the ordinary safeguards of civil law are inadequate.

Having disposed of the practical answer to this question from history, we now come to the judicial answer. In a case arising out of the Dorr rebellion in Rhode Island, the Supreme Court held that "if the government of Rhode Island deemed armed opposition . . . so formidable . . . as to require . . . the declaration of martial law, we see no good ground upon which the court can question the authority." In the Milligan case, which arose in 1864 through his trial and conviction by military commission in Indiana for inciting insurrection, etc., the Supreme Court of the United States held that martial law "was confined to the locality of actual war," and also that it "can never exist when the courts are open and in the proper and unobstructed exercise of their jurisdiction." "If in foreign invasion or civil war the courts are actually closed, and it is impossible to administer criminal justice according to law, then on the theatre of active military operations, where war really prevails, there is a necessity to furnish a substitute for the civil authorities thus overthrown to preserve the safety of the army and society; and as no power is left but the military, it is allowed to govern by martial rule until the laws can have their free course." This ruling was made by a bare majority of five, the opinion of the other four members, as delivered by the chief justice, was to the effect that martial law may be called into action by Congress and is not necessarily limited to the time of war but may be exercised at other periods of "public danger," and the fact that the civil courts are open is not controlling against such exercise, since they "might be open and undisturbed in the execution of their functions and yet wholly incompetent to avert threatened danger or to punish with adequate promptitude and certainty the guilty."

This case was decided by the Supreme Court on the last day of the December term of 1865, but the opinion of the court was not handed down until the first day of the corresponding term in 1866. Congress in the face of this decision almost immediately passed the act approved March 2d, 1867, in which it approved all acts, proclamations, and orders of the President and acts done by his authority between the 4th of March, 1861, and the 1st of July, 1866, respecting martial law, military trials, arrests and trials of persons charged with participating in the rebellion or aiding the same as being guilty of disloyal practices. And the acts done or proceedings had in this connection were to be regarded with the same validity as if they had been done under the previous and express authority of Congress. The civil courts of the United States and of the States were by this act especially barred from taking jurisdiction of or in any manner reversing any of the proceedings had or acts done as mentioned. All officers and other persons in the service of the United States who had acted in the premises were to be held *prima facie* to have been authorized.

Similar indemnity acts, though not quite so sweeping in character, had been passed by Congress on March 3d, 1863, and May 11th, 1866. In respect to these the Supreme Court in 1883, in the case of Mitchell *vs.* Clark, said: "For most of the acts," covered by the statutes in question, "there was constitutional power in Congress to have authorized them if it had acted in the matter in advance. It is possible that in a few cases for acts performed in haste and in the presence of overpowering emergency that there are no constitutional powers anywhere to make them good." . . . "That an act passed after the event which in effect ratifies what has been done, and declares that no suit shall be sustained against the party acting under authority, is valid, so far as Congress could have conferred such authority before, admits of no doubt. These are ordinary acts of indemnity passed by all governments when the occasion requires it."

The act complained of in this case was done in St. Louis by a military commander when that city was not the theatre of war and when all the courts were open and in the discharge of their functions.

Contemporaneously with the indemnity legislation of March 2d, 1867, and subsequent to the promulgation of the opinion in the Milligan case, Congress passed the first reconstruction act and placed the rebel States practically under martial law. This act and the acts of July 1st, 1867, amendatory thereof came before the Supreme Court of the United States in the case of Texas *vs.* White. In its December term of 1868 the court upheld these acts upon the grounds already stated in this paper.

In 1871 Congress passed the so-called Ku-Klux acts, and authorized the suspension of the writ of habeas corpus and the institution of martial law in certain localities in the South. The courts were open and a state of war did not exist.

From this statement of facts it has been argued that

the judicial answer, whether or not martial law may be instituted, is not free from contradiction. It is said that while in 1866, in the Milligan case, the Supreme Court confined the legal exercise of martial law to the locality of actual war when the courts are closed, yet in 1883, in the case of Mitchell *vs.* Clark, it sustained the exercise of martial law power by a commanding general at a time when the courts were open at a locality removed from the theatre of war. Further, that it spoke in the same case with approval of the acts of indemnity passed by Congress in 1863 and 1866. This has been construed by some writers into a recognition not only of the power of Congress to pass laws for the institution of martial law in time of public danger at places remote from the actual theatre of war, but also of the right of the President to act in this respect in cases of imminent peril when Congress could not be called together. An examination, however, of the questions involved in the latter case does not justify the conclusion that the court meant to contradict its decision in the Milligan case, and to lay down a different theory of martial law from that of necessity as there explained.

Under the Constitution it is made the duty of the United States to protect each of the States against domestic violence. Congress has early in the existence of our Government authorized the President in case of an insurrection in any State against the government thereof, on application of the legislature of such State, or of the executive when the legislature cannot be convened, to employ such part of the land and naval forces as he deems necessary to suppress such insurrection. The rebellion of 1861 brought forth permanent legislation empowering the President to call forth the militia and to employ the army for the suppression of insurrection against the Government and for the execution of the laws

of the United States. And a similar power was conferred by the legislation of 1871, for the purpose of
maintaining the civil rights of the people of the States,
when divested by violent combinations and conspiracies
against the laws of the United States. Under these
laws the assistance of the military may be resorted to
in any instance of such insurrection or lawless combination, from an isolated case of riotous obstruction to the
magnitude of the recent Civil War.

History shows us that there are stages of public danger between the normal condition of peace and the
existence of a state of war when the civil machinery
of the Government is powerless to control the public
disorder, and it becomes a necessity to resort to the use
of military force for the security of public safety and
private rights. Under the law the President is constituted the judge of the existence of the exigency arising
in the first instance, and he is bound to act according to
his belief of the facts. When he exercises this authority vested in him, the presumption is that he exercises
it in pursuance of law.

Martial law has heretofore been inaugurated by a
formal proclamation of the President, or Commander-in-
Chief, or declaration of the commanding general. This
notification designates the place or district within
which military authority is to be operative, and to what
extent the courts or civil administration are affected
by it, as well as the directions to be observed by the
community.

The employment of martial law has been likened to
the exercise of the right of self-defence by an individual. Homicide is said to be excusable if committed
by any person in self-defence when bodily harm is
threatened and immediately impending; the citizen is
justified in taking life in the protection of his property

and of his domicile from violence, and in the due prevention of a violent crime or in the suppression of a riot. Necessity is in these cases the basis upon which the legality of the use of force depends. The occasion and justification of the employment of martial law rest upon the same basis.

" It is manifest," Justice Blackburn said, " in the interest of those under its care that every government, whatever its form may be, must possess the power of resorting to force in the last extremity. The want of such a power would place the very existence of the state at the mercy of organized conspiracy. The public safety therefore, which is the ultimate law, confides to the supreme authority in every country the power to declare it when the emergency has arisen."

Martial law is resorted to as much for the protection of the lives and property of peaceable individuals as for the repression of hostile and violent elements. It may become requisite that it supersede for the time existing civil institutions; but in general, except in so far as relates to persons violating military orders or otherwise interfering with the exercise of military authority, martial law does not in effect suspend the local law or jurisdiction or materially restrict the liberty of the citizen.

As the introduction of martial law can be justified only by necessity, it is to be continued only so long as the public exigency on account of which it was proclaimed shall prevail.

Civil and criminal liability follow private wrongs committed under color of martial law and unnecessary force or oppression, or arbitrary force not within the scope of the necessity. The officer whose duty it is to enforce martial law is liable for his acts before the civil courts, where the necessity for its enforcement must be made out.

Closely connected with the subject of martial law is the suspension of the writ of habeas corpus. It has been said that the declaration of martial law is the suspension of this writ.

The writ of habeas corpus is the offspring of the common law. Its benefits and securities were enlarged and guarded by the habeas corpus act of Charles II. It has been looked upon, from the days of the colonists, as one of the great charters of American liberty. Its purpose has ever been to give speedy relief from all unlawful imprisonment, and to enforce upon judicial and other officers the duty of deliverance. It was, therefore, specifically declared in the Constitution that "The privilege of the writ of habeas corpus shall not be suspended unless in cases of rebellion or invasion the public safety may demand it."

For a long time it was asserted that the State courts had jurisdiction to liberate under the writ of habeas corpus persons taken or held by Federal officers in the illegal or undue exercise of a power conferred by Congress. The Supreme Court finally held that a State judge had no jurisdiction to issue a writ of habeas corpus or to continue proceedings under it, when issued for the discharge of a person held under the authority, or claim or color of authority, of the United States by an officer of the Government, and that in such cases the authorities of the National Government have supremacy until the validity of the question involved is determined by the tribunals of the United States.

Without the suspension of the writ of habeas corpus martial law cannot effectually be exercised; such suspension is essentially to the effective making of summary arrests of civilians charged with offences and the holding of them at will or with a view to trial by a military tribunal. The two powers are closely connected; one substantially involves or includes the other. The suspension, however, of this writ does not legalize what is done while it continues; it merely suspends for a time this particular remedy. All other remedies for illegal arrests remain, and may be pursued against the parties making or continuing them.

The question whether, under the provisions of the Constitution relating to the suspension of the privilege of the writ, the President is authorized to order or effect such suspension, was raised at an early period in the recent War of the Rebellion. By a proclamation of May 10th, 1861, the President authorized the commander of the Union forces in Florida to suspend there the writ of habeas corpus if he found it necessary. On August 13th, 1862, he suspended the writ as to persons liable to draft who should absent themselves from their places of residences in order to avoid it; and later on by his proclamation of September 24th, 1862, he further ordered "that the writ of habeas corpus is suspended in respect to all persons arrested, or who are now, or during the rebellion shall be imprisoned in any fort, camp, arsenal, military prison, or other place of confinement by any military authority, or by the sentence of any court-martial or military commission."

It was the opinion of Chief Justice Marshall that the power of suspending the writ was a legislative power and vested in Congress alone. In a case coming before him in 1861 Chief Justice Taney made a positive ruling to that effect which has been concurred in by a series of decisions in the United States and State courts.

Congress by an express provision in the act of March 3d, 1863, specially vested in the President the authority, whenever in his judgment the public safety might require it, to suspend the privilege of the writ in any case arising in any part of the United States.

Under this legislation the President issued his proclamation of September 15th, 1863, suspending the writ throughout the United States in terms similar to those set out in his proclamation of the previous year, already quoted.

The act of 1863 expired with the close of the rebellion in 1866.   A subsequent suspension for a limited period took place in accordance with special authority of Congress in 1871 in the case of the unlawful combinations of the so-called " Ku-Klux" in South Carolina.

It may now be deemed to be settled by the rulings of the courts, the action of Congress, and the practice of the Executive, that the President is not empowered of his own authority to suspend the writ of habeas corpus, and that a declaration of martial law made by him or a military commander, in a district not within the theatre of war, will not justify such suspension in the absence of the sanction of Congress.   The result must be that martial law proper will in the future rarely be initiated in the United States where Congress has omitted to provide for the means for rendering its exercise effectual.   Should, however, evil days come upon us, and an emergency arise requiring in the preservation of public safety the arrest in good faith and the holding of public enemies or other criminals, in temporary disregard of judicial process sued out for their release, the officers and soldiers concerned must, as in the past, look to Congress for relief.

" This is a Government of laws, and all authority exercised must find its measure and warrant thereunder." It is a corner-stone of American freedom that an illegal command is not a justification.   The remedies for abuse of power on the part of the President are found

in his amenability to impeachment; of military officers
and soldiers to their amenability to both civil and military law, and lastly in the army being subject to the
legislative power of the representatives of the people.

The framers of the Constitution were jealous of a
standing army. When the clause to empower Congress
to raise armies was under debate, it was proposed that
the standing army should not exceed one man for every
thousand inhabitants. This ratio should give us to-day,
with our present population, an army of 65,000 men—
we have but 25,000.

The history of the army of the United States during
the past century shows that the jealousy existing
against it has been unfounded. It has ever been the
servant of the people. It has been the pioneer of civilization from the lakes to the Gulf of Mexico and from
the Alleghanies to the Pacific. Under the protecting
shelter of its camps and blockhouses the pioneers laid
the foundations of Pittsburg, Cincinnati, Chicago,
and many other cities, and towns of lesser note too
numerous to mention. It demonstrated its heroism in
many encounters with the savage foe. It carried its
banners victoriously to the hall of the Montezumas, and,
though small in numbers, did its full duty in the War
for the Union.

Trained in the principles of constitutional law as
part of their professional education, and thoroughly in-
doctrinated with the fundamental theory of our institutions, that the military is subordinate to the civil
authority, the officers of our army will ever be ready
when called upon to defend and support the Constitution
of the United States and the laws made thereunder,
and if need be to lay down their lives in the discharge
of this their sacred and sworn duty.

Frederick. W. Seward

FREDERICK W. SEWARD.

Frederick W. Seward was born at Auburn, N. Y., in July, 1830. He is a son of the late William H. Seward. His preparation for college was made at the academies in Auburn and Albany. He graduated in 1849 at Union College, which has since bestowed on him the degrees of A. M. and LL. D.

Entering at once upon his legal studies he was for a time in his father's office, afterward in that of Judges Kent and Davies in New York. He was admitted to the bar at Rochester in 1851. Before the close of that year he was invited by Thurlow Weed to embark in journalism. He joined the staff of the Albany *Evening Journal*, becoming subsequently an associate editor, and a few years later one of the proprietors of the paper. He resided in Albany for nearly ten years, taking active part in public affairs, uniting in the effort to found the Albany University, and being chosen orator to welcome Kossuth in behalf of the young men, when the great Hungarian visited the State capital. He participated in the meetings and movements that resulted in the organization of the Republican party, and the merging in it of the anti-slavery portion of the old Whig party.

He married, in 1854, Miss Anna M. Wharton, of Albany.

In 1861 his father, having been appointed Secretary of State by President Lincoln, desired his assistance in official business at Washington. He went thither during the critical period preceding the outbreak of the Civil War. His was the memorable mission from Washington to Philadelphia to warn the President-elect of the plot for his assassination on passing through Baltimore.

Early in the spring he was appointed Assistant Secretary of State by President Lincoln, and continued in that position during the troublous period of Civil War and Reconstruction. Having especial charge of the consular service, he participated also in the management of diplomatic affairs. His duties were varied and difficult, requiring constant tact and prompt and resolute action.

During the absence or illness of the Secretary of State the assistant takes his place as Acting Secretary; and in that capacity Mr. Seward had charge of the Department of State during periods aggregating several months. He sat in the cabinet council which decided the question of moving the army into Virginia, as well as in that which resulted in the reorganization of the Army of the Potomac after the second Bull Run defeat, and before the victory at Antietam. He was also in the memorable cabinet meeting of April 14th, 1865, when General Grant came in person to report his victory at Appomattox and when the policy of reconstruction was decided upon.

On the night of that day President Lincoln was murdered at Ford's Theatre. At the same hour another assassin attempted to kill Secretary Seward while lying helpless in bed after a carriage accident. His son sought to defend him, and in the struggle both father and son received wounds at first thought to be fatal, and from which neither recovered until after the lapse of many months.

Both the Secretary and Assistant Secretary continued in office during the Administration of President Johnson, and were engaged in the negotiations for the settlement of the Alabama claims, the evacuation of Mexico by the French, the purchase of Alaska, the treaties for St. Thomas and San Domingo, and the opening of diplomatic relations with Japan and China. In 1866 Mr. F. W. Seward and Admiral Porter were sent on a special mission to the Dominican Republic with power to conclude a treaty for Samana if they should find it practicable or expedient.

Retiring from office in 1869, Mr. Seward accompanied his father in his journey across the Continent and his trip to Alaska, where the Indians welcomed the ex-Secretary as "the great Tyee who bought the land," and then through Mexico where they were received and fêted as guests of the nation.

In 1875 Mr. Seward was elected to the New York Legislature. He proposed and advocated the constitutional amendments placing the canals and prisons under responsible heads, and had charge of the bill for the first elevated railroad (the Ninth Avenue line).

In 1877 President Hayes and Secretary Evarts invited Mr. Seward to resume his old position at the Department of State. While there he introduced reforms in the consular service, and took active part in the negotiations which secured the harbor in Samoa to the United States and in those developing commercial and diplomatic relations with Oriental powers.

In 1881 Mr. Seward was one of the commissioners in behalf of the State to participate in the Yorktown Centennial celebration.

In later years Mr. Seward has been residing at Montrose-on-the-Hudson, devoting his time to occasional law business, but mainly to literary pursuits. His "Life and Letters of William H. Seward," in three volumes, was published by Derby & Miller in 1891. His journal of "A West Indian Cruise" appeared in *Godey's Magazine* in 1894.

His lecture at Union College on "American Diplomacy" was delivered in November, 1892.

AMERICAN DIPLOMACY.

By Hon. Frederick W. Seward.

Under the shadow of college walls the classic authors, of course, are familiar reading. In perusing their pages you have doubtless observed that the intercourse between nations in ancient times was largely made up of battles and booty, treason, stratagem, and spoils. The old-fashioned rule prevailed among civilized races then as it does among savages to-day.

> "The simple plan
> That he shall take who has the power,
> And he shall keep who can."

But you have also observed that sometimes the opposing armies were so nearly balanced that their respective commanders had some doubts as to *who* was going to "take," and *who* was going to be able to "keep." Under these circumstances the trumpeters would sound a parley, and heralds would be sent forward to propose terms of peace or conditions of combat. The heralds were allowed to come and go in safety, and hostilities were suspended until their errand was accomplished. These heralds were the precursors of our modern diplomatists.

As the nations grew in size and wealth commerce sprang up between them. New and complex questions arose which could not be settled by a brief interview with a herald. Kings who wanted to prevent bloody and costly wars began to send ambassadors to other sovereigns, to stay long enough at the foreign courts to make such explanations, claims, promises, or threats as were needed. Soon European sovereigns found it to be wise economy to have permanent channels of communication with each other. So, at last, each king in Europe established at his royal neighbor's capital a minister with secretaries and subordinates, forming what in modern parlance is called a "legation."

Now a minister during the Middle Ages reflected the temper of his times. Prejudices of race, religion, and locality were very strong. Sovereigns suspected each other of sinister designs, and generally with good reason. Except in cathedrals and cloisters there was little talk about the "universal brotherhood of man." A minister was expected to be loyal to his king, just and fair to his fellow-countrymen. But when it came to dealing with the dreaded and detested foreigners, he was free to beguile, wheedle, cajole, threaten, or deceive. Volumes even were written to prove that deception was a part of his duty, that he might commendably cheat, from patriotic motives, and unblushingly lie—for the public good. In fact, as Lord Palmerston used to remark, he might break all the commandments in the Decalogue except the eleventh, which was, "Thou shalt not be found out."

But there was progress in diplomacy as in everything else. It began slowly to be realized that nations were not necessarily hereditary enemies, that they had some interests in common worthy of protection. And so out of centuries of experience was gradually evolved that benign and majestic body of jurisprudence known as "the Law of Nations"—the law which is superior to all other laws of human origin; the law to which kings and emperors must bow, and to which even treaties and constitutions must conform; the law written down in no statute book, and enacted by no parliament or legislature, but resting simply on the common consent of Christendom;—the law prescribing the limits of war and peace, defining the duties of belligerents and neutrals, and saying alike to sovereign and subject, "Thus far you may go, but no further."

The winter of 1776–77 was one of the gayest seasons of the brilliant court of Louis XVI. The gilded salons of Paris and Versailles echoed with the festivity of throngs decked in silks, satins, and velvets, diamonds and lace. But the figure that attracted most attention and excited most comment was that of a plainly clothed old man of seventy, who had come to Paris all the way from Pennsylvania. His face was full of benevolence, his manners and speech were simplicity itself. His fame had preceded him across the Atlantic. He was already known as philosopher, savant, inventor, and author— and now he came as a diplomatist. The fashionable world paused in its revelry to look at and listen to the American commissioner, Benjamin Franklin.

The French are quick to perceive the meaning of symbols. They intuitively saw that here was a type of a new departure in diplomacy. Here was a diplomat who wore no court dress, because he came from no court and represented no king. It was impossible to suspect him of any sinister purpose, for he came simply as the representative of other men like himself, who were struggling for self-government and the common rights of man.

The lesson sank deep into the hearts of the French people. In the palace where "le Grand Monarque" had haughtily declared, "*L'Etat, c'est moi!*" now began to be heard murmurs of such words as "Liberté," "Egalité," and "Fraternité." New theories of government began to find favor throughout Europe—especially when Franklin was reinforced and followed by such envoys as Jefferson and John Adams, John Jay, Gouverneur Morris, James Monroe, John Marshall, Elbridge Gerry, Albert Gallatin, Rufus King, and Richard Rush.

A minister of the old régime represented his sovereign. In order to enjoy that sovereign's confidence, he was bound to carry out his purposes, whether good, bad, or indifferent, to keep his secrets, and to follow in his ways, however crooked they might be. Now an American minister represented, not a sovereign, but a sovereign people—a people desiring only to deal fairly with other nations, and claiming nothing but their just rights. Their minister found himself standing on a higher plane of principle. He was the advocate, not only of a country, but of human rights. The Congress itself had solemnly declared, "Let it not be forgotten that the rights for which the American people are contending are the rights of Human Nature." Furthermore, the road to the confidence of the sovereign people lay, not through secrecy, but through publicity. They had no use for treachery or lying. And how could a diplomatist intrigue successfully, under the gaze of a hundred thousand eyes, aided by the searching light of all the newspapers?

The young Republic began its diplomatic career modestly, welcoming immigrants and granting them naturalization and protection, defending its rights according to its ability, claiming respect from Europe by its moderation and justice, and setting an example of independence and self-government to the Spanish colonies of Southern America, which, before many years they, one and all, began to try to follow.

There stood for many years on the chief avenue at

Washington an unpretending two-story brick edifice known as the Department of State. Here the foreign relations of the United States were conducted for the greater part of the century. Here were kept the archives and the correspondence with all foreign governments, and here were prepared the instructions, replies, and treaties which were to determine the nation's foreign policy. From here Oliver Ellsworth and his colleagues were sent out to make the treaty with Talleyrand which averted a threatened war with France. From here Jefferson sent the first written President's Message to Congress. Here Madison prepared the instructions to Robert R. Livingston, as Minister at Paris, to guide him in negotiating the purchase of the great Louisiana territory. Here Decatur and Preble were instructed to break up the piracy of the Barbary powers, to release the captives and make an end of the tribute. From here Monroe and Pinckney set out, to try to stop the impressment of American seamen and the seizure of American ships by the British navy. From here emanated Jefferson's proclamation ordering all British men-of-war out of American waters. Here Secretary Monroe gave the British Minister his passports, and President Madison proclaimed the war with England. Here, soon after, came the Russian Envoy to offer friendly mediation in the conflict, and from here, soon after that, Henry Clay and his colleagues went out to effect the restoration of peace by the Treaty of Ghent. From here was promulgated the celebrated "Monroe Doctrine," that this continent was to be thenceforward free from European dictation. Here John Quincy Adams concluded the treaty with Spain for the acquisition of Florida. From here went out the recognition of the independence of Mexico and the South American republics. Here Lafayette was welcomed, and from here Harrison bore greetings to Bolivar. Here was penned General Jackson's message denouncing nullification by South Carolina. Here Webster concluded his treaty with Lord Ashburton, settling all boundary and extradition disputes with England. And here he made his famous declaration that "Every merchant vessel on the high seas is rightfully considered part of the territory to which it belongs." From here Secretary Calhoun, on the night before President Tyler's retirement from office, sent out a messenger offering annexation to Texas. Here Secretary Buchanan drafted the treaty of peace with Mexico, and from here went out Polk's proclamation of the new treaty of Guadalupe Hidalgo and the acquisition of California and New Mexico. Here Clayton heard the knell of his political hopes, when the bell over his head began to toll for the death of General Taylor. From here went forth the invitation to Kossuth, then exiled in Turkey, to come to the United States on board an American frigate. Here were framed the instructions and treaty through which Commodore Perry was to open Japan to American commerce. Here Marcy penned his celebrated dispatch in the Koszta case, maintaining the rights of American citizenship. And here President and Queen exchanged congratulations in the first messages that ever went over the Atlantic Cable.

During all this period of the gradual growth of American diplomacy, Europe was convulsed by the fiery ordeal of successive wars. Napoleon, for a while, was setting up thrones and seeing them topple down again. Then followed the great gathering of diplomats at the Congress of Vienna,—which sought to reconstruct on old lines, to guaranty the "peace of Europe" and maintain the "Balance of Power," that balance which is always getting unbalanced,—that peace which is always preparing for war! Struggle followed struggle, between diplomatists, sovereigns and armies—on the banks of the Rhine and the Danube, on the shores of the Adriatic and the Baltic, on the waters of the Black Sea and the Red, on the plains of Lombardy, in the marshes of the Crimea, in the mountain ranges of the Alps, the Apennines, and the Balkans. Diplomacy exhausted its skill and gave way to cannon. Cannon in turn proved unavailing and gave way to diplomacy again—each struggle ending only in some rearrangement of the squares on that great chessboard which we call the "Map of Europe."

And here, by the way, we may note the old tradition that the game of chess was devised by an Eastern sage, to amuse the leisure hours of his royal master, and that consciously or unconsciously, he gave it the form of a satire on the monarchical form of government. First, there is the king, ostensibly the ruler, the source and centre of power,—but in fact the weakest point of the whole organization. Unable to move but a step at a time in any direction: surrounded by courtiers and guards, he is constantly exposed to dangers threatening himself and all his court. He lives in dread of hearing from some quarter the ominous warning, "Check." Next there is the piece which we call the Queen, but which in Oriental lands is styled the Prime Minister. With greater power but less responsibility he dominates the board, yet must take constant risks of his own besides sharing in whatever misfortune may happen to the king. This piece typifies that "power behind the throne" which, whether a minister or a mistress, has ruled so many kingdoms. Then come the Bishops, representing the reverend clergy, the established religion of the state. They move on a different line from the other pieces, and apparently an indirect one,—yet are always unexpectedly crossing the paths of sovereign and subject. Then the Knights. These typify the nobility and gentry,—loyal to the sovereign and zealous in his defence, yet careless of the rights of the commen people, leaping over their heads and over all obstacles. Then the Castles, which are the fortifications that mark the limits of the realm. Finally the Pawns, who represent the common soldiers, —unable to do anything save to move forward, in obedience to orders, stimulated by the promise of promotion and preferment, when they have passed through the enemy's lines, but, alas, nine times out of ten, swept out of existence before they get there.

Does not this mimic warfare on the board fairly reproduce what is going forward, on a greater scale, at the court of every sovereign in Asia and in Europe?

But even in the American Republic there was a "power behind the throne"—a power behind the sovereign people, gradually growing until it threatened to undermine their authority and divide their union. This was the slave power, the combination in the interest of maintaining and extending African slavery. Scoffing at "equality of human rights" as an "abstraction," it denied the fundamental principle of republican government. It made race and color the badge of servitude, and set property above humanity. It was a natural and logical sequence that it should adopt European methods,—that it should seek to establish a "balance of power," by an "equilibrium of States," —that it should "filibuster" for new territory in which to plant slavery—and that, when thwarted in its designs, it should threaten disruption and bloodshed. And so came on the "Civil War."

The Civil War brought new confirmation of the old

maxim that "a house divided against itself cannot stand." The foreign dispatches daily pouring in upon the table of the Secretary of State attested the fact. Since the great American Republic had chosen to divide, it no longer inspired fear and hardly commanded respect from foreign powers. Its flag might be flouted, its remonstrances ignored or despised; kings, statesmen, and adventurers were watching for its downfall and preparing to profit by it. Menaces of disaster seemed to start up on every side. One week would come news of an attempt to seize the line of interoceanic communication across the Isthmus of Panama. The next would come intelligence that Spain had taken possession of San Domingo and unfurled again over it the banner of Castile. Next, that France was meditating a like enterprise to overthrow the Mexican republic and establish in its stead a government hostile to the United States. Presently came news of the precipitate action of Great Britain, in the Queen's proclamation, raising the disaffected Southern States up to the level of a belligerent power, before they had either an army in the field or a single ship afloat on the sea. Doubts were freely expressed by British statesmen, whether the Government of the United States had any more cohesiveness than "a rope of sand."

Similar manifestations of unfriendly feeling came from other countries. Rancor and contempt for the unhappy Republic were freely expressed in her hour of misfortune. It was a disagreeable surprise, at the North, to find the depth and fervor of the anti-American prejudice that seemed to prevail in Old World courts. But the explanation was not far to seek. Those who believed monarchy the only safe and strong government, saw in the coming fall of the republic a confirmation of their theories and predictions. Furthermore, the smaller the fragments into which the great American Republic might choose to shatter itself, the less likely any of them would be to disturb the "balance of power" elsewhere.

The diplomatic correspondence, during the war, fills many bulky volumes. The limits of this lecture will allow only reference to a few salient points.

Its key-note was given by the American Secretary in his earliest communication to France, in which he said: "Foreign intervention would oblige us to treat those making it as allies of the insurrection. If several European states should combine in that intervention, the people of the United States deem the Union worth all the cost and all the sacrifices of a contest with the world in arms, if such a contest should prove inevitable."

The first and indispensable step toward convincing European governments that the Union would stand was to show that we believed it ourselves. So there was no word of doubt, no hint of apprehension in the communications to foreign powers. The most fervent faith in success was expressed, at the hour when the prospects for it seemed the darkest. Victories might be trusted to carry their own moral, but tidings of defeats must always be accompanied by assurances that the Union would yet surmount its troubles.

Each week went out from the State Department a concise *résumé* of the progress made by the military and naval forces. This "Circular on the Military Situation," as it was called, soon came to have great usefulness. Ministers of foreign affairs, cabinets, and courts in Europe soon found that its statements were the only ones always reliable, for their own agents in the United States had no such opportunities for ascertaining the precise facts, and the newspapers had a maze of conflicting reports.

Early in the war, it was learned through the Legation at St. Petersburg that Great Britain and France had agreed to take one and the same course on the subject of the American war, including the possible recognition of the rebels. Later, this understanding was distinctly avowed by M. Thouvenel, the French Minister of Foreign Affairs. This alliance for joint action might dictate its own terms. From a joint announcement of neutrality, it would be only a step to joint mediation or intervention: and it was hardly to be anticipated that the Washington Government, struggling with an insurrection which had rent the country asunder, would be willing to face also the combined power of the two great empires of Western Europe. To the minds of French and English statesmen the project was even praiseworthy. It would "stop the effusion of blood" and increase the supply of cotton. It would leave the American Union permanently divided: but that was a consummation that European statesmen in general would not grieve over.

On the morning of the 15th of June, a scene occurred at the State Department which had more influence on the fortunes of the Union than even a pitched battle. The Secretary was sitting at his table, reading dispatches, when the messenger announced:

"The British Minister is here to see you, sir, and the French Minister, also."

"Which came first?"

"Lord Lyons, sir; but they say they both want to see you together."

Seward instinctively guessed the motive for so unusual a diplomatic proceeding. He paused a moment and then said:

"Show them both into the Assistant Secretary's room, and I will come in presently."

A few minutes later, as the two ministers were seated side by side on the sofa, the door opened and the Secretary entered. Smiling and shaking his head he said:

"No, no, no! This will never do. I cannot see you in that way."

The ministers rose to greet him.

"True," said one, "it is unusual, but we are obeying our instructions."

"And at least," said the other, "you will allow us to state the object of our visit?"

"No," said Seward, "we must start right about it; whatever it is. M. Mercier, will you do me the favor to come and dine with me this evening? Then we can talk over your business at leisure. And if Lord Lyons will step into my room with me now, we will discuss what he has to say to me."

"If you refuse to see us together," began the French Envoy with a courteous smile and shrug.

"Certainly, I do refuse to see you together, though I will see either of you separately, with pleasure, here or elsewhere."

So the interviews were held severally, not jointly; and the papers which they had been instructed to jointly present and formally read to him, were left for his informal inspection. A very brief examination of them only was necessary to enable him to say courteously, but with decision, that he declined to hear them read, or to receive official notice of them. Writing to the United States Ministers at London and Paris, he said: "We shall insist, in this case as in all others, on dealing with each of these powers alone, and their agreement to act together will not at all affect the course we shall pursue. This Government is sensible of the importance of the step it takes, in declining to receive the communication in question."

The projected intervention, thus thwarted in the first year of the war, was again and again attempted in some different form during each succeeding year. At one time, the plan was seriously discussed in the Imperial councils at Paris, of putting forward some small power like Belgium to pick a quarrel with the United States, and then the two great empires, suddenly espousing that side of the controversy, would be able jointly to crush the American Government, thus drawn into a trap.

In the *Trent* case, the search of a British packet, and the seizure on her deck of two Confederate commissioners, by a United States naval officer, seemed to give the coveted opportunity for intervention. British navy yards and arsenals resounded with active preparations. Ships were commissioned and troops embarked. Assurance came to London from Paris, that Imperial France would join in the attack upon the American Republic. At Washington the case was complicated by manifestations of popular feeling adverse to the surrender of the prisoners. To give them up, it was argued would be a National humiliation, yet, on the other hand, to refuse, meant war with France, Great Britain and the Confederacy, all at once.

It was a surprise all round when the Secretary of State, in his reply, showed that in surrendering the men, the United States scored a triumph of one of its cardinal principles. "I discovered," he wrote, "that I was really defending and maintaining not an exclusively British interest, but an old honored and cherished American cause, upon principles that form a large portion of the distinctive policy of the United States. These principles were laid down for us in 1804 by James Madison, when Secretary of State in the Administration of Thomas Jefferson, in instructions given to James Monroe, our Minister to England. The ground

9

he assumed then was the same I now occupy, and the arguments by which he sustained himself upon it have been an inspiration to me in preparing this reply. . . . We are asked to do to the British nation what we have always insisted all nations ought to do to us."

When the public had read the document and the newspapers had made their comments, it was seen with popular satisfaction that in returning Mason and Slidell the United States had established beyond peradventure the doctrine for which the War of 1812 was fought; and now had committed England to it also.

As the progress of the war developed new opportunities, redoubled energy and daring were shown in blockade-running enterprises, as well as in sending information and supplies through the Union lines to the insurgents. Great Britain had undertaken to be "neutral" between the two belligerents. But neutrality is always easier to promise than to practise. It was difficult to be impartial. The Southerners naturally hated the blockade. The British, as naturally, shared in that feeling. The South encouraged communication in every possible way with England; while the North had, for its own safety, to impose a vexatious system of passports, police surveillance, frontier guards and blockading squadrons. Arrests and seizures were of frequent occurrence. Then the Secessionists would avail themselves of the protection of European governments for those engaged in these enterprises. Havana, Nassau, and the towns on the Canadian frontier became favorite points of rendezvous. They could meet, consult, and mature their plans without any official surveillance; and could find there many whom cupidity or love of adventure would lead to join them. The authorities, both British and Spanish, were jealous of interference by United States officers with any vessels or persons under their jurisdiction. The vessels and men engaged, if successful, loudly boasted of their connection with the rebels; but when intercepted or captured, declared themselves "neutrals," and claimed the protection of foreign governments.

An infinite variety of questions arose, and the shelves of the Department of State, to this day, groan under the burden of the documents and discussions to which they gave rise. Many of the cases, arising under novel conditions of modern warfare, were without any precedent to govern their decision. Yet it was necessary not only to render exact justice, but to do it in such a way as should not offend the roused susceptibilities either of the American or the foreign nation.

Sometimes a single seizure would give rise to half a dozen different questions; while the Laird rams, the *Florida* and the *Alabama*, came up, in one shape or another, by every foreign mail.

The Queen's proclamation of "belligerent rights" was claimed as convenient screen for all kinds of daring enterprises. They were further encouraged and stimulated by London insurance companies. Those engaged in them often obtained insurance on their vessels and cargo, at Lloyds and other offices, at 15 per cent for running in and 15 per cent for coming out. Insurers were tempted to share in these ventures by the enormous profits, while the shippers and merchants made money if even but half of their vessels got safe into port.

Unusual activity and unwonted industry pervaded the Washington legations of all the maritime powers. The attachés of the British Legation found themselves as busy as hard-working attorneys' clerks. A dozen communications a day would frequently pass between the Legation and the Department. There were vessels

unlawfully detained on suspicion of running the blockade; vessels lawfully captured in attempting to run it;
rebel cruisers receiving aid and comfort in colonial
ports; Federal cruisers in the same ports denied ordinary courtesy; rebel ships escaping the vigilance of
British authorities; British ships complaining of the
surveillance of American ones; prisoners wanting to
be released on taking the oath of allegiance; prisoners
taking it and breaking it as soon as released; seamen
claiming exemption because they were British subjects;
claims of ship-owners for damages; intercepted dispatches; vessels wrongly seized, or rightly seized but
wrongly dealt with; customs regulations not in accordance with treaties; customs decisions not in accordance
with facts; duties that ought to be refunded; duties that
ought not to be collected; foreign subjects claiming
exemption from draft; enlisted soldiers claiming release as "foreigners," after having spent their bounty
money; officers arrested as spies, and spies escaping as
clergymen; rifles shipped as "farming implements"
and gunpowder as "white lead;" rebel munitions of
war claiming to be "arms for the Indians," and treason
able documents pretending to be "Bibles for the
heathen!"

The French Government, like the British, had no faith
that our National Union would ever be restored; and
from time to time manifested its impatience at the continuance of what it deemed our hopeless struggle. On
at least seven different occasions, the preliminary steps
toward intervention were taken, and only checked by
diplomatic address on the part of the United States, or
by news of success of the Union arms.

First was the project of joint action with Great Britain, already described; which was nipped in the bud
in 1861. Then the plan to make common cause with

Great Britain in the *Trent* affair. This was thwarted by the diplomatic settlement. Next, the notice given to the United States that the manufacturing and commercial classes of France were suffering from the depression caused by the blockade, which prevented the export of cotton and the import of French goods at Southern ports. This was checked by the capture of New Orleans and other ports and reopening them to trade, under the stars and stripes. Then came the denunciation of the Federal Government for temporarily obstructing Charleston Harbor, by sinking vessels loaded with stone. It was a surprise to the French Government, when they were answered by American envoys that France herself had done the same thing, and under the Treaty of Utrecht had not only temporarily but permanently closed a harbor that remains closed to-day.

In 1862 the Emperor's address to the Chambers was prepared and contained an intimation that he was about to take steps for active measures to break the blockade. The Secession advocates in Europe were jubilant over the expected announcement, and stock speculators at the London Exchange and Paris Bourse were going to make their fortunes by its effects on the market. At the last moment the Emperor became convinced that the step was a dangerous one, and the threatening paragraph was stricken out.

As the American Minister, Mr. Dayton, wrote, "The Emperor's address came—it was not what they expected! They said that just before its delivery, 'the switch had been turned off,' and forthwith, the British Ministry, the London *Times*, and other portions of the English press ran off along with it!"

In 1863 the Emperor renewed his proposal to Great Britain and other powers for joint interference in the American contest,—saying that if they refused, he would proceed alone. But, before he was ready to do so, came the fall of Vicksburg, and the victory at Gettysburg; and the French Minister at Washington wrote his Imperial master that, in view of these great successes of the Union arms, he had better wait still longer.

The latest and most dangerous, perhaps, of all the French movements was the expedition to set up an Empire in Mexico, overthrowing republican government there and menacing it in the United States. The French Minister of Foreign Affairs — M. Drouyn de l'Huys, in conversing with Mr. Dayton, the American Envoy, assured him that France had no thought of conquering Mexico, or establishing a permanent power there. "In the *abandon* of a conversation somewhat familiar," added Mr. Dayton, "I took occasion to say that, in quitting Mexico, France might leave a *puppet* behind her."

"No," replied Drouyn de l'Huys, "no,—the string would be too long to work!"

In this opinion the Minister was sagacious and wise. But ultimately he was overruled by the Emperor, who had determined to try the experiment with Maximilian. It resulted as Drouyn de l'Huys had predicted. "The string was too long to work," and the unfortunate Archduke finally lost, not only the Empire, but his life.

But all foreign governments were not unfriendly during the war. The Spanish-American republics, though they could not give aid, did not withhold their sympathies. Even the threatening cloud of European intervention was relieved here and there by a ray of sunshine. Sweden and Denmark sent words of sympathy. Italy expressed the friendship that had been expected from her. Prussia sent assurances of just and generous feeling. The President of the only republic in Europe wrote that Switzerland regarded the struggle with the deepest anxiety, adding that "Switzerland passed through a similar crisis fourteen years before, which threatened to tear asunder the then loose connection of the twenty-two Cantons. But, renewed, rose the present republic from that tempest, strengthened internally and abroad. May God grant that the United States of America may also emerge, renewed and strengthened from this crisis!"

Russia was a steadfast friend of the United States during the Civil War. In the volumes of diplomatic correspondence there are very few pages under the head of "Russia," and these contain only messages of amity and good-will. Russia had no grounds of complaint or claims for damages, or, if she had, she never presented them. The plan for an intercontinental telegraph to connect the United States and Russia by way of Bering's Straits, and the survey of the route made under the auspices of the two governments, helped to promote the mutual good feeling.

It was through the Legation at St. Petersburg that information was received of the design of France and England to enter upon a scheme of joint action adverse to the United States. Russia was invited to join in their plans for "mediation" and "intervention," but promptly refused unless the United States should ask her. When the threatened intervention, nevertheless, seemed impending, a Russian fleet appeared in American waters, and passed summer and winter there. Official announcement of its purposes, it was thought, might be embarrassing; and Prince Gortschakoff was a sagacious diplomatist. He simply sent over the fleet, and instructed the Russian Minister to say that it came "for no unfriendly purpose." The Government and people of the United States intuitively understood that while its help might never be needed, yet, if needed, it would be forthcoming. Courtesies and festivities were exchanged, on ship and shore, between the naval officers and the authorities at New York and Washington, whose significance was fully appreciated at London and Paris.

In 1863, grave apprehensions as to the outcome of the War had been excited by the Draft Riots in New York. A diplomatic incident then occurred which was not without its influence on European governments. The foreign ministers were as usual taking their summer recreation at Newport, Cape May, Saratoga, and other places of fashionable resort. The Secretary of State had often told them they could learn little of the true character of the country or its people, unless they left the seaboard and great cities and visited the rural regions of the interior. He saw how difficult it was for them to realize that the country was not becoming exhausted, or that the causes which led to the draft riots in New York might not be at work in every town. When he invited them to accompany him on a visit to his own home in central New York,—" the heart of the North"—several of them signified that they would go with willingness and pleasure. Some of the diplomatic gentlemen started with him in a special car for Washington,—others joined the party at New York. Its number varied at different stages of the journey, but the English, French, Spanish, Italian, German, Russian, Swedish, and Central American representatives continued through nearly the whole of it.

They visited New York and its vicinity. They went up the Hudson, through the valley of the Mohawk, and over the hills into Otsego County. They saw Albany and Schenectady and Little Falls, visited Sharon Springs and Trenton Falls, spent a night at

Cooperstown and sailed on Otsego Lake. They went to Utica and Rome and Syracuse. They stopped at Auburn, visited Seneca Falls and Geneva, traversed Cayuga and Seneca Lakes, saw the mills and factories of Rochester and the harbor of Buffalo, swarming with lake craft and having its elevators in full operation. Hospitalities were showered upon them, more than they could accept. Serenades greeted them in the evening, with kindly invitations for the morrow. But every day's ride was a volume of instruction. Hundreds of factories with whirring wheels, thousands of acres of golden harvest-fields, miles of railway trains laden with freight, busy fleets on rivers, lakes, and canals, showed a period of unexampled commercial activity and prosperity. Then the flag flying everywhere, the drum heard everywhere, the recruiting offices open and busy,—the churches, the hospitals, the commissions and benevolent associations, laboring for the soldiers' care and comfort, all attested the resources of an empire and the self-reliant patriotism of a great republic!

One of the ministers, writing to his government, said: "The resources of the Northern States, instead of being exhausted, seem practically inexhaustible!"

Foreign nations had known at the outset that the attempt to dissolve the Union was made by the slaveholding section. But they did not at first realize the effect of the war upon the system of slavery itself. As slaves began to escape from their masters and form "contraband camps" under the Union flag, it was perceived that the advance of the Union armies operated as an emancipating crusade. The military orders in regard to the protection and enlistment of escaped fugitives, and the Seward-Lyons treaty with Great Britain for the final suppression of the Atlantic slave trade, all tended to define the position of the Government; and when in January, 1863, President Lincoln issued his emancipation proclamation, it was seen that Union success meant the ending of slavery, while Confederate success would be its continuance. Gradually popular sympathies began to array themselves on the emancipating side throughout all civilized lands. This popular feeling was reflected by parliaments and courts, and so tended to modify diplomatic action toward the United States.

Well, the war ended at last. Diplomacy, during its continuance, had been a "sea of troubles." But now the reefs and breakers began to disappear and the waters grew smooth again. From every foreign court came assurances of friendship, all sincere enough, for it could no longer profit any to quarrel with the United States. With peace and a restored Union diplomatic labors were lightened. Suggestions for international action were now all courteously received and duly considered. It had been useless, during the war, to attempt to enforce claims, however just, against foreign governments. Now this class of subjects again received attention. The most feasible and usually the most equitable way of settling such questions is by a joint commission, to examine the claims, fixing the amount found justly due, and rejecting claims found baseless. Each nation appoints one commissioner, and the two select a third to act as umpire. Few nations decline to accede to a mode of procedure so fair and reasonable. Treaties for such adjustment of claims were made with Peru, Columbia, Venezuela, Mexico, and other powers. Even the "Alabama Claims," for depredations by British-built ships flying the Confederate flag, were now listened to with respectful attention, and negotiations commenced for their adjustment by joint commission.

Another important negotiation was that begun with

Germany, to settle the long-disputed question as to the recognition of the principle of emigration and naturalization as an inherent and universal right. Bismarck, on behalf of the North German Union, conceded that principle, and then similar treaties were readily made with other continental powers.

New envoys began to present themselves at Washington from governments that had hitherto deemed it unnecessary to hold diplomatic relations with the American Republic. Ministers came from Turkey, from Tunis, from Japan, from China, from Siam, and from every Central and South American republic not already represented. Treaties with Japan and China were made for the furtherance of intercourse, travel, and trade, bringing those hitherto secluded empires into the circle of Western diplomatic and commercial relationship.

Perhaps the strongest evidence of the change in foreign opinion in regard to the United States was that given by the messages of sympathy after Lincoln's assassination. The world-wide feeling excited by that event found expression in communications from every part of the habitable globe. An avalanche of letters and resolutions of condolence and sympathy poured into the State Department by every mail for weeks and months; emperors, kings and queens, sultans, pachas, and grand dukes, presidents and governors, ministers of state, cabinets, parliamentary and legislative bodies, courts of justice, municipal organizations, diplomatic representatives, colonial officers, boards of trade and health, local committees, public presses, benevolent societies, social clubs, workingmen's unions, trade associations, churches, teachers and schools, all joined in these manifestations of horror at the crime and sympathy with the American people. It was as if an electric touch had brought all the world into union, and revealed the common brotherhood of all mankind. By order of Congress all these were gathered and printed in a great quarto volume of over 900 pages—a unique and interesting historical record. It was entitled "Tributes of the Nations to Abraham Lincoln."

The return of national prestige and power seemed to offer favorable opportunity to make such extension of the national boundaries as had been proved to be desirable or necessary. During the war the Government had labored under great disadvantage for the lack of advanced naval outposts in the West Indies and in the North Pacific. Blockader unners and hostile cruisers had found there shelter, protection, and supplies, while war-vessels of the Union were met by vexatious restrictions. After the close of hostilities, therefore, negotiations were entered upon which resulted in a treaty for the cession of the Danish West India Islands, with the fine harbor of St. Thomas, to the United States. A similar negotiation with the Dominican Republic resulted, first, in a treaty for the harbor of Samana, and then in one for annexation of the island republic. Neither of these treaties, however, were favorably received by Congress; and so the opportunities were lost. A third similar negotiation, that for the cession of Russian America, had a better fate. This treaty was ratified, and though its acceptance was attended with many misgivings and adverse criticisms, the value of Alaska thus acquired is now conceded, so that no one now proposes to give it up.

Renewed and more cordial relations now began to grow up with the other nations of the Western Hemisphere. The Secretary of State, in addressing the President of the Dominican Republic, outlined the national policy in saying: "The United States, like every other structure of large proportions, requires outward buttresses. These buttresses consist of republics like our own, founded in adjacent countries and islands, upon the principle of the equal rights of men. We desire those buttresses to be multiplied and strengthened. You are quick to perceive the use of the main edifice, in protecting the buttress you have established, and thus it happens that the republics around us only impart to us the strength which we in turn extend to them."

Upon these lines the foreign policy of the United States has been continued and is conducted to-day. It has moved steadily in the direction of adjusting or arbitrating all old disputes: settling and closing up all claims. It has sought to promote the extension of American trade by treaties of amity, commerce, and reciprocity of import duties. It has aimed to protect American ships and American seamen and American citizens in all foreign waters and all foreign lands. It has given encouragement to the coming in of worthy immigrants, while seeking to shut out only those who are incapable or unworthy of citizenship. It has sedulously cultivated the friendship of all sister republics, especially those of the Western Hemisphere. And it has aimed to maintain just and peaceful relations with every nation on earth.

It has not only conceived but actually put in force a higher ideal of international relations. It has planted itself upon the ground of absolute justice instead of that of national aggrandizement. It demands nothing but its due. It will take nothing by fraud or force. Even when obtaining indemnity for injuries, if there should be an overpayment the United States will insist on paying it back. This was notably the case, a few years since, with the Japanese and Chinese indemnity funds. And one difficulty was that there was no precedent in

diplomatic history for any such action—no nation before having felt called upon to voluntarily give up cash
in hand, whether obtained by fair means or foul.

Of course the secret is, that it is the people who are
sovereign. However it may be with an emperor or
king, a people have no desire to fill their coffers in any
way but an honest one.

And now, what has been the general effect of American diplomacy? That it has been useful, nay, indispensable to the United States, needs no demonstration.
But it has accomplished more than that. It has paid
back to the Old World its lessons in international law
by valuable lessons of its own. It has demonstrated
that honesty and fair dealing are not only compatible
with diplomacy, but form its highest attribute. Though
the Republic is but a little over a century old, its ministers are everywhere recognized as envoys whose word
may be relied upon, and whose purposes are open and
avowed. This is but one of the many forms in which
our experiment of republican government is impressing the world at large. The protection of the nation
against hostile aggression from abroad, the establishment of the rights of emigration and naturalization, the
settlement of the long-vexed question of the right of
search, the destruction of the slave trade, the expansion of the national boundaries by peaceful means instead of force or fraud—all these are the achievements
of American diplomacy within the century.

Now, all the governments and all the people of Europe are watching the career of the American Republic
—the governments with solicitude, the people with interest and hope. And both are profiting by it. Under
the benign influence of its example, absolute monarchy
has given place to limited monarchy and constitutional
government. Parliaments are taking the place of se-

cret councils, and even thrones are becoming historic symbols, rather than present powers. The world is tending, by slow and gradual steps, toward equality of ranks and rights, toward freedom and self-government, and so perhaps at some distant day to the realization of the philosopher's dream of the ideal government, based on peace and universal brotherhood.

THOMAS FRANCIS BAYARD.

THOMAS FRANCIS BAYARD, the son of James A. Bayard, was born in Wilmington, Del., October 29th, 1828. He was educated chiefly in the Flushing School established by the Rev. Dr. F. L. Hawks, and, being intended for mercantile life, was placed in a business house in New York City. After the death of his elder brother in 1848 he returned to Wilmington, studied law and was admitted to the bar in 1851. He was appointed United States District Attorney for Delaware, but resigned in the following year. In 1855 he removed to Philadelphia, where he became the partner of William Shippen and practised for two years, but then returned to Wilmington. There he continued in the practice of the law until he was elected in 1868 to succeed his father in the United States Senate. In 1861, at a public meeting in Dover, he delivered a memorable speech in favor of peace with the South. He took his seat March 4th, 1869, and being re-elected for a second term, in January, 1875, and again in 1881, served continuously until he became Secretary of State, March 4th, 1885. On the day on which he was elected to the Senate for a full term his father was also re-elected as Senator from Delaware to serve for the unexpired part of his original term. This is the only case of a father and son being voted for by the same legislature to fill the senatorial office. In the Senate he served on the committees on finance, judiciary, private land claims, library, and revision of laws. In October, 1881, he was elected president *pro tempore* of the Senate. He was a member of the electoral commission of 1876–77, and a conspicuous upholder in Congress of Democratic doctrines and State rights. He was voted for in national convention as a candidate for the Presidency in 1880 and again in 1884. On appointing his cabinet in March, 1885, Mr. Cleveland selected Mr. Bayard for the post of Secretary of State. Including his great-grandfather Governor Bassett, he is the fifth member of his family to occupy a seat in the United States Senate. On March 30th, 1893, President Cleveland nominated Mr. Bayard for the post of United States Ambassador to Great Britain.

POLITICS AND THE DUTY OF THE CITIZEN.

By Hon. Thomas F. Bayard.

Mr. President and Gentlemen:—It was in no formal or passing spirit of careless acceptance of a kindly and courteous invitation that I came within the precincts of this venerable school of learning, but a long-standing feeling of attachment and sympathy drew me to the Alma Mater of men who were my close kinsmen, and who long years ago shared in these halls the blessings and pleasures of a liberal education, and from these portals went forth to their duty in life.

Among the possessions which I prize are the diplomas which Union College bestowed upon my brother and my uncle as graduates, and (*honoris causa*) upon my honored father as Magister Artium.

The subject I have been asked to consider is "Politics in the United States," and the view I am to take is that of an American discussing with his fellow-citizens the gist and meaning of their Government. And we can confine our view to no class or occupation of men among us, to no geographical or sectional residence, but the entire body of the people of the United States must be included in the view.

The written Constitution of the Government under which we live contains few definitions, but important among those few is-that of citizenship:

"*All persons* born or naturalized in the United States,

and subject to the jurisdiction thereof, *are citizens of the United States* and of the State wherein they shall reside."

The Declaration of Independence was by the whole people of the colonies, and no colony was named in it, and no individual or class referred to of the "good people," but the people conjointly. From the first they acted as a nation composed of free units, acting under a government localized as to the control of the domestic and daily affairs of life, but generalized where the common defence and general welfare were to be considered.

After the people of the colonies had declared their independence as a conjoint act as "one people" appealing to the Supreme Judge of the world for the rectitude of their intentions, absolving themselves from all allegiance to the British Crown, and dissolving all political connection between them and Great Britain, they concluded their declaration by a mutual pledge of *their "lives, their fortunes, and their sacred honor,"* in firm reliance upon the protection of Divine Providence.

Here is language which permits but one construction, that it was each and every individual in all the colonies who thus jointly and severally personally pledged that which each man could only pledge for himself, "*his* life, *his* fortune, and *his* sacred honor."

Individual conscience made appeal to the Supreme Judge as individual conscience alone can, and thus at the very threshold of American emancipation from foreign control we note the unit of American society— the free individual man, whose responsibility was thus assumed, thus announced, and whose personal liberty, civil and religious, became thenceforward the paramount object—the great end to secure which the new Government was designed.

The purposes and object of the declaration was the

security of personal rights—expressly so—"life, liberty, and the pursuit of happiness." *They* were declared to be the true and only basis of all powers of government of man over man; and no mysterious entity greater and wiser than the free man himself was supposed to be generated by the coming together of individuals in "the pursuit of happiness," and by assuming the name of "the State" to absolve the individual from his personal allegiance to politics or lessen to each citizen his share of duty in framing and upholding the social fabric of law under which he is to find protection and security.

After the Declaration of Independence had been promulgated, the Colonial Congress made recommendation to the respective colonies,—"That each colony shall adopt such government as shall best conduce to the happiness of *their constituents in particular*, and to America in general." And this was accordingly acted upon by each colony separately in the formation and adoption by each of a constitution suitable to the interests and feelings of its own inhabitants.

The Articles of Confederation between the States so called into political existence were formally ratified in July, 1778, to be followed by our present Constitution of a closer union in September, 1787.

This Government extends its powers over every man individually, at every moment and in every locality within the jurisdiction of the United States, and together with the laws and treaties enacted and entered into in accordance with its provisions is the supreme law of the land.

The true sovereignty of our National Government was never better stated than by the late Justice Miller in the case of the United States against Lee, in which a mysterious sovereignty higher than the Constitution and laws had been invoked to overthrow the rights of an individual citizen of the United States suing in its judicial courts. In speaking for the majority of the Supreme Court, Justice Miller said:

"No man in this country is so high that he is above the law. No officer of the law may set that law at defiance with impunity. All the officers of the Government, from the highest to the lowest, are creatures of the law, and are bound to obey it.

"It is the only supreme power in our system of Government, and every man, who by accepting office participates in its functions, is only more strongly bound to submit to that supremacy and to observe the limitations which it imposes upon the exercise of the authority it gives."

The domain of morals and the domain of positive law must not be confused, and their boundaries can always be perceived and respected by regarding the principles of religious and personal liberty, and confining the legislative powers to those public objects and purposes which still leave his individual discretion and self-control free to guide the citizen in his "pursuit of happiness," so far as the liberty and happiness of others are not invaded or impaired by his action.

But let it be remembered, politics is a branch of ethics, and to be enduring must be founded upon the moral law.

There can be no such thing in the true American sense as "*low politics.*" Some other name and definition should be given for that degradation of a civic action, that abandonment of individual duty and responsibility, which seeks to make merchandise of political powers and prostitutes the privileges and opportunities afforded by a free and generous popular system to the behests of corrupt selfishness and infidelity to public trusts.

The cold-blooded and conscienceless dealing with the interest of the masses of a population; the perversion of the intent and object of public laws, public policies, and public interests for the sake of private emolument and personal ambition, has no right in this country of ours to the name of "politics," but should be assigned to the category of other unwarranted, criminal, and dishonest acts.

The politics of the American is a branch of the ethics of the American people and is indissolubly connected with the morality of the American people, so that by easy and logical steps, when we come to discuss "politics in the United States," we find ourselves following the footsteps of our ancestors, until we stand upon the high tableland of patriotic duty and personal responsibility for its performance.

The principle of individual responsibility and freedom was necessarily accompanied by faltering and fickle action in the primary, creative, and tentative steps which slowly led by a rugged pathway onward and upward to the consolidated empire and stupendous results which now on every hand attest its virile growth. But the original and seminal principle must not be forgotten nor departed from, and we must ever be mindful, as we dwell in easy enjoyment upon our splendid inheritance, that as individual fidelity and exertion produced it, so the individual default or folly or crime in relation to political duty may cause its decay and ultimate loss. Folly or carelessness may wreck the splendid fabric which has grown from generation to generation, from early stages of pain, privation, and strenuous labor to its present stately proportions.

Public spirit is but an aggregation of private spirit striving for the general welfare.

There is nothing automatic or mechanical in our

system, but it is especially and generically a *voluntary* government, called into being by human hearts, owing its force to voluntary action created by the love of freedom swelling in the souls of men and impelling them to any personal sacrifice necessary for its success.

Will (*voluntas*) is necessarily an individual emotion, and freedom and independence are synonyms in describing a social arrangement in which it is the essential force.

In a government so generated and so regulated, its safety, peace, prosperity, and permanence must necessarily depend upon the sense of political responsibility and duty in the citizens individually, whether acting as representatives, or as simple integers of the community, and upon the degree of intelligence, care, courage, and conscience which they bring to the task.

A German jurist has well said: " What is sowed in private law is reaped in public law, and the law of nations. In the valleys of private law, in the very humblest relations of life, must be collected 'drop by drop, so to speak, the force, the moral capital which the State needs to operate on a large scale and to attain its ends," and I cannot forbear to supplement this by one of our own Emerson's fine thoughts—

" Things are saturated with the moral law. There is no escape from it. Violets and grass preach it; rain and snow, wind and tides, every change, every course in nature, is nothing but a disguised missionary."

Politics in the United States has been so resplendently marked by this recognition of the personal duties of American citizenship that any self-questioning as to such duty is answered by a glance over our short history as a people, and a consequent realization of the force of individuality left free to exercise its faculties in the political field,

When the Constitution of "a more perfect union" had been framed in 1787 the reaction from the intense exertions of the war, the relaxation of the highstrung heroism sustained through the seven weary years of suffering, and falling upon other years of poverty and depression, produced not unnaturally discontent and disorder even among the most patriotic of the scanty population whose homes fringed the shores of the Atlantic.

The scheme of consolidated union met the objections of those jealous of liberty and fearing power in any shape. Commercial selfishness in some States, local jealousies and personal ambitions in others—all added to that spirit for contradiction's sake, so often epidemic, and swelled the current of opposition so violently that the deepest anxiety prevailed lest the fruits of war for independence should be blighted and lost forever in the dissolution of the Union.

In such a condition of affairs, so critical, so environed with doubt and disaster, "temptations without and corruptions within," when it might be said, indeed as it was said, by no one less than the great and only Washington himself, that the life of the nation was held in suspense, it is now plain that nothing but the popular belief that *he* must be at the head of the new government, and that *his* hand would hold the helm on the new voyage in which the ship of State was headed, sufficed to overcome the flood of opposition and allowed us to make the port of National safety. And when the voyage had begun and storm and tempest threatened to overwhelm the unskilled ship's company, we may well note with grateful admiration how the wisdom, courage, and intellectual power of Alexander Hamilton, a citizen of New York, were unhesitatingly devoted to secure the adoption, and then to put in operation the plan of government, differing from that which he had recommended, but of which he, nevertheless, became the most efficient, unselfish, and influential advocate.

Mr. Worthington Ford's edition of the writings of Washington contains in one of the late volumes the episode of Washington's last presidential term, and if any one wishes to become acquainted with the higher elements of American politics let him read the correspondence of Washington and Hamilton, which discloses the noble patriotism which animated those two great citizens, whose names must forever be linked in the history of the Republic.

There is not in any chapter in the history of politics of any age or country a disclosure more honorable to human nature than this correspondence.

And equally may we note how the calm, clear light of John Marshall's mind cast its rays over the devious and obstructed channel. How this simple great man dropped the musket he had carried at Valley Forge and in the many battles for liberty, and with no other education than that obtained in the schools of his native country in Virginia, and the scanty rays of learning shed from the torch of that modest little rustic college of William and Mary, hastened to dedicate with logic unsurpassed and a luminous force unequalled the great intellectual and moral gifts with which he had been endowed by the Eternal Master to the cause of American politics. How he clothed the skeleton of the Constitution with the nerves and muscles of reason and argument until it became a fortress of strength, the citadel of philosophy and sound law for the guidance and government of a mighty nation.

This is but one page in American politics, and in it we may find the index to our duties. It is the fearless, straightforward declaration of conscientious judgment upon public affairs; it is the abandonment of profitable and private pursuits at the call of duty for the unpaid service of which the country stands in need; it is defiance to the loud outcry of popular passion, or ignorance, or disdain for the stealthy efforts of cupidity and plutocratic seduction—such are the contests going on each day all over the broad land now covered by our National ensign.   This is American politics—and to each citizen is entrusted a ballot that he must cast in favor of or against the true and only means by which the objects for which our Government was ordained can be kept secure in our day, and transmitted to the generations so soon to stand here in our places.

To each generation of men come the duties of their day and hour; in each generation the representatives of the people are to be selected, and upon the people and upon each citizen rests the duty of selection of these representatives, through whom the voice of the people is to be expressed, or whose selection individual responsibility cannot avoid or escape.

This day a question whose importance cannot well be exaggerated looms like a baleful shadow over the welfare of the American people and is advancing rapidly to compel its decision.   It constitutes a great fact in American politics, whose importance cannot be circumscribed by the interests of any class or occupation or any number of classes or occupations of our people. No one political party can or does contain its solution, but to every American, regardless of party affiliations, the responsibility has come, is here to-day, to take a citizen's full share in the determination of a political question fraught with possibilities of disaster, that threatens the integrity of popular institutions, and among them the institution of property itself.

I am sure I do not overstate the imminence of the

danger resulting from a departure from the measure
and fixed standard of values which to-day underlie the
vast superstructure of contracts and obligations soluble
in money, and all forms in which credit is relied upon
from one end to the other of this vast and busy
country.

This is a dominating question to-day in American
politics, and it cannot be dwarfed to the dimensions of
party associations, but is pregnant with importance to
the welfare of all, and therefore proper to be used by
me on such an occasion as this to illustrate my conception of what constitutes the highest duties of American
citizenship.

Since the Seventh Century, before the coming of our
Lord on this earth, the inter-relations of gold and silver
and copper coins have complicated the units of standard
weights, and the opening of large and new mines of
these metals have been the chief cause of fluctuation,
ranging as between gold and silver from 12 to 1 to 25
to 1 (as to-day), and between silver and copper from
250 to 1 to 150 to 1, the present ratio.

Of the need of standard weights and measures for
dealings of mankind, I need not speak. No people,
even partially civilized, but recognize their necessity,
and the higher the civilization, the greater the accuracy, the more delicate the test of truthfulness. Politics
and ethics here are blended. In all times, among all
nations the units of weight and measurement have ever
been held sacred and essential, and their standards
have been religiously guarded—usually in temples for
divine worship and by priestly hands. The Roman
capitol and the temple of Hercules were places of
ancient deposit. In England the crypt of Edward the
Confessor was formerly the sacred place of deposit, and
to-day, at Westminster and a few other carefully

guarded public buildings, the standard of the units of weight and measure are carefully preserved.

The force and meaning of the word "immure" came to my mind the other day in reading of the opening of the solid walls of masonry in the public place of deposit in London and the bringing forth from their "immurement" of the standards of weight and measure for the purpose of comparison with the copies kept for daily use; and then with assurance of their absolute and rigid accuracy, restoring them to the wall in which they were again immured for strict preservation. Every precaution that science can supply, even to conducting the tests in vacuum, lest even the atmosphere itself might diminish accuracy, is resorted to.

Such ceremonials, impressive in their formal solemnity, not merely control the vast commercial exchanges of a great empire, but they comply with the great enduring law of morals, and have a meaning which it behooves us carefully to ponder.

The Biblical injunction contained in the Book of Deuteronomy is thus obeyed.

"Thou *shalt not* have in thine house divers measures, a great and a small; but thou *shalt have a perfect and just weight, a perfect and just measure* shalt thou have: that thy days may be lengthened in the land which the Lord thy God giveth thee."

And to like effect is the proverb of Solomon:

"Divers weights and measures are an abomination unto the Lord—and a false balance is not good."

The coins of nations have valuably assisted in the history of metrology, but alas! coupled with the imperfection that there was always a temptation to lessen their weight, so that commercial weights and the scale of buildings and vases have been the most reliable sources of information. *But the ever-existing necessity of a fixed measure and standard value* has compelled the continued use of coins, when once established, notwithstanding their depreciation, because the standard and measure of value *is essential to regulate every conceivable transaction of the the dealings of mankind.* To palter with it, to allow any doubt to be connected with it, to depart from it is to infect the whole community with suspicion and distrust, and consequently to paralyze business in every department of life; to alarm the timid, stimulate the unscrupulous elements of society, and, in short, undermine the basis of all social and civilized intercourse which is contained in the word "credit."

Advancing civilization is marked by the increasing confidence of mankind in each other. Hoarding of money or articles of value signifies lower civilization, because of the absence of credit, and withdraws from circulation the instrument by which exchanges are most conveniently effected as a common denominator. The common measure of value is the commodity that will best serve in this exchange, and no doubt should ever be permitted to attach itself to the stable value of the coin so used.

But it is plain that a great danger impends, and the fabric of our national credit, and consequently of all private credit, is seriously threatened by the apprehended loss of the present gold unit of value and the substitution of the fluctuating and greatly reduced value of silver.

Surely this is politics of the gravest nature, and when we look to the representatives of the American people, now assembled in Congress, what do we see? What do we hear?

In columns of ably conducted journals of high character I have read from day to day the reported remarks and opinions of a number of Senators and Representa-tives, and with sorrow and dismay I find but a comparatively limited number of expressions indicative of an appreciation of the crisis or of an intent to deal with the question otherwise than cunningly, evasively, and to degrade its treatment below the just level of American politics and down to the level of supposed party advantage, local popularity, ignorant prejudice, or even base pecuniary speculation.

How are we to account for this want of statesman-like forecast, this want of outspoken, fearless, well-considered individual judgments, that were in duty bound to be formed and expressed upon a question of such intense importance, after the manner of our fathers, when events demanded of them the performance of similar duties? Is is not the consequences of the triumph of *the machine in politics*, and the admission of money changers into the temple of our liberties? The most famous political machine in history came into use just one hundred years ago during the French Revolution. It took the name of its inventor, Dr. Guillotin, and it was said that he himself became one of its early and almost countless victims. It was a central feature in the Reign of Terror. But it did not shear off men's heads more readily, it did not more effectually still the voice of manly protest and of personal and independent judgment, than *the political machine* which in our day is in operation in some of the most populous and wealthy States of the Union, and which happily has been lately checked so far in its attempt to control the politics of the nation.

We need a new declaration of personal independence, pledging anew life, fortune, and sacred honor, working in the individual heart and mind and proclaiming itself in political action. This was the foundation principle upon which our Government started, and which was intended to be maintained and protected; and our form of Government does secure it, and will secure it, if it is not tamely, and meanly, and basely abandoned. The higher politics of America do not require fortune nor great talents nor family nor business connections nor official station. Political duties can be followed in private station as faithfully if not as conspicuously as in public; by a poor man as well as by a rich; by a man of plain good sense as by a man more gifted—but it needs a man.

In short, politics requires personal character, The higher the personal character the higher the politics. With conscience and character the natural possession of each living man there will be no want of higher politics.

Let me read you a thought of a great soul, whose eloquent voice is now alas! stilled in death. Hear what Phillips Brooks once said of character:

"The wonders of life are not in deeds but in character. Given the character, the deed does not surprise me. Let me look into the martyr's soul and see the perfect consecration which is burning there, and then there is no wonder in my spirit when I see him walking the next day to the stake as to a festival. The wonder would be if I saw him turn and run away. The wonder is that they should be the men they are. When once they are the men they are, the things they do are not wonderful."

Times change, but principles abide. Each era of history exhibits its own page of glory or shame, and men are found far apart in date, but in close spiritual companionship, brothers in arms enlisted under the standard of truth and justice, an invincible army of immortals,

"The men that may not lie"

fighting for

"The truths that cannot die."

Give me leave to call the names of two who were separated by three centuries, but whose examples teaches the same higher duties of citizenship.

One was Sir Philip Sidney, the soldier, statesman, and poet, whose duty it became to encounter the displeasure of his imperious and high-tempered sovereign Queen Elizabeth. This imperial dame had become strongly inclined to accept the proposal of marriage of a French prince, d'Alençon, afterward Duke of Anjou, and in 1579 had signed a treaty of marriage with him. The match was unpopular with the British people, and for publishing a pamphlet in opposition to it the author and the printer were condemned to have their right hands stricken off, and the cruel sentence was carried into execution. The royal court was much divided in opinion, but fear of royal displeasure and its extreme consequences in those unscrupulous days prevented open protest, until in 1580 Sidney resolved to give plain utterance of his patriotic judgments, and in firm but respectful language drew up a strong and careful protest and argument against the marriage.

It has been well called "at once the most eloquent and the most courageous piece of that nature which the age can boast."

In it he speaks to Elizabeth in the character of a simple gentleman and loyal subject, relying upon no support of party nor representing himself as the mouthpiece of an indignant nation. It is the grave but modest warning of a faithful squire to his liege lady in an hour of danger.

The entire document in its lucid and forcible array of argument would be well worth reading, but my reference to it is to show how the courage and high sense of duty of this English gentleman led him to brave the inflamed passions of the haughty, powerful, and possibly amorous Queen, and avert at great personal risk a greater danger to his country. He faced power and did not hesitate to cross its path in the cause of duty. Three centuries rolled by and in the Western Hemisphere a nation had come into existence speaking the English tongue, and, expanding the principles of civil and religious liberty, had grown into a mighty power, a family of self-governing republics, with population and resources beyond the wildest dreams of the European explorers of the day of Queen Elizabeth.

In the United States of America the prizes of wealth, power, and distinction urge men to fierce and eager contention and beget forces, material and moral, which surge to and fro across the broad land with almost irresistible power.

To face popular displeasure demands even more courage than to encounter the disapproval of a monarch. Popular opinion fills this land and wraps itself around each citizen like an atmosphere. Moral courage, self-sustaining, self-reliant conscience is needed by that man who places himself athwart the current of a decided popular demand.

Yet in a popular government such checks against the volatility of popular will are more supremely essential than under any other form, and the duty of opposition increases in proportion to popular error.

One of these exhibitions of popular excitement began to manifest itself about fifteen years ago, and, unhappily for the welfare of the nation, has not yet spent its dangerous force. I mean the demand for the unlimited coinage of silver money regardless of its intrinsic and merchantable value in relation to gold, and to this I have already referred.

In 1878 the Legislature of the State of Mississippi passed almost unanimously, in compliance with an excited popular demand seeking any device that promised relief from their extreme war-begotten poverty, a joint resolution intructing their Senators in Congress to vote for the bills remonetizing silver and repealing the resumption act, and at that time the late Justice Lamar, being one of the Senators, had formed and expressed an opinion in opposition to these measures.

On February 15th, 1878, Mr. Lamar arose to perform "a very painful duty, but one which was none the less clear," and I will use his own words to describe best his own conduct:

"Mr. President, between these resolutions and my convictions there is a great gulf. I cannot pass it. Of my love to the State of Mississippi I will not speak; my life alone can tell it. My gratitude for all the honor her people have done me no words can express. I am best proving it by doing to-day what I think their true interests and their character require me to do. During my life in that State it has been my privilege to assist in the education of more than one generation of her youth, to have given the impulse to wave after wave of the young manhood that has passed into the troubled sea of her social and political life. Upon them I have always endeavored to impress the belief that truth was better than falsehood, honesty better than policy, courage better than cowardice. To-day my lessons confront me. To-day I must be true or false, honest or cunning, faithful or unfaithful to my people. Even in this hour of their legislative displeasure and disapprobation I cannot vote as these resolutions direct. I cannot and will not shirk the responsibility which my position imposes. My duty, as I see it, I will do, and I will vote against this bill.

"When that is done, my responsibility is ended. My reasons for my vote shall be given to my people. Then it will be for them to determine if adherence to my honest convictions has disqualified me from representing them; whether a difference of opinion upon a difficult and complicated subject to which I have given patient, long-continued, conscientious study; to which I have brought entire honesty and singleness of purpose, and upon which I have spent whatever ability God has given me, is now to separate us; whether this difference is to override that complete union of thought, sympathy, and hope which on all other, and, as I believe, even more important subjects binds us together. Before them I must stand or fall. But be their present decision what it may, I know that the time is not far distant when they will recognize my action to-day as wise and just; and, armed with honest convictions of my duty, I shall calmly await results, believing in the utterances of a great American, who never trusted his countrymen in vain, that 'truth is omnipotent and public justice certain.' "

It was my good fortune and happiness to be upon terms of close personal intimacy with Mr. Lamar, and I was in his counsels when he determined upon this line of action—which, it appeared just then, might be the cause of such displeasure to his constituents as to bring his official life to an end.

But he did not hesitate, and as Phillips Brooks said, "Knowing the man's character, his act did not surprise me," nor did it seem to surprise the brave and generous people of the State of Mississippi, who found in him then, as they always found, before and ever since, a man after their own hearts, and their love and admiration returned him unhesitatingly to his place of trust and honor in the Senate, followed him when he entered the cabinet of President Cleveland and when he took his place on the Bench of the Supreme Court; and to-day they mourn above the new-made grave of their noble and heroic representative the man who dared to displease them when duty demanded it, but who never deceived them nor withheld his sincere judgment.

In our measure or estimate of manhood are we to discriminate among citizens because of their calling and occupation? Is not the same standard for patriotic fidelity and service to be applied to each of us? Is a brilliant uniform requisite for courage, is a commission needed for fidelity? Should a soldier be more faithful and true than his sober-suited fellow-citizen? Was Washington in camp more the Father of his country than in the cabinet?

What would be thought of a council of war or a court-martial in which each man is called upon for his judgment, beginning with the youngest, and a refusal to answer or an evasive attempt to escape from direct reply should be essayed? Would not instant rebuke and disgrace attend such shirking of manly and honorable duty? And are we to have another lower and an opposite standard of morals for our civil life?—when men are selected as civil representatives and yet falter, equivocate, shuffle, or falsify their conscience for fear of losing popular favor or place or pay. And this is true of all countries, and Montalembert, a French publicist, tells us:

"An unwise thirst after salaried public employment is the worst of social maladies. It infects the whole body politic with a venal and servile humor. It creates a brood of hungry suitors capable of every excess to gratify their longings and fit instruments for any base purpose as soon as they are in place."

Such were not the impulses, the objects of the men who made this Government a possibility. It was because their personal characters were enlisted, and

because, being free, their characteristics could be exerted and displayed.   If, as Pope sang, following Homer,

" Whatever day
Makes man a slave, takes half his worth away,"

it is plain that individual liberty is esential for the
permanence of our system, for " corrupted freemen are
the worst of slaves."

Let scorn and wit exhaust their sneers, and jibes, or
execrations, one fact must be admitted, and cannot
truthfully be denied of the party called "the Mug-
wumps" in the political vocabulary of to-day, and that
is, they have exerted themselves for something higher
than the official patronage of the Republic.   Whatever
else they may be, they cannot be accused of office-
begging.   This alone gives them a right to respect,
and in it I discern a principle of political action which
I hail with respect and gratification and welcome as a
refreshing and elevating force in the Republic.

Sir Walter Scott relates that when the old Lord
Auchincleck, father of Johnson's Boswell, was in alter-
cation with the Doctor over the character of Oliver
Cromwell, Old Sam roared out: " Well, sir, what good
did Cromwell ever do the country?" " God, Doctor!"
said the Scotchman, " He gart kings ken they had a
lith in their neck."

And I hold, the man or set of men who lets King
Caucus or the party bosses occasionally know they
have "a lith in their necks" performs important and
necessary public service.

The lesson needs repetition from time to time that
political parties are but means to an end, and that end
the safety, honor, and welfare of the country, and when
that end is forgotten the sooner party dies the better.

Forewarned is forearmed, and the dangers to our

welfare to which I have referred are sufficiently proclaimed.

The forces of repair of construction and conservation are not idle but steadily and efficiently at work all over the land. Chief among them are the educational institutes, covering the country with an intellectual and moral network by which vice and ignorance are trammelled and restrained.

Day by day in the midst of the idle froth of sensationalism published as "news," the records of Vanity Fair, the calendar of crime, the sorrows, sores, and the sins of society, there is found also the glad tidings of new schools endowed, new institutes of education and industry founded, new libraries erected, and kindred benefactions all springing from the awakened conscience of individuals, voluntarily adding to the political strength of our country.

This respected college is an honored factor in the great purposes of our Government, and I feel it an honor and a privilege to be here, humbly but sincerely to add my effort to promote the cause of higher politics in the United States.

MONTGOMERY SCHUYLER.

MONTGOMERY SCHUYLER was born at Ithaca, N. Y., August 19th, 1843. He is the seventh in descent from Philip Pieterse Schuyler, who emigated from Holland to Beverwyck, now Albany, married there in 1650, and became a magistrate and captain of foot in the service of the West India Company. His father, Rev Dr. Anthony Schuyler, is the rector of Grace Church, Orange, N. J. Mr. Schuyler was a member of the class of 1862 in Hobart College, but was not graduated. In 1865 he joined the staff of the New York *World*, then under the editorship of Manton Marble, and his life ever since has been that of a working journalist. His connection with the *World*, mainly in the capacity of an editorial writer, lasted for eighteen years, until the sale of the paper in 1883, when he joined the staff of the New York *Times*, with which he has since been connected. He was early attracted to the study of architecture, and has written much upon that art, especially with reference to its condition and tendencies in this country. He is the author of "Studies in American Architecture" (New York, 1892), and has now in preparation a "History of Architecture in the United States."

ARCHITECTURE.

By Montgomery Schuyler.

The subject that has been assigned to me is that which I should have chosen had I been left free to choose. It is more true, perhaps, of architecture than of any other of the arts that deal with form that the prosperity and advancement of it depend upon the existence of an enlightened public as well as of skilful practitioners. It is true that the public, any public, is enlightened by the efforts of the practitioners, and can be enlightened in no other way. The philosophy of art at least is a philosophy teaching by examples. It is only by familiarity with admirable examples that we come to admire rightly. A sense of responsibility for one's admirations may be called the very beginning of culture, nor can a culture be deemed complete that does not include a discriminating judgment of the works of the oldest and the most pervading of all the arts. It is not to be expected, nor perhaps to be desired, that an educated layman shall possess theories of art and standards of judgment either acquired for himself or derived from others. But it is very much to be desired that he shall have a sense so habitual and automatic that it may well seem to be instinctive of the fitness or unfitness, congruity or incongruity, beauty or ugliness of the buildings that he daily passes, and that in any case must exert upon him an influence that is not the less but the more powerful for being unconsciously felt. Such a sense comes most readily and most surely from the habitual contemplation of excellent works. It is the birthright of a man who has been born and reared in a country in which admirable monuments have been familiar to him from childhood. It is a means of education from which we in this country are necessarily to a great degree debarred, for I suppose it will not be denied that there are many American communities in which one may grow up to manhood without once having sight of a respectable specimen of the art of architecture. I remember standing for some hours in the square upon which fronts the Cathedral of Rouen, one of the loveliest of the legacies the Middle Ages have bequeathed to modern times, and watching the busy throng of Frenchmen and Frenchwomen, the citizens of a bustling modern town, that passed beneath it. There was scarcely one, of whatever rank in life, that did not pause in passing long enough to cast one recognizing and admiring glance at the weatherworn and fretted front. Think what an education the daily sight of such a monument constitutes, how it trains the generations that are reared in its shadow, and how deeply a people so unconsciously trained would fail to admire the very smartest and most ornate edifices of many American towns! It seems to me that something of the same beneficent influence is shed upon the people of New York from the spire of Old Trinity, as it soars serenely above the bustle of Broadway, and stops the vista of Wall Street, or upon the people of Boston by the ordered bulk of the tower of the new Trinity looming so large over the dwellings of the Back Bay.

You may retort upon me that the influence of the cathedral of Rouen is not perceptible in the modern architecture of Rouen; but there is much to be said in behalf of the modern architecture that surrounds Rouen cathedral, as of the modern architecture that surrounds

Notre Dame of Paris, in comparison with the current architecture of our American towns. I shall not be charged with underrating the essential differences between the mediæval and the modern architecture of France and of Europe, or with overrating the modern architecture, because the difference is in a manner the main theme upon which I have to address you. It seems to me one of the most pointed contrasts that the world affords between a living and progressive and a conventional and stationary art. But the modern building, the current building of France, and more or less of Europe in general, is distinguished in this comparison with the current building of American towns—and in either case I am speaking not of the exceptional works of artists but of the prevailing and vernacular work of journeymen—it is distinguished by certain qualities that we must admit to be valuable, by sobriety, by measure, by discretion. Very much of this comes no doubt from the learning of the schools, from the learning in particular of the great school that since the time of the great Louis has dominated the official architecture of France, and the influence of which is transmitted, as we see, to the common workman. You will remember that these qualities—of sobriety, measure, discretion —are the very qualities which Mr. Matthew Arnold finds to distinguish French literature in the comparison with English literature, and which, in that well-known essay of his upon "The Literary Influence of Academies," he attributes so largely to the existence of the French Academy. I cannot help thinking that he exaggerates this influence, and that the undeniable difference is more largely due than he admits to national characteristics and less largely to the machinery of institutions. In the national building, however, the national school of France has without doubt had a great influence. It is an influence which is spread‚ing over the world, and which has already established a distinct cult of its own among American architects, that is at present perhaps the dominant influence in our own architecture—an influence the nature of which I shall ask you to consider. But these excellent qualities which French building shows in comparison with American building seem to me to be also due largely to the existence of relics of the great art of the past. In England, where there has never been any official inculcation of architecture, the current building is characterized in comparison with our own, though in a less degree, by the same qualities that characterize the French building. It is less violent, more restrained, more decorous. And England, like France, possesses those monuments the very presence of which seems to temper crudity and to repress eccentricity, to make impossible the architectural freaks that seem to be spontaneously generated in the absence of their restraining influence.

It is not many years since an English traveller, not an architect, but a travelled and cultivated man of the world, delivered the opinion that there was no country in the world in which the art of architecture was at so low a stage as in the United States. He had just traversed the continent, and there was certainly no malice in his remarks, the spirit of which was entirely amicable. There can be little doubt that his saying simply reflected the impression that an experience like his would be apt to make upon any cultivated European. It is the impression derived not from the buildings that are the boast of a few towns, the exceptional and artistic performances, but from a general survey of the building of the country. The building is doubtless more crude and provincial, as a rule, in the newer than in the older parts of the country; and one main reason for this is that the older parts of the country, the towns of the Atlantic seaboard that comprised the colonies, contained examples of colonial building that were as nearly as the builders could make them examples of the current architecture of the old country. They were not very many in number, nor very extensive in scale, not very durable in construction. But every one of the Atlantic towns possessed one or more of them that have lasted to our own time, or nearly so, and that gave to the builders who lived and worked in their presence examples of measure and sobriety and discretion that tended to preserve them from the excesses of the pioneer builders who had not the advantage of any models whatever.

It is not to be wondered at that some twenty years ago many of the young architects of the country should have become so revolted with the extravagance and the crudity of the current building as to revert to the colonial building for models. And this accounts for the vogue, short-lived as it was, which the so-called Queen Anne fashion of building had in this country. Although the revival of it was imported from England and not developed here, it was connected with this admiration for the colonial work which, though it was commonly tame, was at least never wild. The crudity of much of the work that was done during the Gothic revival set architects to studying the classic detail of the old mansions, although a knowledge of this detail was simply part of the stock in trade of the carpenters and the plasterers who were imported during the Eighteenth Century, and continued to be part of the stock in trade of their successors during the first quarter at least of the Nineteenth. Though Queen Anne, specifically so called, was a very passing fashion, the preference for classic detail, as an orderly and understood assemblage of forms in the use of which it was difficult to attain a positively offensive result, survived Queen Anne, and has been so potent ever since that the present tendency of architecture in this country is a reversion to the Renaissance that has prevailed in Europe for the past three centuries. This tendency has been very powerfully promoted by the increasing influence on this country of the Paris school of fine arts, of which the pupils, filled with its traditions, are every year returning in increased numbers to take part in the building of the United States. Especially has this tendency been stimulated just now by the brilliant success of the architecture of the Columbian Exposition, which was essentially a display, on an imposing scale, of modern French architecture, though it is also true that some of the architecture even of the World's Fair was French not so much after the École des Beaux Arts as "after the scole of Stratford-atte-Bowe."

The attractiveness of the French ideal in architecture is so great that it has imposed itself all over Europe, insomuch that the new quarters of nearly all European cities are becoming imitations of Paris. It is visibly tending to impose itself upon this country also, under the influences to which I have referred, the revolt against the crudity of our unschooled vernacular building and the zealous propagandism of the pupils of the Beaux Arts, and of the architects whom they have in their turn influenced. It would be folly to dispute that the training of the French school, upon which the architectural training of all Europe is more or less modelled, is a most valuable training in qualities and accomplishments that are common to all architecture and that are needed in all architecture. Founded as it is upon the study of the classic orders, it confers or cultivates a perception of proportion and relation, of adjustment and scale; in other words, of that sobriety, measure, and discretion which, in whatever style they may be exhibited, or whether they be exhibited in works not to be classified under any of the historical styles, so plainly distinguish the work of an educated from the work of an uneducated architect, precisely as the literary work of a man who has studied the models of literature is distinguished from that of an uneducated man. One may freely own that the current architecture of Europe is more admirable than the current architecture of America, and that, if that were all, those architects would have reason who urge us to adopt current European methods in the study of architecture and to naturalize, or at least to import, current European architecture. But it is not American architecture alone, it is modern architecture in general that leaves a great deal to be desired as the expression in building of modern life. It is not only our own country, but it is the time that is architecturally out of joint. No thoughtful and instructed person who considers what an expression classic architecture was of classic life, or mediæval architecture of mediæval life, is satisfied with modern architecture, for the reason that no such student can regard it as in the same degree or in the same sense an expression of modern life. The French seem indeed to be very well satisfied with the result of their methods of instruction and practice, but it is worth while to remember that the whole professional and literary life of that French architect whose writings have had the strongest influence upon this generation of readers—I mean Viollet-le-Duc—was a protest against the aims and the methods of the École des Beaux Arts, and the academic architecture which it produced as unrepresentative of modern French life, as

12

unreasonable and untrue. So inveterate and so radical was his opposition to the manner in which architecture was taught at the French national school, the training of which is held up to us as a completely adequate model, that on his appearance there as a lecturer he was mobbed by the students whom he was invited to address and to whom his criticisms seemed to be almost in the nature of blasphemy.

The late Mr. Richardson, whose great services to the architecture of this country no one will deny, who was himself a graduate of the École des Beaux Arts and who brought its training to the solution of American architectural problems, bore interesting testimony in the same direction. He told me that, revisiting France many years after his academic experiences in Paris and when he himself was at the height of his success and celebrity, he had looked up those who had been the most promising of his fellow-students. He found them well-established architects and many of them occupying the position, so much coveted in France, of government architects. But he found them—I do not remember that he made any exceptions but at any rate he found many of them—deeply dissatisfied with the official architecture which was imposed upon them by the necessities of their careers, lamenting that they were not at liberty to transcend the trammels of the official style, and envying him the freedom he enjoyed in this respect as a practitioner in America and not in France. Surely we may very well hesitate before acknowledging that a system which is thus deprecated by theorists on the one hand and by practitioners on the other, as inadequate to the architectural needs of the country from which it is derived and in which it has been naturalized for two hundred years, and as incompetent to produce the architectural expression of French life, may be transplanted with confidence as promising complete satisfaction of our own needs, and as offering us the expression in architecture of American life.

How are we to explain the anomaly thus presented? While every other art is living and progressive, architecture is by common consent stationary, if it be not actually retrograde. In every other art the artists have their eyes on the future. They do not doubt that the greatest achievements of their arts are before them and not behind—

"That which they have done but earnest of the things that they
    shall do."

In architecture alone men look back upon the masterpieces of the past not as points of departure but as ultimate attainments, content for their own part if by recombining the elements and reproducing the forms of these monuments, they can win from an esoteric circle of archæologists the praise of producing some reflex of their impressiveness. This process has gone so far that architects have expected and received praise for erecting for modern purposes literal copies of ancient buildings, or, where the materials for exact reproduction were wanting, ingenious restorations of those buildings. In architecture alone does an archæological study pass for a work of art. The literature of every modern nation is an express image of the mind and spirit of the nation. The architecture of every modern nation, like the dress of every modern nation, is coming more and more to lose its distinctiveness and to reflect the fashion of Paris. It was not always so. The architecture of Greece and Rome tells us as much as antique literature of Greek and Roman life. Mediæval architecture tells us so much more of mediæval life than all other documents of that life that they become insignificant in the comparison, and that from their monuments alone the modern man can succeed in penetrating into the spirit of the Middle Ages. Nay, in our own time the architecture of every country outside the pale of European civilization is a perfectly adequate and a perfectly accurate reflex of the life of that country.

I have spoken of the analogy between architecture and literature. It seems to me that it is not fantastic, and that if we follow it it may lead us to a comprehension of the very different state of the two arts to-day. Nobody pretends that modern literature is not an exact reflex of modern civilization. If we find fault with the condition of it in any country, we are not regarding it as a separate product which could be improved by the introduction of different methods. We are simply arraigning the civilization of the country thus completely expressed. If we find one literature pedantic, another frivolous, and another dull, we without hesitation impute these defects as the results of national traits. The notion that any modern literature is not a complete expression of the national life no more occurs to us than the notion that any modern architecture is such an expression.

Now, modern architecture, like modern literature, had its origin in the revival of learning. The Italian Renaissance in architecture was inextricably connected with that awakening of the human spirit which was the beginning of modern civilization. It is not that classic models have been discarded or neglected in the one art and retained in the other; for down to our own generation, at least, a liberal education, a literary education, has been a classical education. Whatever the baccalaureate degree is coming to mean now, for several centuries it has meant a knowledge of the masterpieces of Greek and Roman letters, as the education of an architect has during the same time implied a knowledge of the masterpieces of Greek and Roman building. A main difference has been that in literature the classical models have been used, and in architecture they have been copied. If writers had hesitated, even while Latin was the universal language of Europe, to use locutions "that would have made Quinctilian stare and gasp," it seems to me quite certain that there could have been no literary progress, while it seems to be almost a tenet of the architectural schools, and at any rate it is a fair deduction from modern academic architecture, that no architectural progress is possible. There, alone in the work of mankind, the great works of the past are not alone useful for doctrine, for reproof, for correction, for instruction, are not even models in the sense in which we use the word in reference to other arts, but are "orders" to be carried out as literally as the conditions will allow, are fetiches to be ignorantly worshipped and invested with mysterious powers.

At the time of the revival of learning the purists were as strenuous in literature as they are even yet in architecture, and for a time as prevailing. The literary classics were to them what the architectural classics still are to the practitioners of official architecture, and the vocabulary of the ancients as sacred a repertory of words as the orders of the ancients a repertory of forms, to which nothing could be added without offence. To them it was not requisite that a writer should express his mind fully; it was not even necessary that he should have anything to say, but it was necessary that his Latinity should be unimpeachable. So long and so far as it was enforced, the restriction to the ancient vocabulary had as deadening an effect upon literature as the like restriction still has upon architecture. Lord Bacon has given an excellent account in a few sentences of the consequences of this "more exquisite travail in the languages original" upon the progress of literature and the advancement of learning. "Men began to hunt more after words than matter; more after the choiceness of the phrase and the round and clean composition of the sentence, and the sweet fulling of the clauses, . . . than after the weight of matter, worth of subject, soundness of argument, life of invention or depth of judgment." The literary purists of the Renaissance were inevitably impatient of men who were preoccupied with what they had to say rather than with their way of saying it, and were especially incensed against the school philosophers "whose writings," to quote Bacon again, "were altogether in a different style and form, taking liberty to coin and frame new terms of art to express their own sense, and to avoid circuit of speech, without regard to the pureness, pleasantness, and, as I may call it, lawfulness of the phrase or word." Substitute "form" for "phrase or word" and you have here an exact statement of the respective positions of the progressive architect and of the architectural purist, and of the reason why it is out of the question that architecture should advance when the teaching and the practice and the judgment of it are confided to the architectural purists.

In literature the restriction did not last long. If it could have lasted it would have arrested the literature and the civilization of Europe, for a demand that nothing should be expressed in new words was in effect a demand that nothing new should be expressed. Such a restriction, when the human spirit had once been aroused, it could not accept. The instinct of self-preservation forbade its acceptance. Men who had something to say insisted upon saying it, saying it at first in barbarous Latin, to the pain of the purists who had nothing to say and did not see why anybody else should have anything to say that could not be expressed in the classical vocabulary; saying it afterward in "the noble vulgar speech" which at first, and until it had been developed and chastened and refined by literary use, seemed cruder and more barbarous still. The progress of mankind being at stake, the purists in literature were overwhelmed. Only the progress of architecture being at stake in the other case, the purists have prevailed and architecture has been sacrificed, with only local and sporadic revolts, and these for the most part within our own century, in place of the literary revolution that was triumphantly accomplished four centuries ago.

It was not accomplished without a struggle. The "more exquisite travail in the languages original," when there was no other but classic literature, had induced in scholars the belief that the masterpieces of that literature would never be equalled. It is, I believe, still questioned by scholars whether the classic masterpieces have been equalled even now; while it is the opinion of scholars that the languages in which they were composed are still the most perfect orders of speech that have existed. It was natural, then, that men who had nothing in particular to say, or at any rate felt no urgent need of expressing themselves, should have deemed that classic literature was complete as well as impeccable, and that its limitations could not be transcended. Fortunately for us all, there were other men who felt, with Browning, that

> "It were better youth
> Should strive, through acts uncouth,
> Toward making than repose on aught found made."

and these men were the greatest scholars, as well as the greatest thinkers of the age. Politian, of whom it has been said by a critic of our own time that he "showed how the taste and learning of the classical scholar could be grafted on the stock of the vernacular," ridiculed the purists in better Latin than their own. "Unless the book is at hand from which they copy," he said, "they cannot put three words together. I entreat you not to be fettered by that superstition. As nobody can run who is intent upon putting his feet in the footsteps of another, so nobody can write well who does not dare to depart from what is already written." And while the Italian scholar was deriding the Italian pedants, the Dutch scholar, who did not even look forward to a time when the vernacular should supplant Latin, yet protested against the imposition of classic forms as shackles upon modern thought. "Hereafter," said Erasmus, "we must not call bishops reverend fathers, nor date our letters from the birth of Christ because Cicero never did so. What could be more senseless, when the whole age is new, religion, government, culture, manners, than not to dare to speak otherwise than Cicero spoke. If Cicero himself should come to life, he would laugh at this race of Ciceronians."

It would be as presumptuous in me as it is far from my intention to disparage academic training, in architecture, or in literature. The men who have done most toward building up these great literatures that are at once the records and the trophies of modern civilization have for the most part been classical scholars, and classical scholarship stood them in particularly good stead when they worked in the vernacular, especially during the formative periods of these literatures, when there were as yet no standards or models but those of antiquity. Perhaps what seems to us the most autocthonous of our literature owed more to this culture than we are apt to suppose. "I always said," Dr. Johnson observes, "that Shakespeare had enough Latin to grammaticize his English." They derived from their classical studies a literary tact that could have been imparted so well in no other way. Certainly the same thing is true of the classically trained architects. Whether they are working in the official style that has been the language of their schools, or have attempted the idiomatic and vernacular treatment of more extended and varied methods of construction than the very simple construction of Greece, which was expressed with consummate art, and the more ambitious and complicated construction of the Romans, which yet is simple compared with our modern constructions and which cannot be said to have attained its artistic expression; in either case there is equally in their work this tact, this measure and propriety that bespeak professional training. It is not the training that I am deprecating, but the resting in the training as not a preparation but an attainment. There is another pregnant saying of Bacon that may well recur to us when we see the attempt to meet modern requirements without departing from antique forms, and to carry out academic exercises in classic architecture into actual buildings: "Studies teach not their own use, but that is a wisdom without them and above them, won by observation." It is as if an educated man in our day should confine his literary efforts to Latin composition. Very curious and admirable essays have been made even in Latin poetry and even in our own time. To see how near one can come to expressing modern ideas in classic language is an interesting and useful exercise, by the very force of the extreme difficulty of even suggesting them and the impossibility of really expressing them. When the modern Latinist has finished this circuitous and approximative process he has produced what—a poem? No, but only an ingenious toy for the amusement of scholars, a "classic design." If he devoted his whole literary life to the production of such things we should be entitled to pronounce decisively that he had nothing to say, or he would take the most direct way of saying it. It would be evident that he was preoccupied with the expression and not with the thing to be expressed, not with the idea but "with the pureness, pleasantness, and, as I may call it, lawfulness of the phrase or word." A living and progressive classic poetry in our day, we all perceive to be merely a contradiction in terms. Classicism is the exclusion of life and progress; and a living and progressive classic architecture is in fact equally a contradiction in terms. Forms are the language of the art of building, and architectural forms are the results and the expression of construction. This is true of the architecture of the world before the Renaissance, excepting the Roman imitations of Greek architecture. It it true even now of the architecture of all that part of the world which lies outside the pale of European civilization. It is only since the Renaissance and in Europe and America that classic forms have been used as an envelope of constructions not classic, and that the attempt to develop building into architecture has been abandoned in favor of the attempt to cover and to conceal building with architecture. This attempt is beset with difficulties, by reason of the modern requirements that cannot be concealed. I have heard of a classic architect saying that it was impossible to do good architecture nowadays on account of the windows. This is an extreme instance, doubtless, but the practitioner of classic architecture must often be as much annoyed by the intrusion of his building into his design, and the impossibility of ignoring or of keeping it out altogether, as the modern Latin poet by the number of things of which the classic authors never heard that he has to find words for out of the classic authors. The versifier does not venture to complain in public, because everybody would laugh at him, and ask him why he did not write English. But the classic architect is not afraid to make his moan, and to complain of the intractability of modern architectural problems, or to excuse himself from attempting a solution of them upon the ground that they do not fit the classic forms. He is not likely to find sympathy in his complaint of the oppressiveness of shackles which, in this country at least, he has voluntarily assumed. Why should we not laugh at him also? He, too, may be recommended to write English, which in his case means to give the most direct expression possible to his construction in his forms, and to use his training to make this expression forcible, "elegant," and scholarly, poetical if the gods have made him poetical; at any rate, "to grammaticize his English" instead of confining himself to an expression that is avowedly indirect, circuitous, conventional, and classic, a "polite language" like the Latin of modern versifiers—*Si revivisceret ipse Cicero, rideret hoc Ciceronianorum genus.*

The repertory of the architectural forms of the past is the vocabulary of the architect. But there is this difference between his vocabulary and that of the poet: that a word is a conventional symbol, while a true architectural form is the direct expression of a mechanical fact. Any structural arrangement is susceptible, we must believe, of an artistic and effective expression. Historical architecture contains precedents, to be acquainted with which is a part of professional education, for many if not for most of the constructions commonly used in modern building. But classic architecture does not contain them. The Greek construction is the simplest possible. The more complicated Roman con- struction was not artistically developed and expressed by the Romans themselves, and the literary revivalists of classic architecture in the Fifteenth Century restricted themselves and their successors to the Roman expres- sion, without very clearly understanding what it was. They were more royalist than the king, more Cicero- nian than Cicero. If we are to accept the statement of Viollet-le-Duc, Vitruvius himself, if he had submitted his own design, as he described it, for the basilica of Fano, in a competition of the École des Beaux Arts at the beginning of this century, would have been ruled out of the competition for his ignorance of Roman architecture. But in any case, the classical building embraces but a small part of the range of constructions that are available to the modern builder. To confine one's self to classic forms means therefore to ignore and reject, or else to cloak and dissemble, the construc- tions of which the classic builders were ignorant, or which they left undeveloped, to be developed by the barbarians. For here comes in another restricting tenet of the schools, that you must not confuse historical styles. No matter how complete an expression of an applicable construction may have been attained, if it does not come within the limits of the historic style that you have proposed to yourself, it is inadmissible. This is not a tenet of the official schools exclusively. It is imposed wherever architecture is practised arch- æologically. In the early days of the Gothic revival in England Gothic building was divided and classified, more or less arbitrarily, and it would fatally have discredited an architect to mix Early English and Middle Pointed, or to introduce any detail for which

he had not historical precedent, and this with regard not
at all to the artistic success of his work but only to its
historical accuracy. It was not until the architects of
the revival outgrew this superstition that their work
had much other than an archæological interest. Any
arbitrary restriction upon the freedom of the artist is
a hindrance to the life and progress of his art. While
it is no doubt more difficult to attain unity by the use
of constructions that have been employed and expressed in different ages and countries than by renounc-
ing all but such as have been employed together before, and have been analyzed and classified in the
schools, the artist is entitled to be judged by the success of his attempt and not to be prevented from
making it. American architects are happy in being
freer than the architects of any other country from the
pressure of this convention. By the introduction of
the elevator, some twenty years ago, an architectural
problem absolutely new was imposed upon them, a
problem in the solution of which there were no directly available and no directly applicable precedents
in the history of the world. That many mistakes
should be made, and that much wild work should be
done, was inevitable. But within these twenty years
there has been attained not only a practical, but to
a great degree an artistic solution of this problem
presented by the modern office building. The efforts
of the architects have already resulted in a new architectural type, which in its main outlines imposes itself,
by force of merit, upon future designers and upon
which future designers can but execute variations.
This is really a very considerable achievement, this
unique contribution of American architects to their art.
While the architects who have had most to do with
establishing it have been learned and trained as well as

thoughtful designers, it seems to me that they have had advantages here that they could not have enjoyed where conventional and academic restrictions had more force. Certainly, in all the essays that have been made toward the solution of this new problem, none have been less fortunate and less successful than those of academically trained architects who have undertaken to meet a new requirement by an aggregation of academic forms, and to whom studies had not taught their own use. But the problem is by no means yet completely solved. The real construction of these towering buildings, the Chicago construction, is a structure of steel and baked clay, and when we look for an architectural expression of it, or for an attempt at an architectural expression of it, we look in vain. No matter what the merits or demerits may be of the architectural envelope of masonry, it is still an envelope, and not the thing itself, which is nowhere, inside or out, permitted to appear. The structure cannot be expressed in terms of historical architecture, and for that reason the attempt to express it has been foregone. The first attempts to express it must necessarily be rude and inchoate. The new forms that would result from these attempts would be repellent, in the first place because of their novelty, even if they were perfect from the beginning; in the second place, because in the nature of things and according to the experience of mankind they cannot be perfect from the beginning, for the labors not only of many men but of many generations have been required to give force and refinement to the expression in architectural forms of any system of construction. If the designer, however, is repelled by the strangeness of the forms that result from early attempts to express what has not been expressed before, if "youth" will not "strive through acts uncouth toward making" but takes refuge in "aught found made," that is the abandonment of progress. The Chicago construction doubtless presents a difficult problem. All problems are difficult till they are solved. But the difficulty is no greater than other difficulties that have been encountered in the history of architecture and that have been confronted and triumphantly overcome. Is there anything in modern construction that is *a priori* more unpromising, as a subject for architectural treatment, than a "shore" of masonry, built up on the outside of a wall to prevent it from being thrust out by a pressure from within? I do not know what the modern architect would do as an artist if as a constructor he found it necessary to employ such a member. In the absence of applicable precedents he would be apt to conclude that so ugly an appendage to his building would not do to show, and to conceal it behind a screen wall nicely decorated with pilasters. But the builders upon whom the use of this member was imposed, not having enjoyed the advantage of a classical education, saw nothing for it but to exhibit the shore and to try to make it presentable by making it expressive of its function. Their early efforts were so "uncouth" that the modern architect, if he had seen the work at this stage, would have been confirmed in his conclusion that the shore was architecturally intractable. The mediæval builders kept at work at it, master after master, and generation after generation, until at last they made it speak. Made it speak? They made it sing; and there it is, a new architectural form, the flying buttress of a Gothic cathedral, an integral part of the most complicated and most complete organism ever produced by man, one of the organisms so like those of nature that Emerson might well say that

"Nature gladly gave them place,
Adopted them into her race,
And granted them an equal date,
With Andes and with Ararat."

The analogy is not fantastic. In art as in nature an organism is an assemblage of interdependent parts of which the structure is determined by the function, and of which the form is an expression of the structure. Let us hear Cuvier on natural organisms:

"A claw, a shoulder-blade, a condyle, a leg or arm bone, or any other bone separately considered, enables us to discover the description of teeth to which they have belonged; so also reciprocally we may determine the form of the other bones from the teeth. Thus, commencing our investigations by a careful survey of any one bone by-itself, a person who is sufficiently master of the laws of organic structure may, as it were, reconstruct the whole animal to which that bone had belonged."

This character of the organisms of nature is shared by at least one of the organisms of art. A person who is "sufficiently master of the laws of organic structure" can reconstruct, from the cross-section of the pier of a Gothic cathedral, the whole structural system of which it is the nucleus and prefigurement. The design of such a building seems to me to be worthy, if any work of man is worthy, to be called a work of creative art. It is an imitation not of the forms of nature but of the processes of nature. Perhaps it was never before carried so far or so successfully as in the Thirteenth Century. Certainly it has not been carried out so successfully since. It has not been for lack of constructions waiting to receive an artistic expression, for mechanical science has been carried far beyond the dreams of the mediæval builders, and the scientific constructors are constantly pressing upon the artistic constructor, upon the architect, in new structural devices, new problems that the architect is prone to shirk. He is likely to be preoccupied with new arrangements and combinations of historical forms. He asks himself, as it has been said, not what would Phidias have done if he had had this thing to do, but what did Phidias when he had something else to do. An architectural form, being the ultimate expression of a structural arrangement, cannot be foreseen, and the form which the new expression takes comes as a surprise to its author. He cannot more than another tell with what body it will come. Take one recent example, the so-called cantilever of modern engineering. Some of you may be familiar with representations of the Forth bridge in Scotland, in which that recent device has been used upon the largest scale thus far and with the most impressive results. There is one of the new architectural forms for which we are unthinkingly calling. Is it conceivable that this form could have occurred to a man who sat down to devise a new form, without reference to its basis and motive in the laws of organic structure? And so it is always with real architectural forms. There have been very voluminous discussions within this century upon the "invention" of the pointed arch, discussions which have come to little because they have started from a baseless assumption. Architectural forms are not invented; they are developed, as natural forms are developed, by evolution. A main difference between our times and the mediæval times is that then the scientific constructor and the artistic constructor were one person; now they are two. The art of architecture is divided against itself. The architect resents the engineer as a barbarian, the engineer disparages the architect as a dilettante. It is difficult to deny that each is largely in the right. The artistic insensibility of the modern engineer is not more fatal to architectural progress than the artistic irrelevancy of the modern architect. In general, engineering is at least progressive while architecture is at most stationary. And, indeed, it may be questioned whether, without a thought of art and, as it were, in spite of himself, the engineer has not produced the most impressive, as certainly he has produced the most charateristic monuments of our time. "A locomotive," says Viollet-le-Duc, "has its peculiar physiognomy, not the result of caprice but of necessity. Some say it is but an ugly machine. But why ugly? Does it not have the true expression of brutal energy?" The modern battleship is purely an engineering construction, developed in accordance with its functions as a fighting machine, and without conscious reference to the expression of these functions. Yet no one who has seen a typical and completely developed example of the modern warship, such as the *Jean Bart*, which has been seen in American waters, needs to be told that it is a more moving expression of the horrors of war than has ever been seen in the world before, that no poet's or painter's dream of

> "that fatal, that perfidious bark,
> Built in the eclipse and rigged with curses dark,"

appears with anything like so much force to the imagination as this actual, modern and prosaic machine of murder. What may we not hope from the union of modern engineering with modern architecture, when the two callings, so harshly divorced, are again reunited, and when the artistic constructor applies his cultivated sensibility and his artistic training, not to copying but to producing, no longer to the compilation of the old forms, but to the solution of the new problems that press upon him—when he shall have learned the use of the studies that teach not their own use.

ALBON MAN.

ALBON MAN was born in Westville, Franklin County, N. Y.,
June 29th, 1826. His father and mother were both born in Vermont
and were descended from old Puritan stock. Mr. Man's father
was Dr. Ebenezer Man; his grandfather, Dr. Albon Man, and
his great-grandfather, Dr. Ebenezer Man, the name of the eldest
son alternately being Ebenezer and Albon. He fitted for college
at the academies in Fort Covington and Malone, Franklin County,
and entering Union College in 1845, graduated in 1849 in both the
literary and scientific courses, and was elected a member of the
Phi Beta Society. After studying law with his uncle, Albon P.
Man of New York, he was admitted to the bar of New York, February, 1852. He was admitted as attorney and counsellor of the
Supreme Court of the United States in January, 1871. Soon after
his admission to the bar he became partner with his uncle, Albon
P. Man; but by reason of the sickness of his father was obliged
to return to Franklin County and establish his office at Malone,
N. Y., where, in addition to practice of the law, he was employed
as a local engineer upon the Northern New York Railroad. He
was elected district attorney of Franklin County in 1860, and in
1861 went out to the war as major of the 98th New York Volunteers. His health was completely broken down by the hardships
of the Peninsular campaign, and after the battles about Yorktown, the Battle of Williamsburgh, and the first Battle of Fair
Oaks, in which he participated, he was obliged to resign his
commission and return to Franklin County, where he had still
been kept in the office of district attorney by the kindness of the
inhabitants. Finding, however, that his health was insufficient
for the practice of his profession, in the month of December, 1862,
he went to Washington and was employed in the Treasury department in various positions of trust in the office of the Treasurer
of the United States, the Comptroller of Currency, and the Secretary of the Treasury. In 1866 he returned to New York City as
treasurer and general manager of the National Bank Note
Company and as the legal adviser of that company. During this

period he made several inventions in aid of the work of the Bank Note Company, including a machine for gumming postage stamps by air pressure and a safety device for checks, bonds, and other securities. He resigned this position in 1869 and engaged actively in the practice of his profession. In 1871 he became the general manager of the Lorillard estates in New York, for which his legal education, as well as his varied business experience, rendered him well qualified. He continued in the management of these large estates for between thirteen and fourteen years, when he resigned the general management, being still continued as a trustee, executor, etc., for several of the estates and as legal and business adviser. During all this period, and indeed from his youth up, he had kept well advised of the current of scientific progress, particularly in the matters of electricity and chemistry. In youth his private room was in his father's office, a detached building where, in addition to a large business office, was another in which were all kinds of chemicals and apparatus. With these he and the medical students of his father were accustomed to perform many kinds of experiments, and when the announcement of practical photography by Daguerre was made, they endeavored with the camera obscura to get pictures, and succeeded in getting a picture of the yard adjoining the office on paper moistened with nitrate of silver, but were not able to fix the pictures which were thus quite evanescent. Perhaps this was the first photograph upon paper. In 1878 he united with the late William E. Sawyer in producing what is believed to have been the first practical system of incandescent electric lighting. Many inventions having reference to this subject were patented by Sawyer and Man conjointly, and by Mr. Man and Mr. Sawyer separately. A fierce legal contest arose in 1879 between the owners of these inventions and those of Thomas A. Edison, which has been continued to the present time. The first electric-lighting company ever organized, the Electro-Dynamic Light Company, was formed by Messrs. Sawyer and Man in 1878. In July, 1892, the honorary degree of Doctor of Philosophy was granted to Mr. Man by Union College. Since leaving the general management of the Lorillard estates, Mr. Man has continued the practice of the law and the management of his own business affairs, much of his time having been given to the legal contests in regard to electricity. Inventors and men of science, among whom he has many friends, are accustomed to call upon him, discuss matters of invention and science, and to take his advice thereon.

IS ELECTRICITY ENERGY OR ONLY MATTER?

By Albon Man, Ph.D.

Shortly before the meeting of the Alumni of Union in the city of New York, in the year 1891, my old classmate, General Daniel Butterfield, called upon me and requested that I would consent (in case his proposition should be accepted) to deliver a lecture upon electricity before the undergraduates, to be one of a series of lectures which he was proposing to endow.

Without much consideration I consented, or half consented, to please my friend. This was the beginning of tribulation. The moment I began to think seriously upon the subject, I found that I had unwittingly entered into obligations such that it was extremely doubtful whether or not I could discharge them with honor or credit to my Alma Mater, my partial friend, or myself. But I had unthinkingly allowed the General to stand sponsor for me (as by reason of his pride in the class of '49 and old-time association and friendship he was only too ready to do), and I must, however unsuited to the task, endeavor to perform the agreement so thoughtlessly entered into by me.

So it is that I am before you to-day, and I have to beg your utmost indulgence while I endeavor to lay before you a few thoughts and guesses upon a subject too large for exhaustive treatment in a single volume, involving for adequate comprehension of its theories the most thorough knowledge of physics, and of the highest and most abstruse mathematics. A subject at once trite and hackneyed, yet most obscure, a realm of science where thoughtful, well-devised experiment is almost sure to be rewarded by new and valuable discoveries of facts that may be of the greatest benefit to mankind. One in which the loftiest flight of the scientific imagination can reach no bounds, yet one in which he who knows only how to join wires or cover them, or wind an armature in a lathe, or set up a battery is called, or calls himself, an electrician.

How can I or any one else in a single lecture say anything that can be of permanent value upon such a subject?

We are met at the outset with the question, What is electricity? and are obliged to answer, No one certainly knows.

It has been supposed to be a fluid or to be two fluids of opposite qualities, only coexistent, with strong mutual affinities and mutually satisfying one the other. It has also been supposed to be a kind of motion in or of some medium such as a universal ether, which pervades and penetrates all things and all space—a kind of energy.

Let us for the present take this latter supposition as a kind of theory upon which to string our thoughts, and try to find a definition of what we mean by energy later on. In doing this you are aware that we shall be going counter to the opinions of the most eminent electricians. We shall probably part company upon this, with Ampère, Faraday, Coulomb, and others, and possibly with Maxwell, and certainly with Lodge. Not with their scientific researches and experiments, but with their opinions. We may find some comfort with Hertz and Tesla, but whether we do or not, we have a right to make our excursion in the realms of thought, and it may not be wholly fruitless.

Before we start upon our excursion and during its course it will be necessary to say something of the laws by which electricity acts, is made to do work, and is estimated, *i.e.*, weighed or measured by its effects.

The school-books of the past have had much to say about static electricity, and very little about dynamic electricity, that is, continuous electrical currents, or the propagation of electrical activity along conductors, and the utilization of such currents in producing light or heat, or driving machinery, or in doing other work; and the public generally, not having the necessary foundation laid in education at school, seem to be utterly incapable of comprehending the matter.

Again, names have been given to the units or elements of electrical calculation, well known by nearly every one and quite frequently used in common conversation, without adequate conception of their meaning. Thus Coulombs, Ampères, Volts, Ohms, Farads, Watts, Joules, etc., are frequently bandied about in talk without knowing what they stand for, and not infrequently are mixed up, jumbled together, or used one for the other. Unless order and comprehension be brought out of this confusion and ignorance, no excursion, such as we propose, can be made with any hope of pleasure or profit.

Those who gave names to electrical units seem to have had in mind that for purposes of calculation electricity might be treated as a highly or perfectly elastic gas or liquid, without weight—imponderable. At least such is my understanding of the matter. Mind, I do not say that they believed electricity to be elastic; indeed such of them as hold that electricity is a substance, a fluid, or two complementary fluids, distinctly hold, as we must do if we agree with them, that it is utterly inelastic.

Perhaps we cannot do better than to quote here from Maxwell (see his life, page 54, third volume). Speaking of the cells of ether supposed by him to be in motion as vortices and so capable of distortion, *i.e.*, elastic, he says: "According to our theory the particles which form the partitions between the cells (of the ether) constitute the matter of electricity. The motion of these particles constitutes an electrical current, the tangential force with which the particles are pressed by the matter of the cells is electromotive force, and the pressure of the particles on each other corresponds to the tension or potential of the electricity."

It will be observed here that Maxwell concludes that "the particles between the cells" of vortically revolving molecules of ether are electricity. And it is these *particles* that are substantial things utterly inelastic; but in our excursion we are treating the motion, pressure, and force between these inter-etheric particles themselves and the tangential force of the etheric vortices—in other words, the energy—as electricity.

To proceed: If we consider these units as the elements of calculation of the effects that would be produced if such a hypothetical gas or liquid were acted on or relieved of pressure, or set in motion or hindered in its movements, and of the work that it would do when so acted on, we may be able to get some clear comprehension of them.

It must be assumed, first, that the total amount of this supposititious liquid or gas, electricity, is to be taken to be infinite in amount in the universe! Second, that it is in equilibrium and so remains distributed according to its laws of distribution, and at rest until acted upon by appropriate force, when it will be set in motion and its equilibrium disturbed; and third, that when set in motion it will do work, which absorbs the force acting upon it, and it is thereby again brought to a state of equilibrium.

The names given to some of these units are:

First Unit, the Coulomb.—A unit of quantity like a quar or a pint of air.

It is evident that a quart or pint measure full of air or other elastic substance will contain more or less of the elastic substance according to the pressure or force by which it is acted on. Thus if the measure were entirely closed, and air was admitted to it under a pressure of a hundred pounds per square inch, it would receive and contain a certain quantity of air or other perfect gas, namely, that due to one hundred pounds force or pressure. But if the force or pressure driving air into the measure were two hundred pounds per square inch the measure would receive or contain twice as much. So in order to establish a unit quantity of air or other elastic substance, we must first establish a unit of force or pressure under which the elastic substance or thing should be placed or exist when measured, unless the substance or thing were ponderable, in which case we might establish a unit quantity by weight.

As our elastic electricity is imponderable, in order to know its quantity we must first know the force or pressure acting on it or under which it exists. And we must also have some measure of capacity like a quart or pint which will always hold the same quantity of electricity under the same force or pressure, or at least have some means of determining the number of units or quantity. We can then scientifically determine and take a certain force or pressure as a unit of force or pressure, and a certain capacity as a unit of capacity.

This has been done. And the unit of electrical force or pressure is our second unit and is called

A volt, after Volta, the electrician.

It is a unit of electromotive force—" E. M. F.," or of the force which tends to set electricity in motion, or according to our supposition to compress it or impart it to anything, or substance, capable of receiving it.

Our third unit is:

A farad, a unit of capacity, named after Faraday.

Different substances of the same mass or of the same cubical or space measurement will under the same electromotive force or electrical pressure ordinarily contain different quantities of electricity. And two things of the same material of equal mass, and equal cubical or space measurements, and acted on by equal electromotive force or pressure but of different temperature, shape, or location as to other things, or other physical conditions, do not necessarily contain the same quantities of electricity. The farad, or unit of electrical capacity, cannot therefore be compared with the vessel or thing used to measure, a pint or quart, etc.

Two pint measures, one of copper the other of iron, would hold substantially the same quantity of air under the same pressure and temperature. They would not, though made of equal weights and equal sizes and kept at the same temperature and under equal electromotive force or pressure, contain the same or equal quantities of electricity. The farad, therefore, is an electrical unit used principally for expressing the ability of different substances or things to accept and hold electricity under certain electromotive force or pressure, rather than for measuring quantities of electricity by being a unit of capacity, though it is necessarily so used in static electricity, and taken into account in long conductors; but in dynamic electricity, the electricity of currents, the transmission of electrical activity along conductors, there is a more convenient method of measurement and expression of electrical quantity.

Current.—To clearly comprehend the ideas of the other electrical units, let us first understand what is meant ordinarily by an electrical current. It will be sufficient for our purpose to say that it is the transmission of electrical activity from its source in a given direction along or over a pathway or conductor, divided or single, leading from the source of activity and returning to it. It is motion in a circle or circuit started and kept up by force applied in one direction of revolution at one point of the circle or circuit, or at many points in the same direction of revolution, in which case it is evident that the direction of the forces being the same, they are all added to each other, no matter what the sizes of the several forces may be; or if some of the forces in the circuit are in direction opposite to the others the direction of the transmission will be that of the superior force or forces.

For simplicity let us take the simple, single circuit in which the force is at one point in one direction, remembering that what is left of the force, after its passage or transmission of electrical activity through the circuit, returns to itself.

We may liken this to an air-pump, connected with an elastic tube, pumping air into the closed tubular circuit at one end of the tube, and drawing air for its supply from the circuit at the other end, not forgetting at the same time that the air has weight and is not in action, therefore perfectly elastic, but that electricity by our supposition is perfectly elastic but has no weight. The air in the tube would have motion in one direction in the circuit. There would be a seeming pulling of air at one end of the pump, and a pushing of air at the other end of the pump, but the pulling and pushing would both be acting upon the same body of air confined in the tubular circuit—and the tendency of each would be to cause the air to circulate in one and the same direction in the tube.   (See Fig. 1.)

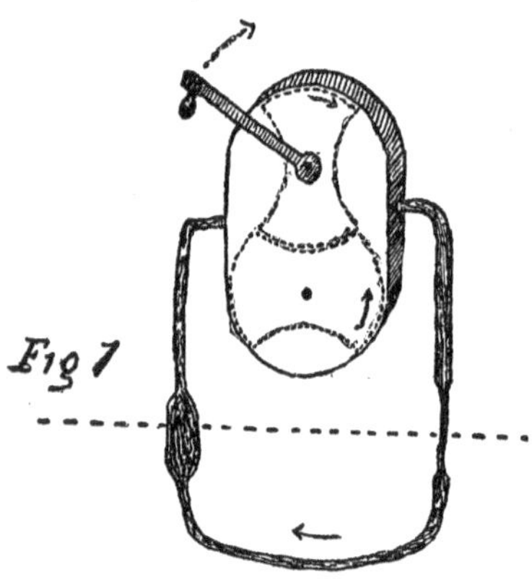

It is evident that the quantity of air, after the pump has got well in motion, that would pass any given point in the circuit in any short time, say one second, would be the same as the quantity passing any other point in the circuit in the same interval of time, and this would be the case notwithstanding the tube in the circuit were enlarged at one point and diminished at other points. The velocity of the air would be different at different points of the circuit, and would vary if the tubular circuit were not uniform in capacity, inversely as the capacity of the tube at the different points.   If the tube were enlarged at one point, the velocity at that point would be diminished; if the tube were made smaller at any point, the velocity at that point would be increased. The total quantity of air passing all points of the tubular circuit in a second of time might be changed by enlargement or contraction at different points of the tube; but still the quantity of air that would pass at any given second of time by one point of the tubular circuit would be the same that would pass in the same second by any other point of the circuit.

The quantity of air passing any given point in the circuit in any given second, of time would depend:

First, upon the amount of force applied to the air by the pump; and, second upon the size and character of the tubular circuit as a whole, *i.e.*, its total resistance to the circulation of air.

As the air we are supposed to be using is without weight and without friction upon itself, if the resistance of the circuit remains constant, and if a given force, say one unit of force, be applied by the pump to the air in the tubular circuit, so long as the force remains constant and continually applied a certain or definite quantity of air will pass any given point in the circuit in every second of time.

The second is the unit of time—our fourth unit.

As our supposed air is without appreciable weight, imponderable, and perfectly elastic, the force will be applied throughout the whole circuit at nearly the same instant of time, and it acquires no momentum by movement. Therefore if we apply twice the force, two units of force to the air of our circuit, twice the amount of air will pass any given point in the circuit in a second or unit of time; and if we apply three units of force, three times the amount of air will pass any given point in the circuit, and so on. The quantity of supposed air which will pass any given point in the circuit in a second or unit of time will increase exactly as the force set to move it increases, if the resistance of the circuit to the circulation of air through it remains constant.

If a unit of force causes a fixed quantity, say one unit

of air, to pass any point of a circuit such as we have im-
agined in a unit of time, it will, if the unit of force or
pressure be continued in the same circuit of steady resistance, cause a unit quantity of air to pass any given
point in the circuit in the next and each succeeding
unit of time during which the force or pressure continues.

Such a flow of air caused by a unit of pressure or
force, in which a unit quantity of air passes each point
of the circuit in a unit of time, would be a unit flow or
current, and the resistance of the circuit which would
permit such a unit flow or current would be a unit
resistance. Such a unit of flow or current corresponds
nearly to the idea of the electrical unit called

The ampere, after the eminent electrician of that
name.

Our fifth unit. It is a unit of current or flow. It is
a compound unit, made up of quantity and time. A
unit quantity of electricity in motion or the passage of
a unit of electrical activity in a circuit in a unit of time
—one ampere. If there be double the electrical activity in the circuit during the second, the unit of time,
it is evident that there is double the flow or current, it
is a current of two amperes; triple the passage of electrical activity per second is a current of three amperes,
and so on. So also the passage of one unit of electrical
activity in a circuit in half a second is a current of two
amperes, in a third of a second three amperes, etc.,
etc., etc. Again, if one unit quantity of electrical activity passes in a conductor in two units (*i.e.*, seconds)
of time, it is a current of one-half an ampere. If in
three seconds or units of time it is a current of one-
third of an ampere, and so on.

The idea of the ampere may be compared to a unit
or measure of water called a miner's inch. A certain

flow or current of water equal, if I mistake not, to the flow or current which takes place through a one-inch orifice under a six-inch head—here the orifice is the resistance, the head of water the force or pressure causing the flow. The head or pressure may be increased if the resistance to flow be increased by diminishing the orifice correspondingly—and still have the same quantity of water flowing in a minute of time—it is still a "miner's inch" of water. Again the head may be diminished if the resistance to flow is correspondingly diminished by increasing the orifice—and still have the same quantity of water flowing per minute— it is still the miner's inch of water. But if the head or pressure be increased, say doubled, leaving the size of the orifice constituting the resistance the same—the flow per minute is doubled—it is two miner's inches. If the head or pressure is diminished, say halved, leaving the orifice the same the flow is halved, it is one-half a miner's inch. If the orifice is increased, say doubled, thereby halving the resistance to flow, the head or pressure remaining the same, the flow is doubled, it is two miner's inches of flow. And if the head remains the same, and the orifice be diminished to one-half, thereby doubling the resistance to flow, the flow is one-half, it is one-half a miner's inch. It is a very convenient unit of measurement for large quantities of flowing water, much more so than any unit of measure of capacity alone could be. It is a compound unit, made up of quantity and time, and corresponds closely to the electrical unit called the ampere in idea, as already said; that is, in its being a unit of flow or current. But in the one case matter, *i.e.*, water, is flowing; in the other, motion or activity is being transmitted, but there is no flow of matter as we are supposing,

Let us now return in thought to our pipe circuit of air,

We have so far considered that the circuit offered a resistance to the circulation of the air. Let us consider what would take place were there no resistance either in circuit or pump. It is evident that as the pump or blower applies or imparts force to the air at one end in one direction, causing the air to move in a circuit returning to the other end of the pump, the current of air in its passage through the pump would impart to the pump as much force as it had received, and the first impulse of force given by the pump to the air would thus go on producing a continuous current of air through the system; and if force or pressure were given to the pump other than that imparted by the air itself, the velocity of the current and the amount of air that would pass any given point in the circuit would go on increasing forever as long as force was being imparted by the pump.

Friction (say resistance) prevents this by absorbing the energy, converting it into some other form or forms of energy, and this is called doing work. The same is true in an electrical circuit, as in our hypothetical air circuit. The resistance absorbs the energy of the force imparted, which tends to set the current in motion or activity. It converts the energy into other forms of energy, *i.e.*, does work. (We are speaking of a simple circuit now, and not one in which a motor or other device driven either by the current of air or electricity absorbs a portion of the energy causing the current and does work outside the circuit.)

The whole resistance of the circuit acts in thus absorbing or converting the energy causing the current into work, and the work done will be distributed in the circuit in exact accordance with the distribution of the resistance. The work done at any point of the circuit will be to the whole work done as the resistance at that point is to the whole resistance of the circuit.

If there be no motor or electro-magnet or electro-plating or the like in the circuit to absorb the energy of the current, and no work is done outside the circuit—such as inducing currents in other conductors or overcoming opposing induction of other currents—then the whole energy causing the current will be expended on the resistance in an electrical circuit and converted into heat, and the falling of one coulomb of electricity, one volt in electromotive force, will produce an amount of heat or do an amount of work equal to

One joule, which is the unit of electrical work, and also a heat unit, and is equal to $\frac{7387}{10000}$ of a foot pound of work. Thus a connection is made between the work done by electricity and other work. It is the same amount of work which is done when a current of one ampere passes for one second of time against a unit of electrical resistance called

One ohm, after another eminent electrician.

This amount of resistance—an ohm's resistance—has been practically determined and ascertained, and lengths of wire having one or several ohms resistance per yard or foot of length are made and sold in the market, and are used as instruments of electrical measurement, as a tape measure or rule is used in measuring length. A certain length of a certain wire is one ohm resistance; double in length, two ohms, etc.

Conductivity is the reciprocal of resistance. If a wire has one ohm's resistance, its conductivity is $\frac{1}{1} =$ one or a unit. If it has two ohms resistance its conductivity is $\frac{1}{2}$ (one-half) unit conductivity. If it has three ohms resistance its conductivity is $\frac{1}{3}$ (one-third) unit conductivity. If its resistance is one-third of an ohm its conductivity is $1 \div \frac{1}{3} =$ three units conductivity, etc.

14

To make clear to our minds still further the idea of electrical resistance as embodied in the unit of resistance, "the ohm," it may be remarked that it excludes the thought of any friction of electricity upon itself in its currents, and includes only the fixed and steady opposition of a conductor to the passage of an electrical current through it, irrespective of the size of the current.

In our air system or circuit, unless we suppose the air devoid of weight and perfectly elastic, the system would offer a certain resistance to the passage of a certain amount of air through it in a second of time. But if we attempted to circulate through the system or circuit double the amount of air per second, we would have increased resistance to each of the volumes of air constituting the double amount, due to friction of the two volumes of air upon themselves. This would not be so in electrical currents. Each additional volume of electricity would meet with the same electrical resistance as though it were circulating alone and by itself in the circuit, and no more.

The unit of electrical resistance may be perhaps illustrated by comparing it to the force of gravity as represented by a one-pound weight being raised by a pulley and rope, and the pulley being prevented by a clutch from revolving except in the direction to raise the weight.

A certain force, say a current, is applied to the pulley to raise the weight. The weight by its gravity offers a certain resistance to force, *i.e.*, one pound, and a certain work is done in raising the weight a certain distance against the force of gravity in a certain time; the clutch now acts on the pulley and prevents the weight from falling.

If we now apply to the pulley double the force by a

double current, it will raise the weight faster and higher—will do twice the work in the same time. But it will be doing it on or against the same resistance, the same weight, the same force of gravity represented by the one pound. The resistance to the current or force driving the pulley is all the time the same one pound of gravity, whether the current is small or great. So the unit of electrical resistance, the ohm, is always the same whether the current be great or small which goes against it or does work upon it. The pulley with the clutch sustaining the weight, when not acted on by the current applied to the pulley, is intended to represent the continued existence of the resistance, ready to be acted on or to resist when force is applied against it, but at rest or inactive at all other times. Such a system might properly be said to have a resistance of one pound, and the resistance could be measured. So a wire is said, though not in use, to have so many ohms resistance—that is, it will offer this resistance to the passage of a current if applied.

This comparison is made to illustrate the fixedness of electrical resistance and its independence of the electromotive force impelling the current, and of the size of the current, and not for any other purpose. Indeed, in our supposed pulley and weight system, the weight would sooner or later be raised up to the height of the pulley and could go no further. Electromotive force would not be so limited.

Again, the force in the pulley and weight is applied to cause mass motion of matter through distance against the fixed force of gravity, while the force in electrical currents acts to cause atomic or molecular motion in the conductor or substance constituting the resistance; and it is the opposition of the atoms or molecules of the conductor to being thus moved that *is* electrical resistance, an opposition probably due to the ordinary motion of the atoms and molecules of matter among themselves or to their balanced attractions and repulsions between themselves when at rest, or both.

Again, in our pulley and weight system, unless we suppose the pulley to be infinitely large, or the arbor on which the rope is wound to be infinitely small, it is evident that the force or current acting upon the pulley must be either actually greater than the force of gravity acting upon the weight, or by mechanical advantage superior to it, in order that the weight should be raised. Otherwise, if it were not for the clutch sustaining the weight, the weight would balance the force applied to the pulley or overcome it, and cause motion in the opposite direction to the applied force of current.

This is not so in electrical resistance.

No resistance however large, unless infinite, can balance an electromotive force however small; and although, when the electromotive force ceases to act, the return of the atoms or molecules of the conductor and surrounding ether to their normal state of motion among themselves or the condition of balanced repulsions and attractions among themselves, before the electromotive force is applied, may, and indeed does, cause a temporary instantaneous reaction, tending to produce increased current, electricity is not supposed to have momentum. Electrical resistance, except for this temporary reaction, can in no proper sense be considered as a force—otherwise it would not be true that any electromotive force, however small, will cause some current, through or against any resistance however large (unless infinite), which is a fact.

Let us return now in thought to our system where we supposed perfectly elastic air to be caused to circulate in a closed circuit of pipe, in which at one point was a pump, by whose force the air is impelled or driven in the circuit of the pipe, and let us introduce a resistance at one point in the pipe by reducing its calibre at that point. Suppose now we have a certain standard of force, called a unit of force, called one volt, and a certain standard of flow or current, *i.e.*, so much air per second, called one ampere, and a certain standard of resistance to flow or current, called one ohm. And that these standards are so taken or chosen that a force or pressure of one volt will cause a flow or current of air of one ampere when the resistance to flow is one ohm. And suppose this to be the condition of things in our air-pipe after the resistance is put at one point as above—viz., that the force is one volt, the flow or current one ampere, and the resistance one ohm.

Now let us further constrict our pipe at the same point so that its capacity at that point is only one-half of what it was when one ampere was flowing—in other words, make its resistance two ohms—it is evident the force or pressure of the pump will not be altered; it will still be one volt, but the flow or current will only be one-half of what it was, viz., one-half ampere, because there is only one-half capacity of pipe at the point of constriction; in other words, if we multiply the number of ohms by 2 (the force remaining constant) we must divide at the same time the number of amperes by 2 to find the current that would then flow; and so if we multiply the number of ohms by 3 or any other number we must at the same time divide the number of amperes by the same number to find the flow or current.

Thus with one volt of force one ohm resistance permits one ampere current:

OHMS.		AMPERES.
1 × 2 = 2 ohms resistance permits ½ amp. cur't		= 1 ÷ 2
1 × 3 = 3 " " " ⅓ " "		= 1 ÷ 3
1 × ½ = ½ " " " 2 " "		= 1 ÷ ½
1 × ⅓ = ⅓ " " " 3 " "		= 1 ÷ ⅓ etc.

Again if the resistance be constant, say for example one ohm, the number of amperes of current will increase exactly as the force increases, *i.e.*, as the number of volts increase, thus:

One ohm resistance permits—

1 ampere of current when the force is 1 volt	= 1 × 1
2 " " " " " " 2 "	= 1 × 2
½ " " " " " " ½ "	= 1 × ½
⅓ " " " " " " ⅓ "	= 1 × ⅓

Our units of current, of pressure or force, and of resistance have been so chosen and taken that when the force causing the flow or current is a unit of force, 1 volt, the current is a unit of current, 1 ampere, and the resistance is a unit of resistance, 1 ohm.

Suppose we desire to increase the number of units of current. As current is a thing caused, an effect of force applied—limited or restrained by another thing, resistance,—we can only change the effect, the current, by changing either the force or the resistance.

Suppose we first change the force 1 volt by multiplying it by any number, say a. We shall then have 1 volt × a = 1a volts, and our amperes will be 1 ampere × a = 1a amperes — our resistance remaining the same, 1 ohm. Suppose we now increase the resistance by multiplying it by any number, say b, we shall then have 1 ohm × b = 1b ohms as our resistance.

We have seen that if we multiply the units of resistance by any number, we must divide the units of current by the same number to find the number of amperes: so our new current, which was $1a$ amperes, will now become $1a$ amperes divided by $1b$ ohms $(= \frac{1a}{1b}$ amperes) and our volts not being affected by a change of resistance, will remain the same as we made it by multiplication, viz., $1a$ volts. It will be observed that the new number of amperes, the coefficient of the current, $\frac{1a}{1b}$, is equal to the number of volts, which we have made $1a$ divided by the number of ohms, which we have made $1b$,—or $\frac{1a}{1b}$ current equals $\frac{1a \text{ volts}}{1b \text{ resistance}}$,—and this would clearly be the case no matter by what number we multiply or divide the volts, or by what number we multiply or divide the ohms; in other words, cause and effect are equal, or in a simple circuit of current returning to itself, the number of units of current are always equal to the number of units of force divided by the number of units of resistance.

This is Ohm's law—the fundamental law of electrical currents.

It is usually stated thus:

$$\text{Current} = \frac{\text{Electromotive force}}{\text{Resistance}}$$

assuming that the student will understand it to mean

$$\text{The units of current} = \frac{\text{The units of electromotive force}}{\text{The units of resistance}}.$$

It is an unfortunate statement or omission in statement. Current can no more equal electromotive force, or electromotive force divided by resistance, than horses or pigs can equal cows. Nor can electromotive force be divided by resistance, more than head of water can be divided by the rigidity of an iron post, or pigs can be divided by cows. They are different things or ideas, and the numerical relation of their units may be compared or their numerical units multiplied together or divided by each other, but not the things themselves. Thus we may say that *the number* of horses on a farm equal *the number* of pigs divided by *the number* of cows; horse, pig, and cow being units—and the comparison, equality, or division being made between *the number of units* of different animals, not between the animals themselves. We cannot say horse equals pig divided by cow, nor in any just sense that current equals electromotive force divided by resistance; but we can say that the number of units of current equals the number of units of electromotive force divided by the number of units of resistance, or that *the number* of

$$\text{Amperes} = \frac{\text{The number of volts}}{\text{The number of ohms}},$$ for it is in reference

to *the number of units* only that we assert the equality exists, when the division is made beween the numbers of other units, not that the units are themselves equal or divided by each other, but only their numerical co-efficients.

I have been thus explicit because I have found that a confusion of ideas existed upon this subject with many persons, going so far as to infer that there might be an absolute and essential equality between current, electromotive force, or resistance, such that one could be substituted for the other, or the actual value of one be expressed in units of the other for all cases.

The ultimate object of all our calculations is to do work, and our mediate thought and speculation is to ascertain how work is done, so as to do it, and to determine the rules for estimating the amount of work in any given case so as to select and proportion our agents to the service required of them. We are discussing electricity with these objects in view.

Let us not make the mistake of supposing it is capable of doing work in and of itself until force is applied to cause electrical motion. It is no more so than still air, or a pond of still water.

Further, it can exist under any pressure or force as can air or water, and only does work when motion or the transmission of activity in some direction through distance is established. It is not then ordinarily a prime mover, but a transmitter, like the belt by which machinery is driven. (I do not mean that it is not legitimate to make use of natural forces to produce electrical energy, or to avail ourselves of natural electrical energies if we can discover them and put them to work.)

We are considering the case of a simple conductor in a circuit returning to itself, in which circuit is a force causing a current of electricity, or electrical activity, through the conductor around the circuit in one direction, and in which there is nothing but the resistance of the circuit (including the resistance of the instrument by which the force is applied, which is part of the circuit) upon which work can be done. We have already seen that the work done in such a circuit is the production of heat, and that a current of one ampere on a resistance of one ohm in one second of time will produce heat equal to one joule, the unit of both work and heat, which is equal to the work of raising one pound $\frac{7373}{10000}$ of one foot against the force of gravity, or equal to o.7373 foot-pounds of work, and that by these means the electrical units may be compared with mechanical units of force and work, or, better, were determined and established of such size or amount—understanding that "force" is that which tends to cause motion in anything, as for instance the force of gravity, to which forces are usually referred in comparison of their amounts.

Let us try and gain some comprehension of what we mean by "work." If we take a unit of mass or quantity of matter, say one pound, we know that pound of matter will be attracted to the earth with a certain force; we may call the force of this attraction a unit of force, a one-pound force, and refer all other forces to it for comparison of their amount or size. If now we raise matter against the force of gravity we do work. If we raise it at all we do a certain amount of work. If we raise it more we do more work. To ascertain the amount of work done, we must know how high we raise it. We need a unit of distance; let us take one foot in length as this unit in distance. We now have a measure of our work: one pound raised one foot against the force of gravity is our unit; it is one foot-pound of work.

If for the force of gravity we substitute a continuing resistance (say friction) that should be the exact equivalent of the force of gravity—*i.e.*, offer as much opposition to the movement of our given mass or pound of matter as gravity does—it is evident that we should do the same amount of work in moving it one foot against this resistance, that we would in raising it one foot against the force of gravity. We may properly say we have done one foot-pound of work when we have thus moved one pound of matter one foot against such an opposition of friction.

We conceive "work" then to be effect of force against opposition in causing motion or activity in matter or a medium.

Force is that which tends to cause motion or action or change of state or condition or place. It implies direction as one of its attributes, and to change the direction of a force implies other force of different direction or work done, or both.

There are many kinds of motion or activity, but for our present purpose we may consider but two kinds, viz. : mass motion in which matter as a mass is moved through distance, and molecular or atomic motion, in which matter as a mass is not moved through distance, but in which its atoms or molecules are set in motion among themselves. For we cannot conceive of motion except something be moved.

That something we call matter.

There are many kinds of opposition to setting up motion or activity or change, such as inertia, friction, other forces, molecular and atomic attractions, chemical affinity, and existing motion or activity of atoms or molecules, etc.

It follows that there must be many kinds of work. We may not yet say that the units of all different kinds of work have been or can be so ascertained as to be comparable with the unit of mechanical work, made up of a sufficient force acting against or in opposition to the force of gravity upon a unit of mass, to cause motion through a unit of distance; but we may, as we have seen, say that the unit of electrical work, the "joule," has been so ascertained, and from this we are indebted to James Prescott Joule, the eminent physicist, who died on the 11th of October, 1889, while these thoughts were being in part written for my own satisfaction, and after whom the unit of electrical work and heat is named.

Force may exist balanced by equivalent opposite force or forces, or be restrained by an infinite resistance without motion resulting, and consequently without work; but a current cannot exist without doing work, unless it can be supposed to go on forever, with the energy imparted to it undiminished. It may indeed use up or diminish opposing force or forces of inferior potency, but unless the force causing the current is balanced or overcome, in which case the motion and current cease, it will do work.

That is, electricity in motion as a current will and must do work. The amount of work, as far as electricity is concerned, depends solely upon the amount of energy, the number of coulombs acting, by the force with which they act, their velocity being always the velocity of electrical transmission. The number of coulombs acting in any given case depends upon the electromotive force and has relation to other things, and is determined by the conditions of the given case.

Resistance in a simple circuit is necessary in order that work may be done, but it does no work. Work is done upon or through it. It may restrain or limit the amount of work by limiting the quantity of electricity passing, but it is a mere opposition, not indeed negative, but passive in idea.

In mathematics it takes on the form of a velocity, and the absolute unit of resistance from which the practical magnetic unit, "one ohm," is derived is a velocity supposed equal to one-fourth the earth's polar circumference in one second.

It might be extremely interesting to inquire why resistance takes on the form of a velocity and what relation the velocity of the atoms of matter or of ether or the velocity of light has to resistance, but I leave this to your more erudite studies of the subject.

Electromotive force, pressure upon electricity, may exist balanced by equal counter electromotive force or pressure, or restrained by infinite resistance, and cause no work; but if not so balanced or restrained by infinite resistance electricity will be put in motion and work will be done.

We see, therefore, that work is the sole product of the electromotive force and quantity of electricity put in motion by the force. We are now ready to find its unit. Do not forget that it is a unit of quantity of work, and that it may be done in a longer or shorter time,—it is independent of time, although in defining it we may say it is *equal* to the amount of work done by a certain current, in a certain time, it is only a quantity or amount of work. As it is made up of electromotive force and quantity, we take the unit of force, 1 volt, and multiply it by the unit of quantity, 1 coulomb, and we have the unit of work: 1 volt coulomb, or 1 joule as it is named.

It is evident that the numerical coefficient of either of the factors may be changed if the other is correspondingly changed, without changing the work, thus:

½ volt × 2 coulombs = 1 volt coulomb, 1 joule, 1 unit of work
2 "   × ½   "   =   "   "   "   "   "   "
4 "   × ¼   "   =   "   "   "   "   "   "

We have seen we must have a resistance in a simple circuit in order that work shall be done, something to do work upon, although the thing that the work is done upon does not enter into the idea of quantity of work.

Suppose we put a unit resistance in our circuit, 1 ohm, and act upon it by electricity impelled by a unit of force, 1 volt, our current would be $\dfrac{1 \text{ volt}}{1 \text{ ohm}}$, equal, as we have seen, to 1 ampere of current. But 1 ampere of current passes 1 coulomb of electricity in one second, so in one second of time we will have impelled a coulomb by a volt—we have 1 volt coulomb of work, 1 joule, a unit of work in a second. So we may say a current of 1 ampere will do in one second an amount of work equal to 1 joule on a resistance of 1 ohm. So also will any equivalent current, as ½ ampere with 2 volts pressure on a resistance of 4 ohms in the same time, one second; for the product of our number of volts by number of coulombs is $\frac{1}{2} \times 2 = 1$ volt coulomb, or joule, and the units correspond to Ohm's law ($\frac{1}{2}$ ampere $= \dfrac{2 \text{ volts}}{4 \text{ ohms}}$). So 4 amperes with $\frac{1}{4}$ of 1 volt pressure will do the same amount of work on 1/16 ohm, for $4 \times \frac{1}{4} = 1$, and 4 amperes $= \dfrac{\frac{1}{4} \text{ volt}}{\frac{1}{16} \text{ ohm}}$, etc., etc.

It will be observed here that we have changed very largely our resistance and yet done the same amount of work in a second, which change became necessary in order that the current should conform to the law of its action—viz., that

$$\text{The number of amperes} = \dfrac{\text{the number of volts}}{\text{the number of ohms}}.$$

But we have not changed the product of the factors doing the work. The number of volts multiplied by the number of amperes has always been equal to 1. So we think we are justified in our statement that resistance does no work and is simply acted on, because we have done the same amount of work in the same time on larger and smaller resistance by factors whose product has been always the same.

It will be asked, How then, with a less force, less electromotive force, tending to move electricity (which you say does no work until moved or put in motion), can it be that a greater work can be done upon resistance than will be done by a greater force, a greater electromotive force, on resistance in certain cases?

Thus according to your statement it is plain that in case of a current represented by the formula 3 amperes $= \dfrac{9 \text{ volts}}{3 \text{ ohms}}$ less work is being done than in the case of the current represented by the formula 6 amperes$=$ $\dfrac{6 \text{ volts}}{1 \text{ ohm}}$. For the product of the amperes by the volts 3×9 is equal to 27, which you say represents the work of the first current, while the product of volts by amperes 6×6 is 36 in the second current, larger than the first, although the electromotive force of the second current is less than the first.

The statement given in illustration is correct, but the question arises from a confusion of ideas. A new idea has been introduced in the question, viz., the rate of expenditure of force—the quantity of force expended in giving motion to electricity in a given time, as one second. This is power—the rate of doing work, so much work per second. Time is the new element introduced, while the unit of work is independent and may be done in longer or shorter time. Besides, an erroneous conception of the unit of electromotive force is shown.

This unit is a unit of pressure, on a unit quantity of electricity or its equivalent, not a unit of the expenditure of energy, going on or taking place at any time or in any fixed time. It is that amount of force which is equal to the amount of force that will cause a certain activity, or quantity of motion, in a unit quantity of electricity; and when this unit quantity of electricity is so set in activity or motion it will do upon 1 ohm or unit resistance 1 joule or unit of work in one second. It is manifest that one-half the amount of pressure per unit of quantity, acting upon double the number of units of quantity, will produce the same amount of electrical motion and the same amount of work in a second; for we have two units of quantity, and one-half pressure on one of the units will produce one-half amount of electrical motion in that unit, and do one-half unit of work, and the one-half pressure on the other unit will also produce one-half amount of electrical motion in the other unit and also do one-half unit of work. The two one-half units of work together make one unit, the same amount of work one unit pressure on one unit quantity will do in a second.

We must understand, therefore, that electromotive force in currents of electricity is the force or pressure upon each unit quantity of electricity passing in the current. It is measured by the unit force or pressure we have defined. And we know that this force must be continually renewed or the pressure will fall in current or dynamic electricity. The motion of the electricity caused by the force will be expended in other motion or work, and new force must be supplied or the motion ceases, the electromotive force or pressure falls or is at an end.

In static electricity, the electricity of Leyden jars and condensers, etc., the electricity is confined, and electromotive force, applied to one unit of the confined electricity, is applied to every other unit so confined, as force applied to one square inch of confined water is applied to every other square inch of water in the confining vessel.

If there is no leak, there is no current either of electricity or water: the force remains applied and the pressure the same, the force does not need to be renewed and there is no expenditure of force, no work done. But if we make an orifice in the vessel containing water, a current flows. The orifice restrains the flow; its want of capacity or size constitutes a resistance. The force sets the water in motion, the water in motion overcomes the resistance of the orifice, work is done, but the force is expended. More force must be supplied to keep up the pressure.

If force is supplied as it is expended the pressure will be kept up, and the flow or current will be constant. That is a flow of equal quantities of water in each second of time. We might take the quantity of water flowing in a second as a unit of quantity, it would be a coulomb of water. We might take this flow per second as our unit of current, it would be one ampere. We might take the pressure per square inch in the vessel, got up by a force that would cause a coulomb to flow in a second of time as indicating that we were using a unit of continuous force; it would be one volt so much pressure per square inch. We might take the amount of work done in a second by such current as our unit of work, it would be a joule. We might reduce our pressure to one-half volt, and make our orifice of double the size, its resistance would be one-half what it was, one-half ohm, but the flow would be the same in one second. One coulomb in quantity per second, 1 ampere in current—the work would be one-half what it was in a second, ½ volt × 1 coulomb = ½ joule, and it would take two seconds to do a joule of work. But if we make the pressure one-half volt, and the resistance one-quarter ohm, we have two coulombs of quantity, and ½ volt × 2 coulombs = 1 joule of work. The same quantity of work done by a different current and different pressure, in the unit of time, one second.

We have seen that we could do different amounts of work in a second, less or more. We can take therefore any length of time less or more in which to do a unit or joule of work. When done it is the same amount of work, it is a joule of work still, it is irrespective of time, it is made up of two factors only, pressure per unit or electromotive force, volts and coulombs in motion. No time comes in question, but it is necessary

15

we should know what amount of work we are doing, the rate of work. To know this we must take time into consideration—so much work in so much time. We must have a unit composed of work and time, work divided by time, a unit of work in a unit of time, a unit of rate of work, like a unit of current composed of quantity of work and time. The actual number of units of work done divided by the number of units of time in which it is done. Our unit of work is composed of pressure and a quantity in motion, volts and coulombs in motion. Combine this with the unit of time and we have the volt-coulomb in motion per second as our unit of rate of doing work. But we already have for the coulomb in motion per second a name, viz., the name of a unit of current, the ampere. So by substitution, our unit of rate of doing work is the volt multiplied by the ampere—the volt-ampere, divided by one second. This unit is named after another scientist.

The "watt," the unit of rate of doing work. The unit of power.

It is made up of three ideas combined: a unit of continuous force or pressure (one volt) acting upon and causing motion in a unit of quantity of electricity (one coulomb), divided by the time during which it is acting (one second).

"Power," the rate of doing work.

"Watt," the unit of electrical power or unit of the rate of doing electrical work.

It is equal to about $\frac{1}{746}$ of a horse-power,—the horse-power being taken as a rate of doing work equal to the raising of 33,000 pounds in one minute against the force of gravity or of 550 pounds one foot in one second. A watt is therefore equal to the raising of about $44\frac{288}{1000}$ pounds one foot in one minute, or $\frac{7373}{10000}$ of a pound in one second, or equal to doing the work of one joule per second.

The one watt multiplied by the number of seconds equals the number of joules. The number of joules divided by the number of seconds in which they are done equals the number of watts.

It will be seen that the words force, work, and power are not in electrical or mechanical calculations synonymous, and that they must not be confounded or used one for the other as they frequently are in conversation. To have clear thought we must have clear definitions of the words we use, at least to ourselves, and it is highly desirable and almost indispensable that those to whom we wish to impart our thoughts, or whose thoughts we desire to receive, should have in mind the same definitions we ourselves have.

There is another word often used in different senses in common conversation, and indeed by many persons laying claim to technical accuracy, which seems to me to require more complete definition. I have reference to the word energy. I find it used as synonymous with work, power, and force—it cannot mean all these. I wish it had been more clearly defined in use.

I take it in thought upon electrical subjects to mean primarily a condition of activity or motion of electricity, or of the medium of electrical activity, which, having reference to quantity also, will do work—and covering the case of a condenser, charged under a certain potential or electrical pressure, although the condenser is not at the time being discharged or its charge doing work outside; nearly akin in its unit to the volt-coulomb, not work done, but the result of work done, and having ability to do work. In its general signification energy is the progeny of previous energy of some kind, and produces energy of some kind, like life that produces life and is the product of life, but indestructible though changeable in character, and therefore continuous and stable in total amount and doubtless infinite in amount in the universe, if the universe be infinite.

Definite amounts of energy may be locked up or stored up and exist as stress in matter or balanced forces, like the energy of the bent spring retained by a catch—like the energy of chemical compounds, or crystallization, or chemical affinities, or repulsion, or attraction of matter upon other matter—ready to flow forth and be changed into other energies when released at some time, but it cannot be destroyed. It will exist as mass or quantity in motion, molecular or atomic motion, heat, electrical activity, or stress, or other form of energy. It is said to be dissipated when we know not, or can not or do not care to observe into what various forms it is changed. In dynamics it may be supposed to be a certain flow or current of energy (activity), being changed into other energy—so much energy per second. And it is in this sense that we speak of it when we speak of the energy of a machine in motion, or of the energy of an electrical current, or of the energy being imparted by heat to a steam boiler, or of the energy given forth by steam in motion from a boiler. The total energy passing or being changed into other energy is the same as the total work. That part of the current of energy that is changed into the form of energy desired in any system is equal to and constitutes the useful work of the system. The rest is supposed to be dissipated, and useful work is what is commonly or generally understood by the word "work."

This view of energy compels us to consider force as simply a result of energy, and in most cases as the manifestation of energy, or a property of energy,—a property in which direction is given to energy, and such direction may be to or from a point outward or inward, toward or from a system, or in a right line of curve, where continuous forces are combined in direction.

There are many ways in which energy may be locked up or stored up so as not to be manifest in present observable force, yet existent and capable, under proper circumstances, of being or becoming so manifest in force and of doing work by producing obvious motion in matter. We can rarely follow completely the mutations or the storage or locking up of energy or its persistence or its release, but an example may not be out of place:

The energy of the sun sets in motion the molecules of water at sea-level. The force is at first heterogeneous in direction among the molecules of the water, the resulting force is from within outward in any small portion, as a drop. Expansion follows. By continued additions of energy the molecules are driven beyond the reach of their mutual attractions in the condition of a liquid and take on the more dispersed condition of a gas—steam. Work is done. The gas occupies more space; it is lighter than air. The energy of gravity causes it to rise to the upper atmosphere, lifts it. More work is done. In the upper atmosphere, which is colder, it parts with its heat or a part of the motion of its molecules, giving energy to the atmosphere surrounding it. The mutual attractions of its molecules are then able to, and do, bring them closer together. The forces are resolved in direction from without inward to a point in a drop until the liquid condition is restored. Work the reverse of expansion, and equal to it, is done, to wit: contraction. The sun's energy given to the drop of water is now in the upper air, but the energy of

gravity which raised it is stored in the drop and represented by the advantage of its position. The space occupied by the gas is lessened; it becomes a liquid. The
liquid is heavier than the air—it falls. The force of
gravity acting on it gives it increasing kinetic energy,
motion, until it strikes the earth, where it parts with
the energy imparted to it by gravity in falling by giving it forth as heat, or producing the heat of impact or
a blow on the earth.

Suppose it falls in a mountain lake, high above its
level, where first acted upon by the sun's heat or energy.
The work done on it—energy used in raising it to the
level of the higher atmosphere—is not all returned to
it by gravity in falling part of the way back to its
former level. What has become of the remainder? The
liquid drop has gained an advantage of position equal
to this remainder. It can do the remainder of the work
done on it in raising it to the upper atmosphere, when
it falls the remainder distance, and imparts it as heat
energy to the earth or its surroundings. Meantime it
is stored up as potential of position in the drop of water
sustained by counter pressure or energy of the bottom
of the lake, in which the drop of water rests. Our remainder energy may therefore be said to be stored up
in the drop of water in the mountain lake. Possibly
with other drops it may turn a mill when it falls, instead of giving its energy forth as heat. Possibly it
may start by evaporation on another round in the upper
atmosphere, and be locked up in ice or snow on the
mountain-top, and be given forth again by the slow
descending glacier, or the destructive avalanche. Yet
no particle of it is or shall be lost.

In our present view energy is a never-ceasing round
of motion,—change, energy ever producing other
energy or energies equivalent in amount; not always,

not usually, perhaps, the same in kind, but equivalent and energy still.

Light and heat are forms of energy, and we are supposing that what we call electricity is a form of energy. The force of gravity is a manifestation of energy of such practically stable and constant character that its unit, the force of gravity on a unit of mass, has been taken as a standard of comparison of the forces of other energies; and the ascertainment of this relation between the units of force of heat and electricity with the unit of force of gravity is called the determination of the mechanical equivalent of heat and electricity.

This is the work performed by Joule (after whom a unit of work, the one joule, is named) and others—the joule being the product of one volt by one coulomb. These units, as well as the one ampere, one ohm, and one farad, are ascertained or taken of such true proportions that they respond in every case to the laws of electrical action, as for instance to Ohm's law, 1 ampere $= \dfrac{1 \text{ volt}}{1 \text{ ohm}}$; and a connection is made between electrical work and mechanical work, so that we are able by the units to compute beforehand, in terms of mechanical work with which we are familiar, more accurately than perhaps in any other science, what will be done by any electrical current.

Let us now review our terms and further define them:

Energy.—Motion of matter.   The product of previous energy.

a. Operative or kinetic energy.

Motion of something, say matter, against opposition or resistance.

b. Stored or potential energy.

When such a condition, state, or position of matter

is produced by energy that, though no present change takes place, yet when the matter shall be released from this condition, state, or position operative energy will result, the energy of the condition, state, or position is said to be stored or potential energy. It is nearly akin to potential.

May we not be justified is supposing that the energy, motion of matter, still exists, and that stored or potential energy is the result of balanced opposing kinetic energies in more or less stable or unstable equilibrium? The solid condition of matter is frequently a condition of storage of energy. Is this and the other conditions of matter always so?

Electricity, a Kind of Form of Energy.—Motion in or of some medium—say in or of a universal ether.

We may, perhaps, get some clearer idea by assimilating or comparing it to the motion assumed to exist in the atoms of gas, according to the kinetic theory of gases: Each atom imbued with motion, the atoms continually clashing together, imparting their energy each to each and receiving energy each from each— bombarding the walls of a containing vessel inside and out with equal forces, when the number of atoms per unit of space inside and out of the vessel is equal, and when they are all imbued with equal energy or motion. (See Fig. 2.)

But when the atoms of the interior of a closed vessel exceed in number per unit of space those outside the vessel, although each atom is imbued with equal motion, the number of impingements of atoms against the inside of the vessel will be greater than that of those outside the vessel upon its outside, and pressure outward is established; or if the number inside per unit of space is less than that of those outside, pressure inward is established. The first would be a case of compres-

sion of gas within the vessel, the second a case of rare-
faction or vacuum in the vessel.   But now, if the num-

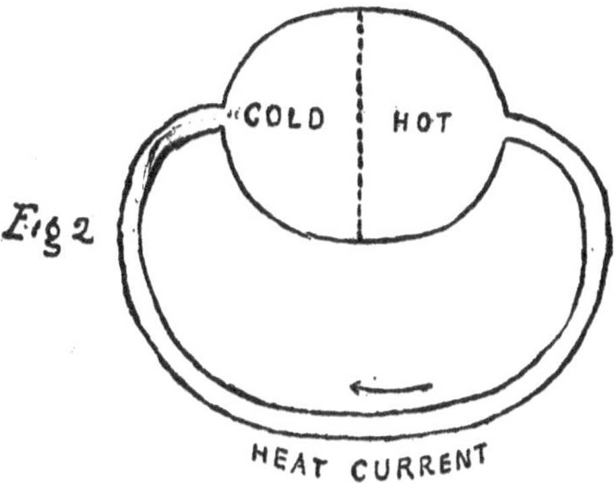

ber of atoms per unit of space within and outside the
closed vessel be the same, but those inside be imbued
with more motion, say by heating them (imparting
heat energy to them), then the number of impingements of atoms on the inside of the vessel will be
greater than on the outside, pressure outward is established, it is a case of excitation of the atoms inside the
vessel.   The reverse pressure, pressure inward, would
be established were the outer atoms excited instead of
the inner ones.

Suppose we take the condition of equal pressure outside and in as the ordinary natural condition of the
gas in the vessel, then all conditions of pressure outward, from compression or excitation of the contained
gas, would be plus conditions of the contained gas: in
which, were an orifice opened in the vessel, a current of
gas would flow from it, and all conditions of pressure
inward from vacuum inside the vessel or excitation of
the gas surrounding it would be minus conditions of

the contained gas; in which, were an orifice opened in the vessel, gas would flow into it.

By putting a diaphragm in the closed vessel with an orifice in it, and pumping gas out of one side and into the other side through a pipe, we might establish a continuous plus condition of the gas on one side of the diaphragm and a minus condition on the other, and a current through the orifice in the diaphragm and through the pipe from the plus to the minus side. And we might use the current of the pipe to drive machinery. Or we might produce a like current of gas temporarily by closing the orifice in the diaphragm and adding heat energy to the atoms of gas on one side of the diaphragm and abstracting it from the other side, until the pressure on one side, due to excitation of atoms by heat, equalled the pressure on the other side, due to a greater number of atoms in a unit of space, moving, however, less rapidly; but when the current of gas has ceased in such a system, there will still be a transference of energy by means of atomic motion of gas from the heated to the cooled side of the vessel—a current of heat, energy, so to speak, through the gas from the plus to the minus side. The plus atoms, continually receiving heat or motion from the source of heat, impart it to the atoms next them, and they to their fellows until it reaches the lowest atoms, which impart it to the heat abstractor; and this difference would depend on the amount of gas acted upon by a given quantity of heat energy.

Heat Resistance.—This current of heat energy would also depend in amount upon the obstructions it would meet by reason of the character of the atoms of the gas, the atoms of some gases being better suited to take on the heat motion, and transfer it to their fellows, than those of other gases. The amount of heat energy transferred in the gas to the final atoms would also depend upon the resistance met in the pipe connecting the plus and minus sides of the vessel, its shape and size, leaving out of view its quality as a receiver and imparter of the motion of the atoms to its surroundings, and also leaving out of view the amount of heat motion converted into other motion in doing work in any part of the circuit, which are not at present being considered.

It must be understood that the foregoing comparison is to be taken as illustrative only—and because it is supposed that some clearer comprehension prevails as to what is meant by *heat* than what is meant by electricity. We are supposing both to be forms or kinds of energy, motion of or in something. Both require a medium. Both have differing quantities or amounts of motion, that may be confined or temporarily located in masses of ordinary matter in a static condition, *i.e.*, in the condition of atomic or molecular motion, confined within the limits of the mass of ordinary matter. Both when so confined are continually giving forth their motion to surrounding objects, and both, when their motion becomes too great, will break the limits of their confinements, perhaps explosively. Both may be converted into mass motion or other energy of equivalent amount. Both may be stored up in a state, condition, or position of matter produced by them, and in which they are not presently manifested. Both may exist as currents of energy, *i.e.*, energy or motion transferred from atom to atom of their medium through distance, or through distance from atom to atom of the conductors, to whose atoms their motion has been imparted, and these currents may be measured by their units of quantity and of force, by also taking into account the opposition or resistance to their flow.

It is asked, What is electricity?

Why not ask what is heat?

The unit of quantity of electrical energy.

The Coulomb.—That quantity of electrical energy or motion which, when imparted to a uniform globular insulated mass of matter of one farad capacity, will produce a pressure or manifest an electromotive force of one volt at any point of the mass.

One Farad.—A unit capacity of an electrical medium, or medium in which electrical energy is or may be manifested, a unit capacity for electrical energy, such that a uniform globular insulated mass of matter of this capacity will manifest a unit electromotive force of one volt at any point, when a unit or coulomb of electrical energy has been imparted to it or abstracted from it.

The capacity represented by that quantity of electrical energy which is required to produce a unit of current, one ampere, against a unit resistance, one ohm, for a unit of time, one second.

Electromotive Force.—Manifestation of electrical energy, in difference of electrical pressure or force.

One Volt.—The unit difference of electrical force or pressure.

The electromotive force equal to that manifested at any point of an insulated uniform globular mass of matter of one farad capacity, when a unit of electrical energy, one coulomb, has been imparted to or abstracted from it. An electromotive force or pressure equal to the continued electromotive force or pressure, while a unit current, one ampere, is flowing against a unit resistance, one ohm.

Resistance.—Static or inherent opposition of matter to the flow or propagation of electrical energy through it, in overcoming which an electrical current is reduced in pressure or electromotive force, the electrical energy being converted into heat.

One Ohm.—The unit of electrical resistance.

The resistance which permits a unit current of electrical energy, one ampere, to flow when the continued electromotive force, or the fall in electromotive force, from initial to returning point of the circuit, is one volt. The amount of resistance in a circuit when the number of units of current flowing are equal to the number of units of electromotive force, *i.e.*, when the number of amperes and volts are equal.

Electrical Current.—Transference of electrical energy through distance.

A flow of electrical energy usually considered as a current only when continuous, in a conductor, making a circuit longer or shorter and returning to itself. A charged insulated body moved in a circuit is a current and will produce magnetism.

The effect of giving direction to electrical energy in or by a conductor, by establishing and maintaining different amounts of electrical activity at at least two points in the conductor, between which the current is considered as flowing, *i.e.*, from the point of greater to the point of less activity; the first is called the plus pole, the other the minus pole.

In static electricity electrical energy is imparted to or abstracted from an insulated receiver, like a Leyden jar or condenser, so as to make electrical activity in the receiver greater or less than that of surrounding objects. Usually some object is placed very near it and connected with the earth, upon which the electricity of the receiver may act by induction through a very short distance, and thus increase the difference of activity between the receiver and this object by driving off the electricity of the object into the earth—make the one more plus and the other more minus, for under our supposition we are compelled to consider that the electrical pressure or electrical activity in all things is normally so high that it is difficult to add to it or subtract from it in an insulated object of any considerable extent, unless we make use of the great capacity of the earth as a receiver, and the repulsion for themselves of electrical activities greater or less than the normal.

But even if this were not the case, we could not continually add energy to an insulated object, allowing none of it to escape or be converted into work or other energy; for the reaction of the energy imparted to the object would soon become so great that we could impart no more to it, and the smaller the object the sooner this point would be reached.

And if we consider the normal pressure of electricity to be so great in all things, we should reach the point when the difference in electrical activities would be so great that we could not overcome it were we to try continually to abstract electricity from an insulated object, and the smaller the object the sooner we should reach that point; or else the insulation of the object would give way, and it would be supplied with energy from outside as fast as we removed it; or in case where the energy were being supplied to the object, it would overcome the insulation and break forth to surrounding objects.

Such high electrical pressure of all things would not in any way militate against the production of currents in a circuit, where we are continually abstracting energy from the one point of the circuit—say the minus point—and giving the same energy to the other point— say the plus point, which is the office of the battery, dynamo, or the like, while the conductor serves to convey or direct the energy imparted to the plus point back again to the minus point.

Right here let us consider the question of the supposed two kinds of electricity: the vitreous or plus, and the resinous or minus, which has been one obstruction to considering electricity as a kind of energy; because the two seeming kinds, notwithstanding the amount of excitation or charge of either kind, always behave toward each other and toward themselves in the same manner, having reference only to whether the kinds acting upon each other are the same or different—the same kinds repelling each other, opposite kinds attracting each other.   How can this be explained upon our supposition that electricity is energy, motion of matter, and of one kind only?

Suppose we assume that there is a normal condition of universal electric energy in equilibrium at any given place, though perhaps differing in amount per unit of space at different places according to some law or laws of the distribution of energy.   Next suppose all conditions of matter in excitation above this normal electrical energy to be plus conditions, and all conditions of excitation of matter below the normal of the place to be minus conditions.   The plus atom above the normal will be emitting or giving forth energy, and the minus atom will be receiving energy; the direction of the currents of energy thus produced will be from the plus atom, and it will be toward the minus atom.   Thus you will see that the directions of the currents between two plus atoms or between two minus atoms will be opposed to one another, and they will therefore repel each other; but between a plus atom and a minus atom the direction of the energy from the plus and to the minus will be the same, they will therefore attract one another.   Thus

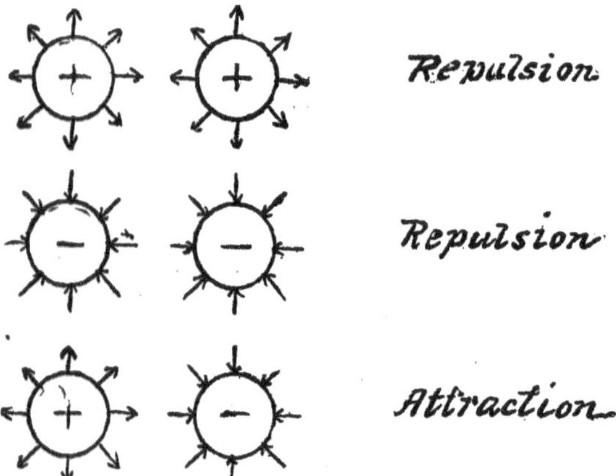

Time will not permit us to go farther into this interesting question at present, but perhaps if you study it carefully you may find that our supposition will explain other phenomena as well as the two-fluid theory will.

Electrical energy in and of itself offers so little that we may say that it offers no appreciable opposition or resistance to being transferred or given direction in a circle or circuit. It is simply giving one direction to existent energy, which theretofore was heterogeneous and balanced in all directions, and this in an imponderable medium, universal ether—a medium in which the planets circulate with so little resistance that astronomers have discovered no retardation in their movements by reason of it, and which is so nearly perfectly elastic that the energy of heat, light, and electricity is propagated in it from the sun to the earth in about eight minutes of time, yet a medium capable of communicating or imparting its motion or energy as heat, light, or electricity to other matter which is ponderable.

This other matter, ponderable matter, does offer resistance to the propagation of electrical energy through it, and of such matter are conductors made.

If, therefore, we abstract electrical energy from one end of a conductor and impart it to the other end, we make a difference of electrical pressure at the two ends of the conductor greater or less, by reason of the obstruction, say resistance of the conductor, and this difference of pressure is called the electromotive force of the circuit.

We have seen that no continuous accumulation alone, or abstraction alone, of energy in or from a finite insulated mass of matter can long go on without reaching the limit of our ability to add or abstract energy—or overcoming the insulation. If we consider motion as the natural condition of matter, and if direction be given to it, it continues until the motion is imparted to or shared with other matter. It follows that motion of matter in a circle or circuit returning into itself, unless it meets with some opposition, goes on forever, at the same rate, whether it is a mass motion, as that of a wheel turning on its axis, or molecular motion of the substance of a ring given a direction of revolution, or vortical molecular motion.

The question arises then, What will give direction to the motion of matter? Opposite equal energy on all sides gives the condition called rest to matter. Abstraction of energy on one side or imparting or applying energy on the opposite side, or both simultaneously, will give it motion with direction, from the positive toward the negative, from the side of applied toward the side of subtracted energy, and in the same line continued. If this line of direction be a circle or circuit or vortex, when the current of energy is once established, to keep it up at the same rate we have in a simple circuit only to abstract at one point and apply

16

at another point energy in the direction of the established current sufficient to overcome the opposition or resistance of the circuit. Imagine to yourselves a uniform field of electrical energy, heterogeneous in direction and balanced or in equilibrium, and therefore not manifest. I mean by this a field of energy in which an equal amount of energy or motion of matter of the field is taking place in each unit of space. Suppose now a body containing a certain quantity of matter, but imbued with a greater or less amount of energy per unit of space, be physically moved through this field of electrical energy: you will see that a disturbance would be caused by the presence of this body within the uniform field of electrical force by the reaction of the differing energies, and that this disturbance would progress with the motion of the body of greater or less energy through the field. Thus mass motion of matter, one kind of energy, would make manifest the electrical energy of the field (if the field was composed of a dielectric or insulator) which before was masked by the equilibrium of the field. Thus Professor Rowland demonstrated that a charged body moving in the air in a circle was equivalent in its effects to an electrical current. Thus, doubtless, the revolution of the dynamo, by cumulating the effects of varying amounts of energy, gives direction to the universal energy and makes it manifest in electrical currents. Let us get rid of our moving mass of ordinary matter, substituting in the place of it a portion of the dielectric of the field, differentiated from the rest of the field by being imbued with greater or less energy than the field at large, and that this differentiated portion of the field has also been imbued with the property of transmitting its increased energy to the dielectric in a certain direction through the field. The effects would be the same as though a charged body were moved through the field. In a medium like universal ether of perfect elasticity and under great tension, and in rapid molecular motion and everywhere existent, suppose we apply a cause (say electrical energy in a given direction) that makes any disturbance of the medium, or distortion in the vortices of the ether before or in front of the cause. There must be corresponding complementary disturbance behind the cause, of opposite sign, and thus we initiate a molecular wave motion in the ether, which would be propagated in space without translation of the mass of the ether, except that due to the first impulse.

We have here all the imagery necessary to radiant electrical and magnetic waves so beautifully made manifest by Hertz and illustrated and perhaps made practically useful by Tesla and others. But for currents we need conductors and insulators or dielectrics or a means of connecting these ethereal waves with ordinary matter,—not that every current is not accompanied by radiant waves, for such is the fact, and induction may be so explained.

Time will not permit of our going into the character or action of insulators or dielectrics, or enumeration of them. We may simply say that the air and ether are such, and that the latter is the supposed and probable medium and storehouse of electrical activity and radiation with which its non-conducting quality not only does not interfere but is a necessity.

Conductors are ordinary matter; we need a connection of the ether with it, a difficult conception since the ether seems to pervade and pass through all ordinary matter without hindrance, even through the earth in its course around the sun. In this I see nothing at present but to have recourse to Maxwell's interetheric particles. But our supposition treating electricity as energy compels us to conceive of them as matter and not electricity. Why not that portion of ordinary matter in some gaseous or ultra-gaseous state so sublimated as to be associated with and acted on by the ether, bound to it and capable of receiving motion from it, and imparting that motion to its fellow ordinary matter. And I refer you here to the experiments of Prof. Tyndall recorded in his eleventh and twelfth lectures "On Heat as a Mode of Motion," in which he shows that different gases have different capacities for taking on the motions of etheric particles and imparting or communicating motion to the ether, and that even the perfume of the flowers has an influence on climate for this reason.

It is a guess, but no more so, so it seems to me, than the ordinary conception of a "bound ether," a portion of the ether bound to or in ordinary matter. And it seems to me our conception is the attaching to, or binding of, the less to the greater, ordinary matter to the ether; while the other seems like binding the greater to the less, the ether to ordinary matter. But we may pass this by, simply remarking that if there be a universal ether (which seems to be proved), there is such a connection between it and ordinary matter that the motions of the one are or may be communicated to or have effect upon the other.

We conceive then that conductors are composed of matter whose molecules are capable of vibrating in the same form and time as the electrical vibrations of the ether (or of the interetheric particles of Maxwell), and so are capable of accumulating such vibrations and transmitting them, and imparting them to other similar matter. In other words, they are opaque to electrical vibrations of ether or the interetheric particles—that is, they take on and cumulate and so use up the electric motion of such particles, while dielectrics or insulators are composed of matter whose molecules are not capable of vibrating in the same time or form as the vibrations of the ether or interetheric particles, and so cannot take on and accumulate and use up the motion of the ether or interetheric particles, and therefore the electric waves of the ether (which fills them and everything else) pass through them without material diminution or loss.   They are transparent to electric ethereal waves, and they cannot take on and transmit the electric impulses of conductors—being out of time with them—but by repeated electrical impulses may respond in other forms of motion such as heat.   Of course I am speaking of perfect insulators and perfect conductors.

Conductivity in this view becomes electric opacity, and insulation electric transparency.   (See Tyndall's " Heat, a Mode of Motion.")

Returning to the consideration of the impulse of energy upon the ether producing a wave in it having direction: if we make that direction a circle or circuit returning into itself (and if the impulse is only a disturbance of universal energy it naturally takes that form or direction), we shall have a wave of disturbance of energy around the circuit in the direction of the first impulse—*i.e.*, the plus direction—which if there be no resistance in the circuit will be eternal.

.We conclude, therefore, that by reason of the high static pressure of electrical energy in all things, to cause a continuous propagation of electrical energy in a circuit we must abstract on one side as much as we put in on the other; in other words, the current must be the same in all parts of the circuit, and such is found to be the fact.   How then are we to consider electromotive force or the manifestation of electrical energy, which is different in different parts of the cir-

cuit, which can only be due to a greater amount of
energy in one part of the circuit than in another? We
must consider it as *difference* of reaction against the static
and normal or resident electricity in the electrical medium, which must first be established before a current will
flow, and in which, if there be any resistance in the
circuit, it must be maintained and kept up or the current
started by it will be used up on the resistance, *i.e.*, converted into other energy, heat.

Suppose, as in Fig. 3, we have an electrical current in
which a is the generator of the current, and suppose
the circuit has no resistance except at R, and that the
resistance at R is five ohms, and the difference in static
electrical energy between the two parts x and y of the
current as established is such that the pressure or force

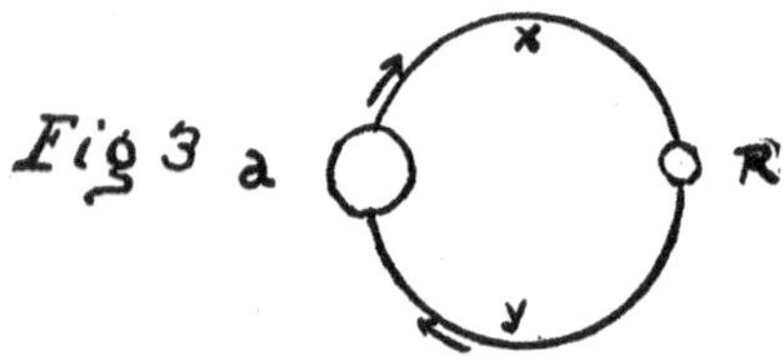

from x toward y through R is manifested as five volts,
i.e., the force of y against x is five volts less than the
force of x against y. We know that a current from x
to y would be established of one ampere, that is, one
coulomb of electrical energy would flow from x to y in
a second if the same difference in electrical energy between x and y were maintained. Now, therefore, if the
generator, a, abstract steadily during one second electrical energy from y amounting to one coulomb of electrical energy in a second and impart it to x, the difference in electrical energy between x and y will be during
this second maintained and the electromotive force or

difference in static pressure will be all the time the same, five volts, and it is manifest that the flow or propagation of energy in every part of the circuit will be the same, namely, one ampere.

We come to the conclusion, therefore, that the office of the electrical generator is to establish and maintain a difference in the static amount of electrical energy between the different parts of the circuit.

Now we know that electrical energy is converted into heat energy and given forth at R.

If therefore y, from which energy is continually abstracted, is insulated, has no supply of energy, the total energy of the circuit must be continually diminished by the amount given forth as heat at R, and we know that this cannot long continue, or the exhausted or minus condition of the circuit would become such that the insulation of the circuit would be ruptured by the difference between static pressure—electromotive force of things outside the circuit and the circuit itself— or the work of removing energy from the circuit against the enormous outside pressure would soon become too great to be continued, unless the circuit were connected at one point only with some great reservoir of energy like the earth, through which energy could be supplied to it.

If both x and y were connected to earth the current would not all flow through the resistance R, but would take the easier path through the earth. Doubtless every circuit, however well insulated, does receive energy from outside things when its potential falls below the normal pressure of outside things—but this will only in part account for the energy imparted or given forth in doing work.

The current is the same in all parts of the circuit.

Whence, then, does this energy come? Mediately

from the generator but directly from the mass of the work or resistance—which takes on or is imbued with energy or motion, by universal energy, by reason of the difference in reaction against universal energy created by the generator.

To cause motion at R energy is abstracted on the y side of the molecule R, and imparted on the x side to an equal amount; the result is motion, increased activity of molecule R. Let us suppose this to be a vortical motion of the molecule (thus—)

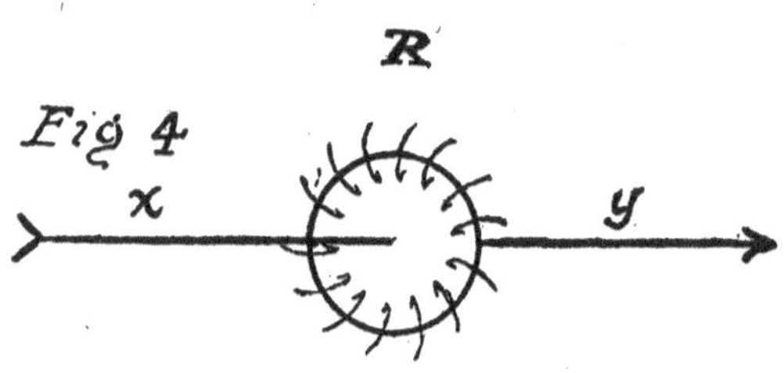

returning into itself. As the position of the molecule is not changed when electrical energy is changed into heat energy, the resistance is the opposition of the molecules of the substance constituting the resistance to being revolved or to taking on heat motion. The generator a takes energy from y, y in turn takes it from one side of R; the generator adds the same amount of energy to x, but has to add this amount of energy to x against the increased activity, or energy of x over y. x imparts to R only the increment of energy due to the work of the generator caused by putting a certain amount of energy per second received from y at a low static potential or activity into x at a higher static potential or activity, and this increment is just equal in amount to the amount abstracted by y from R. For we must remember it costs nothing to circulate the current without resistance or opposing energy. The result is that the total energy of the generator is expended in causing a difference in reaction against universal energy, which in turn acts on the resistance.   It is as though a belt were around R, set in motion by a and pulling on the y side of R and pushing with equal force on the x side of R.   The work done or energy manifested at R, as is the case with every manifestation of energy, requires a difference of potential, a minus as well as plus, else no energy is manifested, no work is done   In other words heat energy, which is that form of energy into which electrical energy is converted when it acts through resistance, requires a minus as well as plus in order to be manifested.

Whatever be the form or character of that motion of matter which we call heat, we cannot conceive of its being initiated unless the force or forces on one side or several sides of a molecule is greater than the force on the other side or sides.   The fact that electrical motion of matter can initiate or produce heat motion of matter proves that it can also retard heat motion of matter, for we have only to have the electrical force equal on both sides, or in opposite directions, to stop the production of heat motion in the molecules.   It follows that heat motion, produced by electrical motion applied on one side or in one direction to a molecule, gives forth electrical motion on the other side of the molecule, for action and reaction are equal; and if the difference in the electrical energy on opposite sides of the molecule remains constant, the heat motion must give forth on one side as much of the electrical energy of the current proper as it receives on the other, the heat manifested being due not to the current but to the reaction of universal energy to which the current is due.

Not that such is the character of heat motion, but in order that we may picture to ourselves how this can be, let us contemplate the following diagram:

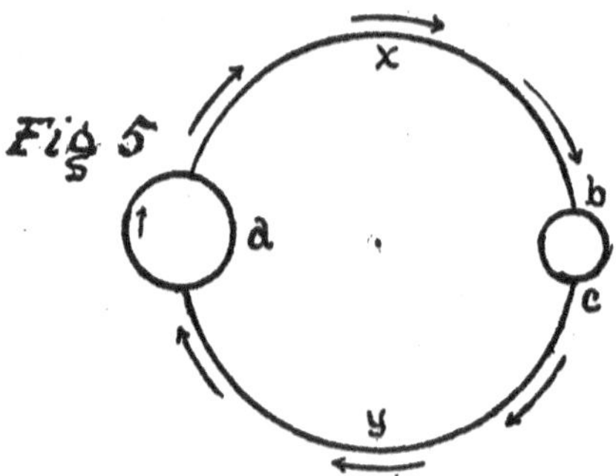

a is the generator supposed so to act as to take energy from y and impart it to x. The energy taken from y leaves it below the normal or universal energy, therefore y receives energy from the resistance R, which is at the normal energy at the point c where it is connected to R, and a current flows from c to y to equalize the energy in y. The same energy taken from y is given to x which is at normal energy. The addition given to x is imparted against the reaction of universal normal energy in and surrounding x, which is existent the same at b one end of x as at a the other. But to equalize the energy in x a current flows along it from a to b. The currents in y and x are equal. The generator is aided by the universal energy up to the normal of universal energy if x and y are at the same potential. The universal energy opposes the addition of energy to x by the generator as much as y favors it. But above the normal of universal energy it opposes by reaction the addition of energy to x, and the energy of y aids less and less as it is reduced below the normal. The energy of the generator is therefore wholly expended against the reaction of universal energy, existent in everything and at every point in the universe, including our circuit and the same or substantially the same everywhere, except as differences of potential are produced or naturally occur in it, when its forms may be changed, that is, work is done.

What then takes place at R?

We have seen that there is a difference in the potential at the two points b and c of R.

What is this difference of potential?

That the activity at b is greater than the activity at c. The reaction against universal energy is greatest at b, least at c. R has resident energy which is of such form and direction, so locked up that it takes force, energy in another direction, to change it into another form of energy. It opposes the change which must take place if a current of energy of different direction or form passes through it. Nevertheless the reaction of universal energy forces the current to pass, a new form of energy appears at R, viz. heat, it is produced by universal energy,—principally stored up in the surrounding ether by the action of the generator, reacting with different forces at b and c.

We have seen that the currents in x and y were only currents of equalization of energy in the conductors, that the whole energy of the generator was expended against the reaction of universal energy. We find now that the work done at R is due to universal energy. We see, therefore, that the current passing y is the same as that in any other point in the circuit, and that it is only mediately and not directly due to the energy of a, the generator; and as it is equal at all parts of the circuit it parts with no energy, or if it does that energy is re-supplied by universal energy.

What then is the medium through which this energy of the work is transmitted?

Universal ether, the medium of the energy of electricity, heat and light.

There must be a current of energy then in the ether corresponding to the work done.

Yes, in the same sense that a current would flow in the ocean, if you dipped up water into a trough on one side and let it run to the other and there flow into the ocean.

It is not meant by this statement that reactions will not be set up in near-by objects or in the ether between such objects and the conductor, by the static condition of the energy of the conductor and by the progressing equalizing flow of electrical activity in the conductor, or that such reactions will not in turn affect the static condition and flow of electrical activity in the conductor for such is the case. But only that such action or reaction, in the sense of our present discussion, may be disregarded as the waves in the ocean are in our last comparison.

It is well known that modern thought of the most brilliant intellects has inclined to consider electricity as an incompressible fluid or fluids, with or without inertia, and the ether as a dielectric or insulator of grea, rigidity, absolutely filling all space and without porest but with electricity entangled in it as water is in a jelly, or as a constituent or a complementary part of the ether itself, or in fact the ether itself, and conductors as holes in the ether, and that upon such theories an immense amount of ingenuity has been expended which may plausibly explain the phenomena of electricity, such as charge, induction, current, magnetism, potential, etc.

These theories are by no means underestimated, and many of those regarding the action of electricity are doubtless very near the truth, and greatly aid in thought upon the subject and comprehension, whether exact truth or not.

It is only when we come to the question whether electricity shall be considered as a form of energy, a kind of motion of matter, or matter itself, that we hesitate. Even those who accept the latter as the true supposition are in the end led up to a consideration of universal vortex motion of ether, which in itself is a condition of universal energy.

The great objection in my mind to this fluid or material theory of electricity is that is seems to limit us to consider the ether as non-porous, so to say; solid; giving room to nothing else within it, impermeable, nothing beyond it or beside it, not made of it.

The conception limits infinity in that direction. Its authors have discovered the foundations of the infinite universe. Excuse us if we hesitate to accept such far-reaching but yet limited theories. Until absolute demonstration shows that the phenomena of electrical action cannot be explained by supposing electricity to be a part of universal motion of matter, energy, let us hesitate to accept them and change the order of the universe in past thought—namely, that within the ether we have found, may be, another and subtler ether, and so on to infinity; and that in like manner other and subtler energies may and probably do exist which we have no senses to perceive and as yet no instruments to disclose, but which may be found out and used in the future as electricity now is.

We may have reached the limit of our present ability to conceive in thought forms or kinds of motion, and the effects of different or other forms or kinds, or the combinations of different kinds; but until necessity compels us, let us not assume that we have found the underlying foundation-matter of which the infinite universe is composed.

To return from our digression. We have seen that the current in the conductor is only a current of equalization of energy in the conductor; it does no work on resistance, but the work is done by universal energy.

Let us take an illustration. Suppose an ox on a treadmill raises water to a height whence by a level trough it flows to a distance, keeping a certain grade or level of itself in the trough; at the trough's end the water strikes against a wheel which it turns, and thence goes to the reservoir from which it was raised. Would you say that the ox was turning the wheel, or only doing work against the universal energy of gravitation? Or that the current in the trough or in the circuit, everywhere the same, was directly caused by the ox or was doing the work of turning the wheel? Or would you say that gravitation was causing the current and doing the work?

Nevertheless, the work done when a current is flowing has a certain relation to the current, *i.e*, is equal to the current quantity multiplied by the electromotive force quantity. This shows simply that there is a simple ratio, as one to one, between the effects of adding energy in causing a flow of equalization against no resistance and the effect of adding energy when causing reaction of universal energy against resistance. So we may use this flow of equalization as one of the factors of work or rather power. It is this current of equalization that is known as "current" in electro-dynamics.

Its unit is one coulomb per second, one ampere.

This current is not due to absolute or equal energy, equal potential, however high, but to the difference of energy, electromotive force. It may and does exist as well in a field of low energy as in one of high energy. It is restrained by resistance (which we have likened to the natural energy of the conductor, the motion of the atoms or molecules of the conductor according to their laws of motion in the system of universal energy) until the motion of the atoms of the resistance, overcome by the reaction of the energy imparted by the generator to the surrounding ether, takes on another form of motion, heat motion, energy, work, when impelled by the reaction of the same energy imparted to and given forth by the ether, it flows on (if it may be said to flow, which we do not know) in equal quantity, in equal time, proportioned to the difference of potential created by the generator in the surrounding insulating or dielectric ether and the resistance of the circuit.

You will perhaps have perceived that my thoughts upon the subject have led me to conceive of electricity as a vibratory motion of matter, and its transmission to be of the nature of wave movement. That its proper medium is the ether, a kind of matter (such I understand was Maxwell's opinion, the weight of ether of the size of the earth is estimated at less than two pounds) and that only in transmission, when sharing its motion with other matter, and not when its vibrations are in equilibrium, is work done.

What then is a wave?

Lodge says, "A disturbance periodic both in time and space." I suppose we must have something to be disturbed. Put therefore "matter" or "a medium" between "disturbance" and "periodic," and we have "a disturbance in a medium or matter periodic in both time and space." The disturbance moves relatively to its position at any fixed time; it is periodic; it recurs at intervals longer or shorter; in space and time is periodic; it takes time to occur.

The wave's length may be hundreds or thousands of miles or less than any distance we can measure. Its time greater than that of the lowest audible sound-wave, 16 to 32 per second, or four hundred to eight hundred billions per second, as in light vibrations, or quicker.

We have thus far spoken of electric vibrations of such wave-lengths and frequency that the atoms of all conducting matter are able to respond to them in taking on their motion, as a stretched string responds to its own note only, and have guessed that resistance was the opposition of the natural energies of the atoms or molecules of conductors to being overcome by the electrical wave-motions, and was therefore constant. *Such* electricity of sufficient quantity and force is destructive to life and overcomes chemical affinities and organized structures.

But Hertz has made manifest, and Tesla has shown us in practical use, electrical energies of enormous potential and wave frequency, yet to which the human organism and everything else, except good conductors, are nearly or quite transparent as they are to magnetism.

Though of enormous electromotive force, these energies pass through us without injury and without our feeling them, but heat and light up lumps of carbon in a vacuum and cause visible waves of ether in vacuum tubes.

It is because our molecular cells are not attuned to vibrations of such great frequency and short wave-length, and our molecules are not disturbed or broken up by the response of the ultimate atoms of which they are composed to these particular waves. (See Lecture 12, "Heat as a Mode of Motion," Tyndall.)

The strings of a musical instrument only respond to the sounds produced by other sonorous bodies, which in wave-length and frequency correspond to the waves constituting the sounds they are capable of producing.

Is this electricity or some other form of energy into which electricity runs when its potential and wave frequency are enormously increased and wave-length shortened?

Does the same thing occur in heat?

Is there an enormous temperature at which heat becomes innocuous to organized structures or at which they become transparent to it?

Does heat become mainly light at such potential?

Is our sun of such temperature, or what is the character of its energy, and in what form is it given forth?

We know that whatever be its form or kind it is capable of being transformed into radiant heat and light, the forms in which we receive it. We see every day mechanical energy transformed into electrical energy, and that, at any distance from its source, again transformed through resistance into light and heat in the electric lamp.

These are only a few of the questions that present themselves to us upon our supposition that electricity is a form or kind of energy, motion of matter. You naturally inquire if electricity is a manifestation of electrical energies of varying amounts in the field of universal energy. What is magnetism?

Faraday and Maxwell, particularly the latter, have demonstrated that it is the rectangular component of an electrical wave: the lines of stress or tension at right angles to the direction of a current. A physical illustration will be found in a washbowl filled with water if the plug be withdrawn at the bottom. The

17

universal energy of gravity will cause the water to fall through the hole, and the same force of gravity will cause the water in the bowl on all sides to rush toward the centre of the bowl from which the water has fallen through the plug-hole; some inequality perhaps directs the opposing currents from opposite sides of the bowl, one to one side of the axis of the plug-hole, the other to the other side of the axis. The result is that the water in the bowl will flow in circles around the axis of the plug-hole. This circular motion represents magnetism, the flow from the plug-hole represents current; both are caused by the energy of gravity, acting in one direction, *i.e.*, toward the centre of the earth.

Why does the magnetic strain or wave always revolve around the current in the same direction with reference to its flow? Perhaps it is due to the direction of magnetic currents of the earth.

I have been unable to picture to myself a cause with which I am wholly satisfied.

Perhaps you can do so.

Why are so many substances transparent to the magnetic wave and at the same time conductors of current?

I see no reason why the magnetic impulses due to electrical transmission should necessarily be of the same form or wave-length and frequency as the current impulses; if they are not this would explain why substances transparent to the one are opaque to the other.

But I have already spoken too long and must stop. If I have said anything that may lead you to think of this subject, even to correct my errors, my object will have been accomplished. Why should you not?

The field is large and beautiful, full of fruits, and mines of precious ore.

Why should you not enter and gather and enjoy and

store up for others?   Who among you will be the future Coulomb, Volta, Ampere, Ohm, Faraday, Watt, Joule, Maxwell, Thompson, Tyndall, Hertz, or Tesla?

We have said little or nothing of static electricity, as little of radiant electrical energy. The course of thought and work was first in the domain of static electricity, then and recently on currents, and is now on radiant energy.

The first is necessary to any complete comprehension of, or thought on, the second and third. You know the rich rewards in honor and profit which have come to those who have pursued the subject and deduced their laws of action and harnessed the energies for man's use.

The domain of radiant energy, wave-motion, is just being entered on. In it, by giving direction, we get rid of the law of the inverse square of the distance in propagation (if we desire to do so), as well as the necessity of conductors. We come back to and make use of all our knowledge of mechanics, chemistry, acoustics, optics, and heat. We see in imagination (hardly that, better with the eye of science) all space filled and vibrating with motion, energy of various kinds, unseen by our natural eyes, unheard, unfelt, untasted, of forms yet unknown, but some of which we can make manifest by instruments and appliances devised by human reason and thought and subjugate them for practical work and usefulness. Yet how few of the many kinds which reason seems to teach us must exist! Who of you will find and help in bringing under control new forms, shall we say, of light or electricity, or heat or sound, or chemical affinity, or who will demonstrate the cause of gravitation or nervous energy, by which your hand receives its commands from the brain, or that subtler energy, the physical basis of thought or

cerebration by which directly or mediately you influence others?

Perhaps you think it all too practical, with nothing
of beauty or pleasure in it. Go to the operas; listen to
the music of the orchestra; apply your acoustics; remember that the pleasure you experience comes from
waves of energy in a medium; close your eyes and
imagine the shell forms of sound-waves expanding outward from their sources, filling all the space with forms
of beauty and grace, chasing one another small and
great, crossing and intercrossing without interference
with perfect harmony, superposed and riding one upon
the other in seeming glee and sport, or moving in the
solemn dirge in stately procession, or clashing or
warring in the battle-piece or in the expression of
anger. If your knowledge of acoustics do not increase
your pleasure, and give to you an added and heightened
appreciation of music, it will be because you have failed
to picture the beauties of form, order, and sequence of
energy which cause the motions of brain substance
which you enjoy as sound. But sound is only one of
the lower energies. When you can appreciate the
higher and more subtle and take in your mind's eye
more of the harmonies and music of truth and nature
and God, then shall your satisfaction and enjoyment
correspondingly increase.

SOME UNITS AND DEFINITIONS—AS EXHIBITED ON BLACKBOARD DURING LECTURE.

1st Unit. Q.	Coulomb.	Quantity unit.
2d Unit. EMF. or E.	Volt.	Pressure or force unit.
3d Unit. K.	Farad.	Unit of static capacity to receive electrical energy.
4th Unit. S.	Second.	Time unit.

5th Unit. C.	Ampere.	Flow unit, $\dfrac{\text{quantity unit}}{\text{time unit}}$
6th Unit. W.	Joule.	Unit of work—1 volt $\times$ 1 coulomb, 1 volt-coulomb.
	Work.	Change of one form or kind of energy into another form or kind.
7th Unit. R.	Ohm.	The unit of resistance to flow or to transmission of energy.
		A length of wire or other conductor offering a unit's opposition to the flow of electrical energy.

RESISTANCE.

	(A Guess.)	The opposition which the normal energy of matter offers to the transmission of electrical energy, and by which electrical energy is converted into heat energy.
	Conductivity.	The reciprocal of resistance.
	Ohm's law.	The number of amperes equals the number of volts divided by the number of ohms.

$$1\,C = \frac{1\,V}{1\,R}.$$

	Power.	The rate of doing work. $\dfrac{\text{Work}}{\text{Time}}$.
8th Unit. P.	Watt.	The unit of the rate of doing electrical work. The unit of electrical power.

$$\frac{1\text{ volt} \times 1\text{ coulomb}}{1\text{ second}}.$$

	Wave.	"A disturbance (in or of a medium) periodic both in time and space" (Lodge). Progressive disturbance in or of a medium.
	Energy.	Motion of matter.
	Force.	The result of energy—in most cases the manifestation or a property of energy. Difference in amount of energy. It implies direction.
Electromotive force.		Manifestation of electrical energy in difference of electrical pressure.

WILLIAM ALEXANDER HAMMOND.

William Alexander Hammond, M.D., Surgeon-General of the United States Army (retired list), and distinguished as a physician, surgeon, and specialist, was born at Annapolis, Md., August 28th, 1828. His father was Dr. John W. Hammond, of Anne Arundel County, Md., whose ancestors had large grants of land in that county from the Crown and from Lord Baltimore.

Dr. Hammond's mother was Sarah Pinkney, whose ancestors came over from Normandy to England with William the Conqueror, and whose names are still to be found on the roll of Battle Abbey.

He was graduated at the medical department of the University of the City of New York, and entered the United States Army in 1840 as assistant surgeon, with the rank of first lieutenant.

In October, 1860, he resigned to accept the professorship of anatomy and physiology in the University of Maryland, but at the beginning of the Civil War he again entered the army and was assigned to the organization of general hospitals in Hagerstown, Frederick, and Baltimore. Afterward the United States Sanitary Commission urged his appointment as surgeon-general of the army, and in April, 1862, he received this commission with the rank of brigadier-general. He instituted radical changes in the management of his office, established the Army Medical Museum by special order, and suggested the plan of the "Medical and Surgical History of the Rebellion." Charges of exceeding his authority and of infringements of the regulations of the service were made against him by Secretary Stanton and he was dismissed from the army in August, 1864. He at once removed to New York, where he settled in the practice of his profession, and made a specialty of diseases of the nervous system. In 1867–73 he was professor of diseases of the mind and nervous system in Bellevue Hospital Medical College, and then was elected to a similar chair in the medical department of the University of the City of New York. He remained there until 1882, when he became one o the founders of the New York Post-Graduate Medical School, and has since delivered lectures on his specialty in that institution. Dr. Hammond has also delivered lectures in the medical department of the University of Vermont, and in 1870 became physician at the New York State Hospital for diseases of the nervous system. In 1878 a bill was submitted to Congress authorizing the President to review the proceedings of the court-martial, and, if justice demanded, to reinstate Dr. Hammond. This measure was passed by the House unanimously and by the Senate with but one dissenting vote. In August, 1879, it was approved by the President, and Dr. Hammond was restored to his place on the rolls of the Army, as surgeon-general and brigadier-general on the retired list.

Besides contributing to current medical literature, he founded and edited the *Maryland and Virginia Medical Journal*, was one of the originators of the *New York Medical Journal*, and established the *Quarterly Journal of Psychological Medicine and Medical Jurisprudence*, becoming its editor. His medical works in book form include "Physiological Memoirs;" "A Treatise on Hygiene with Special Reference to the Military Service;" "Insanity and its Medico-Legal Relations;" "Diseases of the Nervous System," which has been translated into French and Spanish, and many others. He has also edited "Military, Medical, and Surgical Essays," prepared for the United States Sanitary Commission, and translated from the German Meyer's "Electricity in its Relations to Practical Medicine."

Dr. Hammond is also the author of several novels, including "Robert Severne, his Friend and Enemies;" "Lal;" "On the Susquehanna," etc.

In 1888 he removed from New York to Washington, D.C., where he still resides.

BRAINS AND MUSCLES: THEIR RELA-TIVE TRAINING AND DEVELOPMENT.

By Dr. William A. Hammond.

It was with great pleasure that I accepted the kind invitation of the president of your Alumni Association and the founder of this course of lectures, General Butterfield, to address you on the important subject of the relations of physical exercise to the mind and body in some of the prominent occupations of the active man. It is not to be expected that I shall enter at length into the consideration of the anatomy, chemistry, and physiology of the subject; but there are a few prominent points in these connections which it is essential should be understood in order that you may fully appreciate the views which are to follow. For, though you may already have a general idea of the matters to which I refer, it will not, I am sure, be time thrown away, if I endeavor to bring them specifically to your attention on the present occasion.

In order that a person may have the capacity for physical exercise, he must possess three kinds of anatomical organs—nerve centres to provide the force by which the muscles are to be made to contract, nerves to transmit this force, and muscles, by means of which the force is manifested in the movements in the body and limbs. All these organs, however, would be useless unless there were the force to which I have referred to put them in action, and this force is the mind. And by mind we are to understand, not only the force that comes from the brain, but that also which is evolved from other parts of the nervous apparatus, the spinal cord and certain collections of gray nerve tissue, called ganglia, found in various parts of the body. Without this force the organs in question would be in about the situation of an engine without the steam required to set it in motion. The organism is complete, its cylinders, pistons, and valves are in order; but it is dead, for the force that makes it a thing of life is not there. Now this force in the animal body is produced by the action of what is called gray nerve-substance. In the brain this is placed chiefly on the outside to the depth of about a twelfth of an inch, and is hence called the cortex; but in the spinal cord it is in the interior of the organ, extending its whole length, and being shaped something like a capital letter H. I used to say in my lectures to medical students that if I should ever be disposed to make for myself a god, I would select a piece of gray nerve-tissue as the object of my adoration. For it is the most wonderful substance, so far as we know, in the whole universe, surpassing in its grandeur sun and moon and stars and everything else of which we have any knowledge. It is the substance that makes man what he is, that causes him to perceive, to experience emotions, to conceive ideas, to exert his will—in short, to evolve his mind. And though it is found in all animals, high and low, it is in none in such great quantity or in such a high state of elaboration as in that being who stands at the head of all animated nature.

But the gray nerve-tissue forms but a small portion of the nerve substance of the brain and of the spinal cord. There is another which constitutes the greater part of both these organs, and this is the white substance. The nerves themselves consist entirely of this matter. It has nothing to do with the production of force. Its office is to receive impressions from without and to convey to the muscles and organs of the body the power by which their functions are performed. It places the gray substance with which it is in intimate contact in relation with the external world.

I have said that the brain is not the only organ which serves for the production of mind. If you have ever seen, as I have in the course of physiological investigations, a decapitated frog perform acts showing the possession of perception, intellect, and will, you would at once admit the correctness of my statement—a statement which is certainly not in accordance with the preconceived ideas of many of you, and which would possibly be called in question by some physiologists. If the side of such a frog be gently tickled with a straw, the foot of that side is at once used to push the straw away; if that foot be held so that it cannot be employed, the foot of the other side is brought into action to accomplish the purpose. If the animal be placed in a vessel of water, it swims almost as vigorously as if the brain were still in its proper place, and if it meets with an obstruction, it turns aside to avoid it, or if unsuccessful in the effort, ceases its swimming movements. All these efforts show intelligence and indicate that there are other sources of mind than the brain. I have seen a snake crawl to its hole, a distance of several feet, after its head had been cut off, showing that the knowledge it had acquired before mutilation was still present and available for the object in view. The tail of a turtle will vibrate, if pinched, for several months, not only after the head of the animal is removed, but after the entire contents of the shell have been scooped out and made into soup for the delectation of a London alderman or a New York epicure. And in the New York

Sun of a recent date I find an incident described which bears directly on the point under discussion. A sea turtle was captured by a party of gentlemen on the Gulf shore in Texas, and its head was cut off preparatory to the animal being cooked. Much, however, to the surprise of the party, the decapitated turtle endeavored to escape by making for the water. Several times it was turned around, but in every instance it discovered the direction in which the water lay and made efforts to reach it. The writer states that he has several times witnessed a repetition of the procedure, and calls attention to the fact that water-snakes exhibit the like action when decapitated.

I call to mind how, upon one occasion, a rattlesnake behaved to a teamster who had cut off its head with a stroke of his whip-lash. The snake remained coiled, and the man bent over it to examine the animal more closely. Suddenly the coil straightened, and the headless and bloody trunk struck the curious observer full in the forehead. The man fainted from the nervous shock, and the snake crawled away to hide under a sage-bush.

These manifestations are not so striking in warm-blooded animals, but even in them they are not entirely absent. You have all probably seen a chicken, after its neck has been wrung, walk several steps in quite a determinate manner before falling and dying from loss of blood.

A man, however, without a head, is not of much use, but this is mainly due to the fact that the act of decapitation necessarily involves the loss of such a large quantity of blood that the death of the whole body ensues almost at the very instant. Nevertheless, I can recall to your minds many examples in which while the brain, though present, is quiescent or otherwise en-

gaged, actions are performed which can only be the result of some degree of mentality. Take for instance
the fact (of which doubtless many of you have personal
experience) that a young lady will engage her brain in
conversation with her sweetheart, while at the same
time she performs a difficult piece of music on the
piano. She cannot do this with a composition that she
has not thoroughly learned, for then she requires all
the mind that the brain and spinal cord can give her;
but when the music is well mastered she can employ
her brain with her young man and her spinal cord with
her piano. You have all, doubtless, while walking or
reading, occupied your higher mental faculties with
something very foreign to directing your steps in crossing streets or jumping gutters and turning corners until
you reached your own doorsteps, or in paying attention
to the novel you may be perusing or the abstruse volume on mathematics you are studying, and yet you
have never made a mistake in your route or failed to
turn over the leaves regularly as you reached the bottom of the pages without your having the slightest con-
sciousness of what your legs have been doing in the one
case or your hands in the other. No idea of the scenes
that have been enacting before you, or of the incidents
or problems of your books, has been formed. Your
brain has been otherwise employed; your spinal cord
has moved your legs and your hands.

The main point I wish to impress upon you in citing
these facts is this—that there is a force that comes from
the brain and that there is another, and a lower order
of force, that comes mainly from the spinal cord. As
a consequence there are two kinds of physical exercise
—that to which the whole mind is given, and which is
therefore active, spirited, determinate, conscious; and
that into which the higher qualities of the mind do not

enter, and which is therefore automatic, spiritless, and almost, if not entirely, merely mechanical. I simply mention these facts now in order to indicate the principles I desire to lay before you; but as they constitute the essential feature of my remarks, and are the basis of the advice I shall have to give you, I shall consider them at greater length when I have touched a little more fully upon some of the primary conditions associated with all physical exercise.

In order that force of any kind should be developed, matter of some description must undergo a change of form. To obtain steam and the force due to its expansion we ordinarily employ some highly carbonaceous substance, such as coal, wood, or petroleum, by the combustion of which it is decomposed, heat is evolved, the water is raised in temperature, and steam is formed. To obtain the force known as galvanic electricity we can take a plate of carbon and one of zinc and immerse them in sulphuric acid diluted with water. The acid at once attacks the zinc, a new compound of sulphate of zinc is formed, the water is decomposed into its ultimate elements, and through this double action galvanism results and passes off by means of the attached conductors. Then it may in its turn decompose a solution of gold and gild a trinket, flash a telegraphic message to a distant part of the earth, aid the physician in the restoration of a paralyzed muscle, or stimulate an optic nerve, the conducting power of which has been lost, and thus give back the eyesight that otherwise would never have returned.

This law that force results from decomposition of matter is just as absolute, so far as the nervous system of man and other animals is concerned, as it is in its relations to inorganic matter. With every thought, however trifling it may be, a certain amount of gray nerve-tissue is decomposed, and the products of this destruction entering the blood are carried off by the skin, the lungs, the kidneys, and other excretory organs, and discharged from the system as effete material to enter into new combinations, and perhaps to reappear in the course of no very long period of time in the form of potatoes, or turkey, or beef, and again to be deposited as new gray nerve-tissue. Thus the sequence of composition and decomposition continues while life lasts— yes, and after life has departed and the whole dead body returns to the earth from which it came.

And thus the change goes on, not only with every thought that is conceived, with every motion that is felt, with every perception of sight, or hearing, or touch, or taste, or smell that puts us in relation with the external world: with every act of the will, gray nerve-substance is decomposed and new matter, primarily derived from the food we take, is deposited from the blood to take its place.

But this is not only true of the force-producing centres; it is equally a fact with the various organs of the body on which the force acts. Thus the liver secretes bile, and a portion of its substance is destroyed with every drop of the fluid that is formed; the heart beats to send the blood, which is to preserve life, to every part of the body, and with each throb a certain part of the cardiac substance dies; the tears flow, started by some overwhelming passion, and the glands which separate them from the blood weigh less after than before the emotion which put them in action is experienced; a finger is bent, a word is spoken, an eyelid trembles, and the muscles that acted to accomplish these results part with a portion of their fibres. These are not fanciful statements. They are based upon exact experiments and are not subjects on which physiologists differ,

Thus I took the gastrocnemius muscle (the one forming the calf of the leg) of a recently killed frog, weighed it accurately on an extremely delicate balance, then hermetically inclosing it in a glass tube, also accurately weighed, and connecting its nerves with the electrodes of a galvanic apparatus, caused it to contract rapidly until its irritability was altogether lost. Then removing it from the tube, I weighed it again and found that it had very appreciably lost weight.

The fact that physical exercise diminishes the weight of the body you can establish for yourselves by a very simple but perfectly conclusive process. Weigh yourselves on a delicate balance, then exercise strongly for an hour or so, and weigh yourselves again. You will find in every case that you have lost weight. Of course there would be some loss owing to the exhalations from the lungs and skin, but the extent of this can be determined by weighing again after a like period of time has elapsed, during which the body has been kept in a state of quiescence.

Several years ago, when I was more enthusiastic in such matters than I am now, I performed upon myself a series of experiments for the purpose of ascertaining the effects upon the body of rest and mental and physical exertion, and as these have a direct bearing on the subject of my remarks, perhaps you will allow me, if I promise to describe them in non-technical language, to quote some of the results to you.

I found from these observations continued over a period of ten days, that the average weight of the body, as determined upon a balance capable of turning with the hundredth of a pound, was 196.33. I then (the food and all other factors remaining exactly the same) endeavored to ascertain the effects of what to me was unusual physical exercise. This consisted of the lifting of a weight of one hundred pounds ten feet in a minute for three periods of fifteen minutes each at intervals of an hour. This course was continued, as in the standard series of experiments, for ten days. The body was weighed every day, and the average showed 194.13, a loss of 2.20 pounds. Thus the nerve centre originates the force by which a muscle is made to contract. A nerve transmits this force to the muscle and the action ensues. In no essential respect is the process different from that in the sending of a telegraphic message. The battery supplies the electricity, a wire carries it to the recording instrument, and the act is accomplished.

All this will serve to give you an idea of the mechanism of physical exercise and of some of the consequences of muscular contraction, pure and simple, without the interference of any disturbing factor. But did you ever notice in your own experience what a very stupid thing physical exercise, for the mere sake of exercise, is? If you want to see the weariness, the utter despair, excited by this kind of exertion, look at a dog who is turning the wheel of a churn. Or, better still (though perhaps you would experience a difficulty in finding examples in this country), study the faces of the men who are working a treadmill. Apathy, disgust, the sluggish will barely exciting the still more sluggish muscles, the facial expression scarcely more eloquent in expressing mental exhaustion than are the bowed back and semi-flexed limbs indicative of the loss of muscular energy. And if you want a still more striking picture of the degradation of objectless physical labor, look over the earlier pages of Charles Reade's novel "Never Too Late to Mend."

I remember when in the first years of my military experience I was stationed as a medical officer at the little New Mexican village of Cebolleta. A favorite punishment of the commanding officer, when the soldier's offense was not so grave as to require a court-martial, was to cause him to carry stones from one pile to another, a distance of perhaps fifty feet, and when the one was exhausted and the other piled up, to carry them back again, and thus to continue for a period, according to the nature of the breach of discipline he had committed. Nothing was so much dreaded by the men as this punishment; they would have preterred almost anything else. Bread and water for a week, deprivation of liberty, stoppage of pay, even "bucking and gagging" were less unpleasant to them. And yet it was physical exercise, not cruel, not even severe, but painful from its monotony and objectless character.

I have, as have also many of the patients who have come under my professional care, made repeated conscientious attempts to do a certain amount of systematic muscular exercise every day. We have struggled with Indian clubs, dumbbells, lifting-machines, and many other contrivances warranted by their inventors to bring every muscle of the body into action; but it has been weary work, and has been rarely carried on for longer than a few weeks. In my own case I know of nothing more stupid, tiresome, tedious, fatiguing, irksome, than such exertion. It leaves the mind and the body in a state approaching collapse, and one half-hour of it is more exhausting than a whole day spent in hunting, or in some such exercise affording mental stimulus. It always seems to me that it is just so much time thrown away, for we cannot even think when we are swinging an Indian club or putting up a dumbbell. So far as any influence upon mental or physical well-being is concerned, I could never see that it was of the slightest service. In fact, it has always been to me, and to many others whose experience has come to my knowledge, an unmitigated nuisance.

Even walking in the open air without having some definite object in view, or something entertaining in the surroundings, acting as a stimulus to the mind, is a more or less wearisome business. But a promenade down Fifth Avenue, or Broadway, where the houses, the people, the equipages, the shop windows, and the varied incidents necessarily resulting from crowded streets give constant succession of mental excitations, is quite another thing, and one returns from such a walk with the body invigorated and with the mind in a state of elasticity and contentment that nothing else in the whole course of my experience with physical exercise can surpass. If a sudden demand be made for an undue exertion of muscular power, or if some intense mental effort be required, both body and mind are ready for their work, which is performed with a degree of readiness and thoroughness that mere physical exercise without the mental interest could never effect.

In this lie the many differences that exist between the exercise of the person who takes it solitary, perhaps in his bedroom or in a gloomy gymnasium, and one who with some other object in view than that of stretching his legs or contorting his body brings into action both his mind and his muscles in the open air while walking through the ever-changing streets of the city, with a thousand objects of interest around him, or taking a tramp through a region of country new to him, with its varying scenes of mountain and stream and forest, and inhaling such air as can only be had away from the crowded haunts of man. I am not quite sure, however, but that there is more diversion and more recreation (and I stop for the moment to call your attention to these two words, "diversion" and "recrea-

tion") in Fifth Avenue than there is in the Adirondacks
or the Rocky Mountains. I have tried them both very
thoroughly, and I think I have a right to speak with
some degree of positiveness on this point. However,
this is, after all, a matter of taste and education; but
as for me, I confess to liking houses and men and women better than I do trees and chickens and cows.

But, after all, nothing is more desirable in the way of
muscular exertion than to engage in some athletic contest, that not only draws upon the body for all its muscular tact and vigor, but that also calls into exercise the
faculties of the mind in all their categories of perception, intellect, emotion, and will.

The ancient Greeks and Romans well understood the
facts upon which I have laid stress. They thoroughly
knew the advantages of mental stimulation as the ac-
companiment of physical exercise, and hence their
youths were encouraged to enter into contests with
each other for supremacy in running, wrestling, throwing the discus, or boxing with the cestus. Every prize-
fighter knows that he is more fatigued after an hour's
contest with a dummy in the shape of a hollow rubber
ball or a cushion of some kind than he is after a stand-
up fight with the gloves for the same period with an
active antagonist against whom he is obliged to employ
not only his muscles in all their activity and strength,
but his perceptions in their utmost acuteness, his intellectual faculties in some of their most highly developed
forms, his emotions to spur him on in the hope for victory, and his will to set his muscular mechanism in
action and to cause it to functionate with its most intense degree of agility and power.

Exercise, for the mere sake of exercise, is to many
persons the very quintessence of weariness, and it is
impossible to believe that it can in such cases be pro-

ductive of the maximum of benefit which muscular exertion is capable of affording. Fatigue ensues much more quickly and is more pronounced than when the mind is exercised simultaneously with the body. A young woman will go through an amount of muscular exercise in a ballroom that would be impossible for her in the performance of some laborious task in which she took no pleasure. I have no doubt that some of you have experienced like results after rowing in a sham boat in the gymnasium and a spirited contest on the Mohawk with a man rowing against you, and thus calling into exercise all the ambition, the judgment, and firmness, the will power that the gray nerve substance of your cerebral cortex could evolve.

And then on the ball-field, what a splendid arena there is for the exercise, not only of all the physical strength and endurance you possess, but also of those higher mental faculties that such rivalry will always call forth in an American youth, and in the exercise of which he fits himself for the struggle that is before him! That is the kind of exercise that the professional man and the scholar require.

I am quite sure that there is a variety of physical exercise which is not practised as much in this country as it ought to be, and which of all others stands pre-eminent as the kind most efficacious in developing the muscles, and at the same time calling into action those mental faculties, the degree of development of which makes the difference between the man of strong and noble mind and the one of feeble and mean mentality. I refer to fencing. It is pre-eminently an exercise of the mind and body, one that requires in the highest degree not only strength but activity and quickness of movement, while at the same time the mind, in all its faculties, is kept alert, not only so far as attack is concerned, but in studying every muscular movement and every idea of the adversary, so as to anticipate his intended onslaughts before he can make them.

It has been well said by a recent writer on fencing that "the beneficial effects of moderate fencing to persons of weak constitutions, or of studious and sedentary habits, have been attested by medical practitioners of the first eminence. To the public speaker the practice of the fencing-room has been found to impart an ease and freedom of gesture attainable by no other exercise. For, while the use of the foil and the broadsword diffuses ease, elegance, and grace all over the body, and imparts to the look and gesture an appearance of intellectual vigor, it teaches invaluable lessons of patience and self-command, and contributes to. discipline the temper. 'Perhaps there is no exercise whatever,' says Mr. Roland ('Theory and Practice of Fencing'), 'more calculated for these purposes (developing and cultivating bodily strength and activity) than fencing. Riding, walking, sparring, wrestling, running, and pitching the bar are all of them certainly highly beneficial; but-beyond all question, there is no single exercise which combines so many advantages as fencing. By it the muscles of every part of the body are brought into play; it expands the chest and occasions an equal distribution of the blood and other circulating fluids through the whole system. More than one case has fallen under the author's own observation in which affections of the lungs and a tendency to consumption have been entirely removed by occasional practice with the foil.'"

The will travels through a nerve to a muscle at the rate of about seventy feet in a second. A muscle cannot move at a rate of speed the one-tenth part of this. We conceive an idea and exert a volitional impulse upon an arm, for instance, much quicker, therefore, than we can obey the command and move the limb. In fencing, and, indeed, to a less extent in all athletic contests, those who can form a correct idea of the purposes of their adversaries, who can send the will through their nerves with the greatest rapidity, and whose muscles obey their behests with most promptitude and power, will be the winners. Is it not, therefore, apparent that such exercises train both mind and body for the battles of life, and that it is not unreasonable to assert that, other things being equal, the best fencer or ball-player will carry off the most prizes when he contends for scholarly, professional, or business success?

Mere physical exercise cannot of itself prepare a man for any higher position in the social scale that that of "a hewer of wood and a drawer of water" for him who knows how to use his brain. Those who spend their early lives in physical labor, and rise to high estate, do so in spite of their muscles. The brain asserts its superiority, and muscularity is relegated to the background. Lifting heavy weights, following a plough, or breaking stone, do not develop the brain. Such occupations enlarge the muscles and increase their strength, but the professional man or the scholar does not expect to make his mark in the world by his muscular power. It is his brain that is to be strengthened, and his muscles require no more exercise than is sufficient to keep them in a healthy state of repair, to preserve them from rusting as it were; and this they get in the daily routine of normal life without any special means being taken to procure it.

I think that a daily walk of three or four miles in the open air at the rate of about three miles an hour, with such swinging of the arms as nature has provided for in arranging the gait of man, is sufficient. If this is taken on a gymnasium track, or in an enclosed and artificially heated piazza, it will lose some of its good effects, but will still serve the purpose of promoting that metamorphosis of muscular tissue—that removal of old substance and the deposit of new to take its place, which it, in common with all the other structures of the body, requires for its well-being.

But the man who uses up his nerve force in producing muscular contractions runs the risk of not having enough for the other requirements of the system. In such circumstances a condition exists which may be well represented by the simile of the man who has steam power to let. Some of it goes to a silversmith, we will say, some to a printer, some to a miller, some to a man who has an office building with elevators in it. Now, if the silversmith uses up more steam power than his due proportion, all the others suffer. The printer cannot print his books or the miller grind his grist, and the elevators refuse to budge. So it is with man. Excessive use of nerve force in one direction causes imperfect action in other organs; the heart beats feebly and irregularly; the gastric juice, not being secreted in sufficient quantity, leads to dyspepsia; the brain, giving an undue amount of nerve force to the muscles, has not enough for its higher functions, and thus it is that those athletic men who make athletic exercises the main object of their lives are rarely, if ever, noted for great intellectual power. The ancients recognize this fact, and hence Samson, the strong man of the Bible, and Hercules, the athlete of profane history, were poor, simple-minded fellows, easily imposed upon, and, like most other amiable men (men, not women; all women should be amiable), deficient in mental vigor.

It is a matter of daily experience that when the muscles are exercised beyond the point to which they are accustomed, a sensation of fatigue is felt which becomes more intense, and even painful, if the exertion be continued. Make the experiment of trying to hold out your arm at a right angle to the body for five minutes, and if you have not habituated yourself to this effort, you will obtain a very clear idea of muscular fatigue. In such an action the deltoid muscle, which forms the rotundity of the shoulder, is the one mainly brought into use, and it is here that the pain is chiefly felt. What is the cause of this pain? Is it the direct result of the contraction of the muscular fibres? In a word, is muscular fatigue produced solely by muscular contraction, or is there some other factor acting as a causative agent? If solely and immediately due to the action of the muscles, why do we not always feel it when we have exercised them to an extreme degree? Recent investigations go to show that there is another cause, and that is that the muscles, in contracting, suffer, as we have seen, a certain amount of destruction; lower grades of substances result, and some of these are poisonous, and acting upon the muscles before the blood has time to carry them to the excretory organs of the body, exercise a poisonous effect and give rise to that sense of painful fatigue which we all know so well.

Such poisonous substances are produced in the life course of every person through the action of the several organs of the body, and if not promptly removed from the system lead to the development of one or more of those diseases by auto-infection which have just begun to be studied, and which are of such surpassing interest to the physician. Now, it is scarcely a matter for doubt that when muscular exercise is carried on with disgust, or at least without pleasure, these poisonous agents are formed in great abundance and removed with less celerity than when the mind co-operates with the body to give zest and interest to the work. The convict laboring at the crank or on the treadmill readily breaks down, and perhaps dies, poisoned by the excretions from his own muscles. Ought not such facts to have their weight with social economists in their search for the best methods not only of punishing, but of reforming criminals? And when they are sufficiently recognized by the medical profession and the public, we shall have less of so-called neurasthenia and nervous prostration, and very much less of that terrific insomnia with which so many brain-workers are afflicted— for the brain, like the muscles, has its diseases produced by overwork.

And now, my friends, I must bring these imperfect remarks to a close, though there are other important features of the subject that, were there time, might well engage our attention. But I cannot end without requesting you to bear in mind that I am no enemy of proper physical exercise. I am, however, opposed to the apotheosis of muscle at the expense of brain. A man cannot be great in two opposite directions. There is no instance on record of a great athlete being at the same time a great scholar or professional man. We do not go to the Corbetts, the Mitchells, or the Sullivans for the presidents of our colleges, for our eloquent preachers, our learned jurists, our wise physicians, our skilled and gallant generals or admirals. The mental force of man has its limit of quantity, and no one, strive as he may, can exhaust it in physical labor and yet have enough left with which to achieve mental greatness. If I have succeeded in impressing this fact upon your minds, and in pointing out to you what kind of muscular exercise is best, I shall feel that I have been of some service to you, and that my friend did not err when he asked me to participate in the course of lectures he has so worthily established.

A. B. CORNELL

ALONZO B. CORNELL.

ALONZO B. CORNELL, the twenty-fifth Governor of the State of New York, was born at Ithaca, N. Y., January 22, 1832. He was the eldest son of the eminent philanthropist, the Honorable Ezra Cornell, founder of Cornell University, who was intimately associated with Prof. S. F. B. Morse in the original development of the magnetic telegraph in America. Educated at the Ithaca Academy until the age of fourteen, when he became a telegraph operator, young Cornell entered upon the activities and responsibilities of a business career, in which he soon became conspicuous for success and rapid promotion, and early attained an enviable position in the telegraphic profession.

After more than twenty years of active experience in all the various grades of telegraph service, from operator to general superintendent, Governor Cornell was in 1868 elected a director of the Western Union Telegraph Company, and has since been continuously re-elected to that position at each successive annual meeting of the stockholders of that great corporation. For the past twenty-five years he has been a member of its Executive Committee, and since 1883 chairman of the Law Committee. For seven years he was senior vice-president, and in 1875 was designated by the directors acting president, and discharged the onerous duties of that position during the prolonged absence of President Orton in Europe.

Aside from his continuous telegraphic service, Governor Cornell has been extensively interested and occupied in the management of various railway and steamboat enterprises in the United States and also in South America. He has had large experience as a national bank-director and officer, as well as in life insurance corporations. He is the president of the Cornell Public Library at Ithaca, and has been one of the trustees of Cornell University from its foundation in 1865, devoting much valuable service to the safe and judicious development and administration of that great institution of learning, which has in its brief history attained eminent rank among the foremost universities of the entire world.

While pursuing a life of ceaseless activity in business affairs, Mr. Cornell found time to devote much attention to political duties. He became affiliated with the Republican Party at its original formation, and has ever since exerted potent influence in its counsels both local and general. For many years he was chairman of the New York Republican State Committee until elected governor in 1879. He rendered notable service to his party in effecting its reorganization in New York City in 1870–71. His management of the Republican campaign in 1872, resulting in the re-election of President Grant, won him eminent repute as a sagacious and efficient political organizer. The results of that exciting canvass were largely credited to the inspiration of his vigorous leadership. His services were generously acknowledged by many leading Republicans of the United States, who united in tendering him a magnificent souvenir testimonial, which is one of his most valued possessions. He was one of the New York State delegates-at-large to the Republican National Conventions of 1876 and 1880, was a member of the Republican National Executive Committee from 1876 to 1880, and has been a member of the Union League Club of New York since 1867.

As supervisor of Ithaca, New York State Capitol Commissioner, Speaker of the Assembly, Surveyor of Customs for the port of New York, and United States Naval Officer, Mr. Cornell rendered notable service as a public official. In each of these positions he exhibited an independence of character and capacity for executive duties which in many respects rendered his gubernatorial term one of historical importance in the annals of the Empire State. His defiance of President Hayes' celebrated civil-service dictum and its subsequent results will afford future historians a theme for discussion of one of the most romantic episodes in American politics.

At the age of forty-seven, with twenty years' experience in political antagonisms and important official service, Mr. Cornell was in 1879 elected to the chief magistracy of the State of New York by a majority of more than forty thousand over his leading opponent. His extended personal acquaintance and great familiarity with public affairs, combined with his resolute personality, were rare qualifications for the exercise of executive duties, and, consequently, his administration proved more beneficial to the State and the people than to personal or political friends.

Inaugurated governor of New York January 1, 1880, Governor Cornell urged upon the Legislature reformation of the State revenue laws, and under his administration laws were enacted and projected which have added largely to the resources and revenues of the State. Under his recommendation women were rendered eligible to vote and hold official position in the school boards of the State. The admission of women to the direction of school-affairs has already exterminated monstrous abuses of bribery formerly existing relative to the supply and change of school books. He brought the State prisons to a self-supporting basis, and conducted them upon thorough business principles free from all political influence or dictation. He abstained from the use of the pardoning power which had often been a discredit to other administrations. His appointments to office were notable for fitness and qualification for duty required, and it is gratifying to record that no scandal ever resulted from any appointment made by him in the conduct of the gubernatorial office.

The most prominent characteristic of Governor Cornell's administration was the sturdy and independent exercise of the veto power. Friends and foes admitted the resolute and impartial hand with which he protected public interests from spoliation; special legislation sought for selfish private interest was firmly resisted, and improvident appropriations were ruthlessly vetoed. The National Guard was reorganized into a strong, compact, and efficient body by the dismissal of inefficient regiments and companies, thus leaving the military fund available for the support of a smaller but more useful force. A State camp of instruction was established by him, which has become a pattern of militia instruction in many States. His military administration was the beginning of a new era in the militia of the United States.

The New York State Board of Health and the State Railway commission were products of Governor Cornell's urgent recommendation and have proved highly advantageous to the public welfare, He put a stop to the enormous expenditures for newly projected public buildings. During his term the Woman's Reformatory at Hudson was the only new public building undertaken. He enforced an economy in public expenditures below that of any governor's term within the past thirty years. In 1882 he recommended a modification of the usury law, as applied to demand loans, which was enacted by the Legislature and has resulted in equalizing the importance of New York with London, as one of the chief monetary centres of the world, to a greater extent than any other event in our history.

Political events following the presidential election of 1880 resulted in the resignation of the two New York Senators from the United States Senate. This action divided New York Republicans into bitterly hostile factions, and naturally brought the Democratic Party into control of both Senate and Assembly at the election of 1881. Despite the political embarrassments thus forced upon Governor Cornell in the last year of his term, his administration had given the people such satisfaction that there was a general demand for his renomination by the Republican party. He was actively opposed by secret agents of the Federal administration and a coterie of politicians who had failed to secure favors from the Governor.

A decided majority of delegates to the Republican State Convention at Saratoga in 1882 were elected in favor of Governor Cornell's renomination, but the minority faction, by the use of discreditable means, including both bribery and forgery, were enabled to so manipulate the State Committee as to secure control of the temporary organization of the convention adverse to the Governor's friends. Using this advantage, they arbitrarily unseated nearly forty regularly elected delegates and thrust into their places bogus contestants, thus fraudulently reversing the true complexion of the convention as originally elected.

Thus the deliberately expressed choice of a large majority of New York Republicans was ignored, and the renomination of Governor Cornell, which had been so confidently expected, was defeated by a small majority, and the rival candidate was formally nominated. These extraordinary proceedings of the State Convention aroused the deepest indignation among Republicans throughout the State to such an extent that the successful candidate, although of eminent personal respectability, was repudiated at the election by a majority of 192,000, and the Republican Party was plunged into an abyss of degradation from which it required years of patient toil to redeem it.

THE ELECTRO-MAGNETIC TELEGRAPH.

By Alonzo B. Cornell.

Mr. President and Gentlemen of Union College:—
Having enjoyed the honor of three years' service as
an *ex-officio* member of the governing board of this
venerable and useful institution, the earliest of the
long list of colleges chartered by the Regents of the
University of the State of New York, it is very gratifying to be permitted to meet you on this occasion. The
subject assigned me for discussion, the early history of
the electro-magnetic telegraph, the greatest, perhaps,
of all the instrumentalities of modern civilization, is
particularly agreeable, in view of my prolonged iden-
tification with it. Commencing as a telegraph operator at the age of fourteen, while the system was yet
struggling in the weakness of its humble origin, it has
been my privilege to be continuously connected with
its development and management to the present time.

The opportunity of addressing you on this subject
upon the invitation of my lifelong friend, your distinguished alumnus and generous patron, General Butterfield, is all the more gratifying from the fact that his
father and mine were actively associated together forty-
eight years ago in constructing through this beautiful
and romantic valley the first line of telegraph established between the cities of New York and Buffalo.

Before entering upon the definite consideration of
the subject chosen for this occasion, a brief review of
local historical facts and incidents may perhaps pre-

pare our minds for a keener appreciation of the striking contrast between the conditions of life within the Mohawk Valley four generations ago and those of the present day, with which we are all so familiar. When, in 1777, the State of New York assumed a republican form of government and adopted its first constitution, white civilization had been dominant in the Mohawk Valley as far west as Johnstown and St. Johnsville for more than a hundred years, but the rocky gorge through which the Mohawk flows at Little Falls afforded a barrier of defence that enabled the Indians of the Six Nations to hold in check the western migration of the white people for an entire century. It now seems beyond comprehension that the untutored son of the forest could thus, for such a period of time, arrest the onward progress of Christian civilization. It is indeed one of the most remarkable circumstances relating to the wonderful history of American development.

Not until the successful termination of the Revolutionary War did the hardy pioneers gather strength to venture beyond the rugged gateway of the Mohawk Valley for the purpose of residence. The earliest white settlements west of that ancient frontier were established at Herkimer and at Whitesboro, three miles beyond the present city of Utica, in 1784, and within the following ten years permanent communities were located at Auburn, Ithaca, Bath, Canandaigua, Geneseo, and Batavia, which soon became thriving and important towns. The great cities of Buffalo, Rochester, Syracuse, and Utica were the results of the later development of commercial facilities afforded by the improvement of the internal waterways by the State. How difficult it is for us to realize that in the days of good old Governor George Clinton the western frontier was only fifty miles from Schenectady, where now we may any day pass to the great and glorious West, bounded only by the Pacific shore, at the speed of a mile a minute, and may commune with our friends by instantaneous means regardless of distance!

Although electricity has been a positive and important element in and about our terrestrial sphere during all the indefinite ages it has been travelling in space in tireless revolutions around the sun, it is but comparatively few years that mankind have realized any definite knowledge of its real nature. The ancients were filled with amazement and terror at the extraordinary manifestations of ill-omen so frequently observed in the heavens, and all sorts of conjectures were entertained, suited to the fancy or imagination of terrified beholders. Only one hundred and fifty years ago it was a generally accepted theory in England that atmospheric explosions of electricity were caused by the ignition of fine particles or dust of sulphur which had accumulated in the air, and that earthquakes were the results of similar causes within the caverns of the earth. How absurd it now seems that within five generations the most enlightened people of the world, as we have been taught to consider them, should have been the willing victims of such simple delusions.

The earliest systematic and really successful student of electrical phenomena, of whose researches and experiments we have any trustworthy record, was the illustrious American philosopher, Benjamin Franklin, whose experiments commenced at Philadelphia in a very crude and simple way in 1746. His investigations were conducted with such precision and results so carefully noted for future comparison that within two years he discovered and clearly proved the identity of lightning and electricity. He also produced an electric battery composed of series of metallic plates which

19

displayed evidences of decided electric impulse. In 1749 he devised the lightning-rod, by which, as described by him, "ships and houses were to be protected from injury," by arresting the fatal currents discharged by electric explosions of nature and conducting them over a metallic pathway safely to the earth. Franklin's lightning-rod came into almost universal use, and has continued to the present day precisely in the form it was originally designed, according to his own language, "having several bright points to attract the electric current."

Franklin was not only a marvel of industry, but was also an observing investigator and prolific writer. Instead of preserving in secret his discoveries, he promptly published to the world all the knowledge gained, and by this practice soon attracted the attention and induced the co-operative investigation of scientific men throughout America and Europe. Thus mankind gradually became familiar with the mysterious attributes of that vital provision of nature which has so recently become one of the most useful, powerful, and intimate agencies of the human race. On one occasion, when criticised for wasting time in trifling experiments with his kite, endeavoring to draw the electric fluid from the clouds, Franklin made the remarkable prophetic declaration that "Electricity will yet become the quick-winged messenger of both the thoughts and feelings of man." This terse and vivid prediction of both the telegraph and telephone was made a century prior to the development and realization of those wonderful instrumentalities of the present age; and it is difficult for us to realize the extremely slow advance of human knowledge which thereafter ensued in reference to electric science. It was more than fifty years after Franklin's invention of the lightning-rod before man had made, and brought into general use, any practical discovery or invention in electricity.

During the early years of the present century but slight advance was made in the development of electrical science, although there were many persons, both here and abroad, engaged in experimental work, and there was considerable increase of literature bearing upon the subject. It was reserved for another illustrious American to accomplish the next important and decisive step in the pathway of progress. In the year 1828, Joseph Henry, then Professor of Physics at the Albany Academy, afterward a professor at Princeton, and subsequently for many years Secretary of the Smithsonian Institution at Washington, made the highly important discovery that by winding a plain iron core with many layers of insulated wire, through which the electric current was passed, he could at pleasure charge and discharge the iron core with magnetic power. Thus Henry produced the electro-magnet, which was the beginning of the mastery by man of the subtle fluid. He also discovered that the intensity and power of the electric current were materially augmented by increasing the number of the series of battery plates without increasing the quantity of metal used in their construction.

These discoveries of Henry were, beyond all question, the most important in real and intrinsic value ever made in the progress of electric science, as they form the solid basis upon which all subsequent inventors have been enabled to accomplish successful results in their various fields of endeavor. It is conceded by all familiar with the history of electrical progress that the name of Professor Joseph Henry is to be honored and cherished as one of the very foremost of scientific discoverers of any age or country, and it must remain

a cause of sincere and permanent regret that of all the
fabulous wealth that has resulted from the advancement of electrical science, this modest and unselfish
inventor should have passed hence without ever having
realized any substantial reward for his great work.
Not only so, but he was never awarded the appropriate
acknowledgment to which he was so eminently entitled
for the inestimable benefits his discoveries conferred
upon his countrymen and upon the world at large.

The possibility of utilizing Professor Henry's electro-magnet for the purpose of transmitting intelligence
to a distant point was conceived by still another American, Prof. Samuel F. B. Morse, of New York, during his passage on board the packet ship *Sully*, from
Havre to New York, in the winter of 1832. Incidental
discussions between himself and Dr. Jackson, a fel-
low-passenger, in reference to recent electrical improvements on both sides of the Atlantic, led Morse to
the conclusion that intelligence might be instanta-
neously transmitted over a metallic circuit to a distant
point, and he thereupon determined to devote himself
to the solution of the problem involved. The following day he exhibited a rough sketch of a plan for recording electric impulses necessary to convey and express intelligence. He pursued the subject with great
devotion during the remainder of the voyage, and after
arrival in New York began the construction of the necessary apparatus to accomplish his purpose. Morse was
by profession a portrait painter of more than ordinary
merit, and was obliged to continue his artistic labors
for a livelihood. He was a graduate of Yale College,
where his attention had first been attracted to electrical
experiments. He was thus, in a measure, prepared for
carrying forward the important work he had undertaken, and pursued his labors with great assiduity.

Devoting every spare moment to the pursuit of his object, which was slowly attained by reason of his lack of mechanical skill and ingenuity, it was not until 1837 that he had so far succeeded in his efforts as to be prepared to make application for letters patent to enable him to secure and protect his rights of invention in the electro-magnetic telegraph.

In explanation of the slow progress of his experimental work, Professor Morse, in writing to a friend, said: "Up to the autumn of 1837 my telegraphic apparatus existed in so rude a form that I felt reluctance to have it seen. My means were very limited, so limited as to preclude the possibility of constructing an apparatus of such mechanical finish as to warrant my success in venturing upon its public exhibition. I had no wish to expose to ridicule the representative of so many hours of laborious thought. Prior to the summer of 1837 I depended upon my pencil for subsistence. Indeed, so straitened were my circumstances, that in order to save time to carry out my invention and to economize my scanty means, I had for months lodged and eaten in my studio, procuring food in small quantities from some grocery, and preparing it myself. To conceal from my friends the stinted manner in which I lived, I was in the habit of bringing food to my room in the evenings, and this was my mode of life for many years." After the continuance of this heroic struggle for more than five years, Morse found himself compelled to seek the aid of more accomplished mechanical skill than he possessed to perfect his apparatus, and was obliged to surrender a quarter interest in his invention in order to obtain sufficient pecuniary aid for this purpose.

Having thus succeeded in obtaining, at such serious sacrifice, the requisite financial assistance to enable him to perfect the mechanism necessary to demonstrate his invention, Professor Morse lost no time in completing his apparatus and presenting it for public inspection. On the 6th of January, 1838, he first operated his system successfully, over a wire three miles long, in the presence of a number of personal friends, at Morristown, New Jersey. During the following month he made an exhibition before the faculty of the New York University, which was an occasion of much interest among the leading scientists of the metropolis. Shortly thereafter the apparatus was taken to Philadelphia and exhibited at the Franklin Institute, where he received the highest commendation from the Committee of Science and Arts, with a strong expression in favor of Government aid for the purpose of demonstrating the practical usefulness of the system.

From Philadelphia, Morse removed his apparatus to Washington, where he was permitted to demonstrate its operation before President Van Buren and his Cabinet. Foreign ministers and members of both houses of Congress, as well, also, as prominent citizens, were invited to attend the exhibition and manifested much interest in the novelty of the invention. A bill was introduced in Congress making an appropriation of $30,000 for the purpose of providing for the erection of an experimental line of telegraph between Washington and Baltimore, to illustrate, by practical use, its general utility. The bill was in good time favorably reported from the Committee on Commerce, but made no further progress in that Congress. Similar bills were subsequently introduced and diligently supported in each succeeding Congress, but it was not until the very closing hour of the expiring session of 1843 that the necessary enactment was effected and the appropriation secured.

The plan of construction devised by Professor Morse

for the experimental line of telegraph to be erected between Washington and Baltimore, under the Congressional appropriation, provided for placing insulated wires in a lead pipe underground. This was to be accomplished by the use of a specially devised plough of peculiar construction, to be drawn by a powerful team, by which means the pipe containing the electric conductors was to be automatically deposited in the earth. This apparatus was entirely successful in operation, and the pipe was thus buried to the complete satisfaction of all concerned, at a cost very much lower than the work could have been accomplished in any other manner. Two wires were to be used to form a complete metallic circuit, for at that time it was not known, as was shortly afterward discovered, that the earth could be used to form one-half of the circuit. For purposes of insulation the wires were neatly covered with cotton yarn and then saturated in a bath of hot gum shellac, but this treatment proved defective in insulating properties, for when ten miles of line had been completed the wires were found to be wholly useless for electric conductors.

No mode had then been devised for the treatment of india-rubber to make it available for purposes of insulation, and gutta-percha was wholly unknown as an article of use or commerce in this country. Twenty-three thousand dollars of the Government apropriation had been expended, and the work thus far accomplished was an acknowledged failure. Only seven thousand dollars of the available fund remained unexpended, and this was regarded as wholly inadequate to complete the undertaking under any other plan. The friends of the enterprise were quite in despair, and for some time saw no other alternative than to apply to Congress for an additional appropriation. This, however, was regarded as almost hopeless, and the difficulty of the situation was extremely embarrassing. An amusing incident was related of the means used to keep from public knowledge the desperate situation. Professor Morse finally visited the scene of activity where the pipe laying was proceeding, and, calling the superintendent aside, confided to him the fact that the work must be stopped without the newspapers finding out the true reason of its suspension. The quick-witted superintendent was equal to the occasion, and, starting the ponderous machine, soon managed to run foul of a protruding rock, and break the plough. The newspapers published sensational accounts of the accident and announced that it would require several weeks to repair damages. Thus the real trouble was kept from the public until new plans could be determined upon.

After long and careful consideration, Professor Morse very reluctantly decided to erect the wires on poles. This plan was, at first, considered wholly objectionable, under the apprehension that the structure would be disturbed by evil-minded persons. It had, however, become manifest that this was the only mode of construction that could be accomplished within the remaining balance of the appropriation, and, finally, upon ascertaining that pole lines had already been adopted in England it was determined to proceed in this manner. The line was thus completed between Washington and Baltimore, about the 1st of May, 1844, and proved to be successful and every way satisfactory in its operation.

Shortly after the completion of the line the National Democratic Convention, which nominated Polk and Dallas for President and Vice-President, assembled in Baltimore. Reports of the convention proceedings were promptly telegraphed to the capital city, where the telegraph office was thronged with members of Congress, interested in the news. These reports created an immense sensation in Washington and speedily removed all doubts as to the practical success of the new system of communication. A dispatch from the Honorable Silas Wright, then United States Senator from New York, refusing to accept the nomination for Vice-President, was read in the national convention and produced an extraordinary interest from the fact that very few of the delegates had ever heard of the telegraph, and it required much explanation to satisfy them of the genuineness of the alleged communication.

Having thus established beyond all reasonable question the practical utility of the telegraph as a superior means of public and private communication, Professor Morse and his associates offered their patents to the United States Government for the very moderate price of $100,000, with a view of having the system adopted for general use in connection with the postal establishment. This proposition was referred to the Postmaster-General for consideration and report. After due deliberation that officer reported that "although the invention is an agent vastly superior to any other ever devised by the genius of man . . . yet the operation between Washington and Baltimore has not satisfied me that, under any rate of postage that can be adopted, its revenues can be made to cover its expenditures." Under the influence of this report Congress very naturally declined the offer of the patentees, and the telegraph was thereupon relegated to the domain of private enterprise. The result was that the patentees finally realized for their interests many times the amount of their offer to the Government.

During the autumn of 1844 short exhibition lines were erected in Boston and New York, for the purpose of familiarizing business men of those cities with the characteristics of the new invention, but they attracted little attention, and the promoters had much cause of discouragement on account of public indifference. For the purpose of arousing more attention to the system, appeals were made to the public press for favorable notice, which were also generally declined. The proprietor of one of the most prominent and enterprising of the New York daily papers distinctly refused to encourage the establishment of telegraph lines for the reason, as he freely acknowledged, that if the new method of transmitting intelligence were to come into general use his competitors could use it as well as himself, and he would therefore be deprived of his present advantage over them for procuring early news by the use of an expensive system of special dispatch then maintained by his paper. Two years later he refused to join other papers in receiving the Governor's message by telegraph from Albany, and was so badly beaten by his rivals in this instance that his paper has ever since been one of the most generous patrons of the telegraph.

Early in the year 1845 a corporate organization was effected for the extension of the telegraph from Baltimore to Philadelphia and New York, under the name of the Magnetic Telegraph Company, for which a special act of incorporation was obtained from the Legislature of the State of Maryland. Nearly all of the capital of this company was subscribed by Washington people. Baltimore and Philadelphia furnished only a few hundred dollars, while New York contributed nothing. Slow progress was made toward the construction of the line on account of the difficulty of obtaining the right of way either upon railways or highways, and it was not until January, 1846, that the line was completed to the west side of the Hudson River, which formed an impassable barrier to further progress for a considerable period. No method of insulation had yet been devised that would permit the operation of an electric conductor under water, and it was doubted whether a wire could be maintained for a span sufficient to cross the river overhead. Finally, however, high masts were erected on the Palisades near Fort Lee, and on the heights at Fort Washington on the New York side, and a steel wire was suspended upon them. This plan was successful, except that occasionally the wire was broken by an extraordinary burden of sleet in the winter season. This method of crossing the lower Hudson was continued for more than ten years, when it was superseded by submarine cables.

It will be of interest incidentally to Union College to-day to know that when the project for the telegraph line from New York to Buffalo was broached General Butterfield was a student here. While home at vacation, his father questioned him about his studies and whether he had learned anything about the electric telegraph. In response the General gave a full description of the experiments and apparatus used here by Professor Pearson, in illustrating the inventions of Henry and Morse, in such an effective way as to convince his father of the practicability of the telegraph, the commercial value of which he already appreciated. John Butterfield thereupon enlisted heartily in the telegraph enterprise, in which he soon became a master spirit. The lessons taught here to-day in the advanced work of electricity and the practical application of scientific knowledge can have no clearer illustration of the great value attached to a thorough understanding of them by students.

During the year 1846 incorporated companies were

formed under which telegraph lines were extended from New York to Boston, Buffalo, and Pittsburgh, and within the next three years nearly every important town in the United States and Canada, from St. Louis and New Orleans to Montreal and Halifax, was brought into telegraphic communication. Thus, after fifteen years of struggle with all the pains of poverty, often lacking even the common necessaries of life, Professor Morse and his faithful co-laborers had the supreme satisfaction, in 1847, of knowing and realizing that the telegraph system had finally achieved not only scientific success, for this had been proven years before, but that financial success, ample and complete, had come to pay them richly for all the dark days and wearisome years through which they had passed.

Once generally established, the telegraph won its way to popular appreciation very rapidly. It was in harmony with the spirit of the age, and it was not long before every town of any considerable importance regarded telegraphic facilities as an indispensable necessity. The small cost soon induced the construction of rival lines, regardless of the rights of the patentees, and within a very few years unwise competition began to bring many lines to a condition of bankruptcy. The weaker concerns soon passed through the sheriff's hands and found purchasers only at an extreme sacrifice, at the bidding of the more provident and conservative proprietors of competing lines. . Instead of inducing a more prudent course, these disastrous results only served to feed the spirit of rivalry, and general insolvency seemed to threaten the permanent prosperity of the telegraph business, in consequence of the wild and reckless competition which appeared to be inherent in the nature of the business.

This extremely unsatisfactory condition of telegraph

rivalry drifted on from bad to worse until 1854, when, from dire necessity of self-preservation, a few of the more prudent and far-sighted proprietors of telegraph property were induced to combine their interests with some of their competitors and thus avoid the ruinous policy which had been so rapidly exhausting their vitality. Accordingly the principal telegraph lines in Ohio, Indiana, Michigan, and some of the neighboring States were brought into fraternal relations and formed the nucleus of the Western Union Telegraph Company.

The new policy soon brought prosperity in place of waste and improvidence. Profits were devoted to the purchase of additional lines, thus enlarging their domain and strengthening their position. Prosperity increased with rapid strides, and the beneficial effects of extirpating wasteful rivalry and building up a substantial system with superior facilities and provident management gave the new organization a dominating influence among the telegraph companies of America. The same general policy has been pursued to the present time, and has resulted in the establishment of a prosperous corporation of magnificent proportions, carrying on a useful and beneficent business under a greater number of governmental jurisdictions, great and small, than any other corporate organization in existence. The Western Union Telegraph Company now has 190,000 miles of pole lines and cables, with 770,000 miles of wire in use. It has 21,000 telegraph offices, and transmitted last year nearly 70,000,000 messages. Its employees number about 40,000 persons, and its gross earnings last year were $25,000,000.

The project of connecting the American continent with Europe by telegraphic communication, which had for some years been freely discussed, finally took practical shape by the organization of a company for the purpose of laying a transatlantic submarine cable in 1856. The necessary capital was provided without difficulty during the following year, and preparations for placing the cable were finally completed and undertaken during the summer of 1857, but after 300 miles of cable had been submerged, an accident prevented further operations and work was suspended for that season. The following year the enterprise was resumed and the cable successfully laid, but before it had been put into practical operation the electric impulses were lost, and public faith in the possibility of establishing transatlantic communication was very generally abandoned. After a lapse of seven years the project was again renewed, and preparations were made for laying a new cable of greater strength and security, which was satisfactorily accomplished in 1866, and brought into complete and successful operation. Subsequently, numerous other cables were added, until at the present time nearly or quite a dozen submarine cables are in constant operation between Europe and America.

During the long interval of suspension of efforts to provide cable service across the Atlantic following the failure of 1858, the desire for communication with the Old World rapidly increased and finally found expression in practical form for overland lines across the continents of America and Asia, to be connected by submarine cable through Bering Strait. This project was finally adopted by the Western Union Telegraph Company, and in March, 1864, it issued a call for the necessary capital for the undertaking. The entire capital required was promptly subscribed, and the enterprise was pressed forward with much enthusiasm. Elaborate expeditions were speedily organized for operations by land and sea. Hundreds of miles of trackless forests were opened for the construction of lines, and the great undertaking was well on toward completion when, in the autumn of 1866, the unexpected success of the Atlantic cable brought the overland enterprise to a sudden and ignoble end. It was universally recognized that many thousand miles of continental lines could not be maintained in competition with ocean cables, and though several millions of dollars had already been expended, the project was promptly abandoned.

For the development of the telegraph enterprise in America no thanks are due to the wealthy capitalists. As a rule they would not listen to suggestions of investing their money in what was contemptuously termed rotten poles and rusty wires. They wanted something more substantial and conservative as the basis of their investments. An early pioneer and builder of telegraph lines, whose name is now held in grateful memory for deeds of philanthropic beneficence, visited the city of Chicago in 1847 to solicit subscriptions to the capital stock of a company then engaged in construction of the first line of telegraph between that place and the city of Buffalo. He presented a carefully prepared prospectus showing an estimated earning capacity of the projected line of $100 per day. The merits of the contemplated enterprise were freely canvassed at a meeting of bankers, at which one of the most prominent declared that any man who ever expected to see $100 per day paid for telegraphing west of Buffalo must be crazy and unworthy of belief. This oracular declaration prevailed, and the project was ignominiously rejected by the wise men of Chicago. Fortunately, citizens of smaller towns, like Ypsilanti, Kalamazoo, South Bend, Kenosha, and Racine, took a more sensible view of the proposed enterprise and the line was built despite the contempt of Chicago capitalists. Now, however, the men of Chicago pay more than five thousand dollars per day for their telegraphing at rates far lower than would have been thought possible in that early day.

The true spirit of enterprise, which has so grandly developed the resources of our imperial domain, has generally been found to prevail among people of modest means. Thus, nearly every dollar of capital contributed toward the establishment of telegraph lines in this country came from the offerings of people in very moderate circumstances. In this connection, therefore, it is extremely gratifying to state that very few enterprises of any kind returned such generous recompense for the amount of capital invested as the telegraph and telephone lines in America. Considering the apparently temporary and short-lived character of the structures erected for these purposes it seems difficult to comprehend the truth of this statement. An experience, however, of more than forty years in the history of telegraph development on this continent affords abundant assurance of this declaration.

The method of telegraphic communication devised by Professor Morse has been continued in general use in this country with such improvements as have meantime been developed as the results of experience. Instead of requiring a separate wire for each circuit as formerly, four independent circuits are now operated over a single wire by the use of the quadruplex apparatus. This plan effected an important advance, inasmuch as it increased the transmitting capacity of a wire from thirty words to about one hundred words per minute.

Two other methods of telegraphy were introduced into public use about forty years ago as competitors of the Morse. One was the House printing telegraph, by which the message was delivered on a long strip of paper, plainly printed in Roman characters. The other was a system devised by Prof. Alexander Bain, which recorded dots and lines, similar to the Morse telegraph alphabet, by the chemical discoloration of the recording paper. While both were operated with reasonable success, neither of them was able to continue in competition with the simplicity and efficiency of the Morse sounder, and both were long ago abandoned for general use. The Wheatstone system of automatic transmission was imported from England several years ago and is used to a moderate extent for long circuits in this country, but it is too complicated to anticipate that it will ever become adopted for general purposes.

Efforts have been many years in progress to develop a successful system of automatic telegraphy by which much faster transmission of messages could be attained. Several different kinds of apparatus have been produced by which one or two thousand words per minute have been sent over a single wire several hundred miles in distance. The difficulties of adjusting and operating the delicate mechanism requisite for this purpose prevented the final success of those heretofore introduced to public use. Many telegraphers of great experience believe that these difficulties are really insurmountable. On the contrary, others who have devoted much attention to the subject claim that important advances have recently been made in this direction and indulge confident expectations of the early and complete success of automatic telegraphy. Should these anticipated results be accomplished, great changes must follow in the future development of the telegraph business. Enlarged capacity of transmission thus achieved would materially economize the relative expense of line maintenance and consequently cheapen the present necessary cost of service.

Extensive use is made of the telegraph by the United States Government for weather reports. Advices are received at Washington three times a day from a hundred or more points of observation scattered over our entire domain. These reports are digested at the central office by experienced agents and then transmitted for general distribution. Besides the regular telegraph service for which the Morse apparatus has withstood all serious competition for half a century, several other systems have been introduced, designed for various kinds of special service. A printing instrument specially adapted for reporting stock quotations and miscellaneous news has come into very general use in all the principal cities. No broker's office or banking house is considered to be fully equipped for business without such an instrument continually ticking off the various stock-exchange transactions or current news of the day, ranging from the latest railway accident to the details of a popular horse-race or college ball game. Another extensive use of telegraphic facilities of the present day is the employment of special private lines rented by bankers, merchants, and manufacturers, giving direct and exclusive communication with branch houses and correspondents in distant cities. Between New York and Chicago alone more than thirty different special wires are leased to private parties at a rental of $16,000 per annum each. Telegraph signals are also employed in large cities to call messengers for special use, as well as for sending fire alarms, calling policemen, ambulances, and for many other objects.

Probably the greatest special field of telegraph utility in this country is in the operation of railways. No line of railroad is now considered to be adequately equipped for business unless provided with telegraph facilities with which to direct the details of the movement of trains. On the great trunk lines of railway in the vicinity of busy terminals, where service is very frequent, all trains are kept constantly under the control of a telegraph dispatcher, always at the instrument ready for instantaneous communication with every train on the road. By such means trains can be moved with entire safety at very frequent intervals. Thus the capacity of roads for the dispatch of business is vastly enlarged, and accordingly their earning power is greatly augmented. In view of the present universal use of the telegraph in railway operations, it is interesting to recall the extreme reluctance and prolonged delay with which railway managers were at first induced to adopt the telegraph service in their operating departments.

The first railway train run under telegraph orders was on the Erie Railway in 1849, from Middletown to Port Jervis, and the incidental circumstances are quite interesting. The west-bound express arrived at Middletown on time, where it should have met the east-bound express, which did not appear. After an hour's delay, Charles Minot, superintendent of the road, who was a passenger on the waiting train, went over to the village telegraph office and wired the railway agent at Port Jervis to inquire when the east-bound train had passed. Receiving a reply that the train had not yet reached Port Jervis, Minot directed the agent at that place to hold the belated train at his station until the train should arrive from the east. Returning to the depot Minot ordered the conductor to proceed accordingly. The conductor refused to move forward, and the superintendent suspended him from duty and assumed charge of the train himself. He then ordered the engineer to go ahead, which he refused to do. Minot thereupon suspended the engineer from duty, mounted the engine himself and proceeded in safety to Port Jervis, where the missing train was found awaiting the arrival.

With this experience Superintendent Minot devised and promptly put in operation a plan for the movement of trains by telegraph orders, which has ever since been in use on the Erie road. The extreme conservatism of railway management of that period can be readily appreciated from the fact that it was nearly ten years after the Erie road adopted its railway telegraph system before similar facilities were provided on the New York Central Railway. It is only fair to say, however, that the example of the Erie road was followed very promptly by many other roads, and that the Central was one of the latest to adopt the new mode of operation.

Within the last thirty years the telegraph has become one of the most potent and important instrumentalities of active warfare. Since 1860 no great army has been put into actual service of hostility or defense in any country without the co-operation of the telegraph, with a single notable exception. When General Sherman entered upon his phenomenal campaign of marching through the Confederate States, from Atlanta to Savannah, he severed all connections of both railway and telegraph with his base of supplies, and entrusted the successful maintenance of his expedition to the material of his commissary train and the chances of reprisal and supply in the country through which he was to march. The boldness of the movement and its complete success render his expedition one of the marvellous achievements of all history. Every well-equipped army of the present day includes a telegraph contingent supplied with all material necessary to build a telegraph line, where none exists, as rapidly as the army moves. Small poles easily driven in the earth, upon which wires may be readily stretched, enable an army commander to keep constant communication with his base of supplies, as well as with the seat of government and other necessary points of communication. With such facilities, military operations are vastly energized and economized, and rendered in every way more effective and commanding.

Enlarging our view to the domain of national and international affairs, it is difficult to place a limitation upon the possible importance of instantaneous communication between great governmental authorities in solving and composing difficulties arising suddenly under unexpected emergencies in distant parts of the world. Prompt correspondence and timely explanations may easily correct misapprehensions and embarrassment, which, under the mischievous influence of wasted time, might easily drift into irritating and possibly serious complications that would endanger the peace of nations. The modern development of naval armament, now so prevalent with all powerful nations, and the consequent readiness with which naval commanders may complicate their governments by hasty or injudicious action, render vitally important the possibility of quick communication with every quarter of the globe. Never was the need of preventive measures more imperative than now, when in these days of profound peace ironclad representatives of all nations are traversing every sea with the means of first-class warfare constantly and instantly available.

One of the most remarkable features of telegraph experience is the fidelity of the service in preserving the almost absolute inviolability of telegraphic messages. The Western Union Telegraph Company transmits about 70,000,000 messages per annum, or about 200,-000 daily. Complaints of the exposure of the contents of messages are very rare indeed. Of all the vast number of dispatches thus confided to the telegraph fraternity, it is my belief that not twenty-five complaints of the disclosure of their contents come under the observation of the officers of the company within a year's time.

Another extraordinary feature is the small number of complaints of erroneous transmission or failure to deliver dispatches where adequate addresses are furnished. Probably less than one thousand faults of this character are made known per annum, which is at the rate of not more than one for each seventy thousand messages. This record seems almost incredible, but it is based upon the actual experience of the company's administration and affords a memorable tribute to the fidelity and correctness of the service, for which the company is indebted to an army of more than thirty thousand employees.

As an educating medium the telegraph service has been of inestimable value to thousands of young persons employed in its operation. As a general rule, the most expert and accomplished telegraph operators are those who have commenced their professional work between the ages of twelve and sixteen, equipped with the simple rudiments of common-school education. The quickening and expanding influence upon the minds of such youth gained by the painstaking transmission of telegraph messages is really marvellous. They thus become familiar with endless forms and details of business and unconsciously acquire a breadth of knowledge otherwise unattainable. Those who pa-

tiently and cheerfully devote themselves to useful purposes rapidly become qualified for promotion into many
other kinds of business. It is estimated, by those competent to form an opinion on the subject, that a large
majority of all the railway superintendents in the
United States were formerly telegraph operators, and
indeed, it is a well-known fact that the railway administration service has been very largely recruited from
the same source. This is also true in great measure in
the express business, while many former telegraphers
have become bank officers and managers of various
kinds of important business.

These results are obviously due to the fact that the
telegraph service is an exact science, requiring the utmost care and precision in its operation. Thus habits
of accuracy and reliability are acquired and become
such marked characteristics as to render telegraph operators of good habits in especial demand for the performance of important and responsible duties. In
this view it becomes interesting to contemplate the
advantages derived from telegraphic experience for
the large numbers of youth who are entering upon
the activities of life through the medium of such employment.

Not alone in the elevation and advancement of members of its own profession has the telegraph exerted an
important educational influence, but also in its effects
direct and remote upon mankind in general. The collection and publication by the daily press of the current news of the world have produced important results
in the diffusion of general information and in the unlimited promotion of intelligence among all classes of
people. It has stimulated the popular desire for knowledge and consequently induced more prevalent habits
of reading and study, thus exerting a powerful and

increasing influence upon the practical education of mankind.

This theory is forcibly illustrated by the notable increase of newspaper circulation, as well as by the great advance in periodical and book publication within recent years. The rapid growth of public libraries throughout the country, commanding the eager attention of earnest readers, affords also visible evidence of the beneficial effects thus happily promoted. Further and still more convincing testimony is afforded by the ever-increasing patronage of educational institutions, and especially in the gratifying fact that higher institutions of learning are gaining in the attendance of students even more rapidly than common schools, and far in advance of the relative increase of population.

No definite calculation can possibly be made as to the comparative degree of influence the use of the telegraph has exerted in the development of business affairs, but it is universally recognized that there has been an enormous change caused by the extended intercourse of mankind. It is manifestly evident that the opportunity of instantaneous communication throughout all Christendom has increased man's capacity for the transaction of business manyfold. The mind wanders in hopeless speculation when we undertake to estimate the different conditions now existing, compared with what would have been our situation without the telegraph.

In this country, spread over a continental domain of enormous distances, the advantages of electric communication are indeed beyond calculation. Business transactions of the gravest importance are carried on between commercial centres, however distant, with all the advantage of neighborly proximity, and the facilities of distant markets are rendered available beyond the conception of those not familiar by actual experience with the extraordinary opportunities thus offered. Social and domestic relations are more closely united, and in endless ways public interests are favorably affected by the constant availability of ample means for rapid and frequent communication with friends and neighbors, near and remote.

My purpose has been to deal with the history and traditions of the telegraph solely as a business enterprise, and hence no attempt has been made to enter upon a scientific or technical treatment of the subject. For the same reason no reference is made to the manifold uses of electricity in other departments of its application. Whoever desires information in these particulars will more readily find satisfaction by conference with the professor in charge of your department of physics, who, in his laboratory, can afford every facility of illustration without difficulty or delay. The phenomenal development of study in electricity in colleges and universities within recent years is one of the most remarkable phases in modern education. Hosts of bright young men and women are devoting themselves to investigation in this extremely interesting science, and there can be no reasonable doubt that the early future has in store for us wonderful results. We are only yet in the infancy of electrical inquiry, and the rapid acquisition and dissemination of intelligence now prevailing in this domain must surely and speedily raise us to higher levels of knowledge than have so far been attained.

Americans may well have pardonable pride that their country produced three men who, by common consent, have led all the world in the pathway of electrical science, which has worked such marvellous changes in the affairs of mankind. Nothing within the realm of hu-

man endeavor has conferred as much of elevating influence upon our race as the advance in this occult science, for which this trinity of men are justly entitled
to the highest honor. FRANKLIN, the profound philosopher, whose penetrating mind and keen observation
made him the pioneer of electrical development; HENRY,
the accomplished and painstaking investigator, by patient and exact experiment was led to the most important of all electrical discoveries, the production of the
electro-magnet; while MORSE, by the practical application of the electro-magnet for conveying intelligence
over great intervals of space, conquered time and distance.   The names of these three illustrious American
inventors will continue familiar to all future generations as of those who have incomparably honored their
country and all mankind.

Truly Yours
Andrew Carnegie

ANDREW CARNEGIE.

THE story of Mr. Carnegie's career illustrates the value of the principles he inculcates. Born in Scotland in 1837, when only ten years of age his family moved to the United States, locating at Pittsburgh. There the boy found employment firing a stationary engine. Not at this occupation long, he became a messenger in the telegraph service, then in its infancy; learned to telegraph, and soon became an expert operator. Illustrating his position at this time (thirteen years old), let us quote his own words given in an address at a dinner to our late American Consul at Dunfermline, Scotland:

"I awake from a dream that has carried me away back to the days of early boyhood, the day when the little white-haired Scotch laddie, dressed in a blue jacket, walked with his father into the telegraph office at Pittsburgh to undergo examination as applicant for position of messenger boy. . . . Well I remember when my uncle spoke to my parents about it, my father objected, because I was then getting one dollar and twenty cents per week for running a small engine in a cellar in Allegheny City, but uncle said the messengers' wages were two dollars and fifty cents. . . . If you want an idea as to heaven upon earth, imagine what it was to be taken from a dark cellar, where I fired the boiler from morning till night, and dropped into the office, where light shone from all sides, and around me books, papers, and pencils in profusion, and oh! the tick of those mysterious brass instruments on the desk annihilating space and standing with throbbing spirits ready to convey the intelligence to the world. This was my first glimpse of Paradise."

The aptitude, industry, and readiness to serve his employers were recognized. The Pennsylvania Railroad needed a good operator, and he was selected.

But fourteen when his father died, he now was sole support of his mother and brother. While hardly more than a boy he was made Superintendent of a division of the road. Brought into intimate relations with Col. Thomas A. Scott, the famous president of the Pennsylvania Company, they were associated in various enterprises, including the development of oil lands, from which the yield was enormous. At that time the present sleeping-cars were unknown. Woodruff had invented a design, and Carnegie, recognizing its merit, joined the effort to have it adopted by railroads, forming a very successful company for that purpose.

When the rebellion broke out, Mr. Carnegie, then a superintendent of the Pennsylvania road, was called to Washington by the War Department and placed in charge of the military railways of the Government under Assistant Secretary of War Thomas A. Scott, and entered Washington upon his locomotive. Transferred to Alexandria, Va., he operated the lines during the battle of Bull Run, and was on the last train from Burke Station after the defeat. Serving the Government until his health broke down, he resigned and returned to Pittsburgh, travelling in Europe for a year, which entirely restored his health. Returning, he devoted himself to his iron and steel business.

With money already made, and twelve hundred and fifty dollars borrowed from bank, he organized the Keystone Bridge Works at Pittsburgh. In a short time he became chief owner of the Edgar Thomson Steel Works, and the Homestead and the Union Iron Works.

Public interest exists as to the relations between Mr. Carnegie and his workmen. The men are paid on a sliding scale based on the price of products; the rates paid are determined by committees, in which the workmen have due representation. The men are encouraged to take a financial interest in the business, and are paid six per cent. on their investments with the company.

Mr. Carnegie has been a student as well as a worker and accumulator of riches. With but rudimentary education, he has become a facile writer, a ready, forcible speaker, well informed on social, political, and philosophical questions, the practical matters so closely related to human progress and happiness. As an author he has achieved marked success. His "American Four-in-Hand in Britain," intended originally for personal friends alone, has had large public circulation; and the sale of his "Triumphant Democracy" has already exceeded forty thousand copies. Other pamphlets from his pen include:

"Home Rule in America," political address to the Glasgow Junior Liberal Association (pamphlet).

Three articles upon "The Gospel of Wealth," "American Hatred of England," and "The A B C of Money," *North American Review*.

"The Advantages of Poverty," and "The Gospel of Wealth," *Nineteenth Century*.

"Impending Elections in England and America," and "Some Facts about the American Republic."

These publications have commanded wide attention.

Great as have been Mr. Carnegie's achievements in many directions, the crowning glory of his life is the philanthropic spirit which dominates it.

There is no complete list of his gifts, but the following is a partial exhibit of his generous deeds:

Dunfermline, $200,000; Edinburgh Free Library, $250,000; Pittsburgh Free Library and Art Gallery, $2,000,000; Allegheny Free Library, $375,000; Braddock Free Library, $200,000; Johnstown Free Library, $40,000.

The aggregate amount of his gifts is estimated by General Butterfield at over three million five hundred thousand ($3,500,000) dollars. To Carnegie Music Hall, New York City, one of the best of its kind, named after him, he donated a large share of the fund for building.

This sketch gives partially the salient points of Mr. Carnegie's remarkable career.

He is a most domestic man, and finds at his own fireside his happiness in the companionship, affection, and congeniality which bless his union.

He has a host of earnest, warm friends who are attached to him by his genial, sterling, lovable nature. He is unassuming and modest in demeanor.

He devotes himself to literary work, enjoying well-earned leisure in the possession of the fortune created wholly by his own brains, and is respected and admired by the world at large for his pre-eminent capacity and conspicuous worth.

WEALTH AND ITS USES.

By Andrew Carnegie.

Gentlemen:—It is always interesting to address young men, and when these are students of old Union College, with its great traditions, it is a privilege indeed. I am to speak to you upon that all-engrossing theme, "Wealth," which, as Mr. Gladstone has recently said, is the business of the world. That the acquisition of money is the business of the world arises from the fact that, with few unfortunate exceptions, young men are born to poverty, and therefore under the salutary operation of that remarkably wise law which enacts for their good: "Thou shalt earn thy bread by the sweat of thy brow."

It is the fashion nowadays to bewail poverty as an evil, to pity the young man who is not born with a silver spoon in his mouth; but I heartily subscribe to President Garfield's doctrine, that "The richest heritage a young man can be born to is poverty." I make no idle prediction when I say that it is from that class among you from whom the good and the great will spring, and that the reputation of Union College in the future is to be not only maintained, but enhanced. It is not from the sons of the millionaire or the noble that the world receives its teachers, its martyrs, its inventors, its statesmen, its poets, or even its men of affairs. It is from the cottage of the poor that all these spring. We can scarcely read one among the few "immortal names that were not born to die," or who has rendered

exceptional service to our race, who had not the advantage of being cradled, nursed, and reared in the stim-
ulating school of poverty. There is nothing so ener-
vating, nothing so deadly in its effects upon the
qualities which lead to the highest achievement, moral
or intellectual, as hereditary wealth. And if there be
among you a young man who feels that he is not compelled to exert himself in order to earn and live from
his own efforts, I tender him my profound sympathy.
Should such an one prove an exception to his fellows,
and become a citizen living a life creditable to himself
and useful to the State, instead of my profound sympathy I bow before him with profound reverence; for
one who overcomes the seductive temptations which
surround hereditary wealth is of the " salt of the earth,"
and entitled to double honor. [Applause.]

One gets a great many good things from the New
York *Sun*, the distinguished proprietor and editor of
which you had recently the pleasure, benefit, and honor
of hearing. I beg to read this to you as one of its
numerous rays of light:

"OUR BOYS.

"Every moralist hard up for a theme asks at intervals:
What is the matter with the sons of our rich and great
men? The question is followed by statistics on the
wickedness and bad endings of such sons.

"The trouble with the moralists is that they put the
question wrong end first. There is nothing wrong with
those foolish sons, except that they are unlucky; but
there is something wrong with their fathers.

"Suppose that a fine specimen of an old deerhound,
very successful in his business, should collect untold
deer in the park, fatten them up, and then say to his
puppies: 'Here, boys, I've had a hard life catching

these deer, and I mean to see you enjoy yourselves.'
I'm so used to racing through the woods and hunting
that I can't get out of the habit, but you boys just pile
into that park and help yourselves.' Such a deerhound
as that would be scorned by every human father. The
human father would say to such a dog: 'Mr. Hound,
you're simply ruining those puppies. Too much meat
and no exercise will give them the mange and seven-
teen other troubles; and if distemper doesn't kill them,
they will be a knock-kneed, watery-eyed lot of dis-
graces to you. For heaven's sake, keep them down to
dog-biscuit and work them hard.'

"That same human father does with great pride the
very thing that he would condemn in a dog or a cat.
He ruins his children, and then, when he gets old, pro-
fusely and sadly observes that he has done everything
for them, and yet they have disappointed him. He
who gives to his son an office which he has 'not de-
served and enables him to disgrace his father and
friends, deserves no more sympathy than any Mr.
Fagin deliberately educating a boy to be dishonest.

"The fat, useless pug-dogs which young women drag
wheezing about at the end of strings are not to blame
for their condition, and the same thing is true of rich
men's sons. The young women who overfeed the dogs
and the fathers who ruin the sons have themselves to
thank.

"No man would advocate the thing, perhaps; but who
can doubt that if there could be a law making it impossible for a man to inherit anything but a good education and a good constitution, it would supply us in
short order with a better lot of men?"

This is sound. "If you see it in *The Sun* it is so."
At least it is in this case.

It is not the poor young man who goes forth to his

work in the morning and labors until evening that we should pity. It is the son of the rich man to whom Providence has not been so kind as to trust with this honorable task. It is not the busy man, but the man of idleness, who should arouse our sympathy and cause us sorrow. "Happy is the man who has found his work," says Carlyle. I say, happy is the man who has to work and to work hard, and work long. A great poet has said: "He prayeth best who loveth best." Some day this may be parodied into: "He prayeth best who worketh best." An honest day's work well performed is not a bad sort of prayer. The cry goes forth often nowadays, "Abolish poverty!" but fortunately this cannot be done; and the poor we are always to have with us. Abolish poverty, and what would become of the race? Progress, development, would cease. Consider its future if dependent upon the rich. The supply of the good and the great would cease, and human society retrograde into barbarism. Abolish luxury, if you please, but leave us the soil, upon which alone the virtues and all that is precious in human character grow: poverty—honest poverty—

I will assume for the moment, gentlemen, that you were all fortunate enough to be born poor. Then the first question that presses upon you is this: What shall I learn to do for the community which will bring me in exchange enough wealth to feed, clothe, lodge, and keep me independent of charitable aid from others. What shall I do for a living? And the young man may like, or think that he would like, to do one thing rather than another; to pursue one branch or another; to be a business man or craftsman of some kind, or minister, physician, electrician, architect, editor, or lawyer, and after the remarkable address to which you have had the privilege of listening from one of the most distinguished of editors, I have no doubt some of you in your wildest flights aspire to be journalists. But it does not matter what the young man likes or dislikes, he always has to keep in view the main point: Can I attain such a measure of proficiency in the branch preferred as will certainly enable me to earn a livelihood by its practice.

The young man, therefore, who resolves to make himself useful to his kind, and therefore entitled to receive in return from a grateful community which he benefits the sum necessary for his support, sees clearly one of the highest duties of a young man. He meets the vital question immediately pressing upon him for decision, and decides it rightly.

So far, then, there is no difference about the acquisition of wealth. Every one is agreed that it is the first duty of a young man to so train himself as to be self-supporting. Nor is there difficulty about the next step, for the young man cannot be said to have performed the whole of his duty if he leaves out of account the contingencies of life, liability to accident, illness, and trade depressions like the present. Wisdom calls upon him to have regard for these things; and it is a part of his duty that he begin to save a portion of his earnings and invest them, not in speculation, but in securities or in property, or in a legitimate business in such form as will, perhaps, slowly but yet surely grow into the reserve upon which he can fall back in emergencies or in old age, and live upon his own savings. I think we are all agreed as to the advisability—nay, the duty—of laying up a competence, and hence to retain our self-respect; in the words of Burns:

> To win Dame Fortune's kindly smile,
>   Assiduous wait upon her,
> And gather gear by every wile
>   That's justified by honor;

> Not to hide it in a hedge,
>   Nor for a train-attendant ;
> But for the glorious privilege
>   Of being independent.

Besides this, I take it that the sophomores, and even not a few of the freshmen before me, have already decided, just as soon as possible, to ask "a certain young lady" to share his lot, or perhaps his lots, and, of course, he should have a lot or two to share. [Applause.] When a bridegroom recently at his marriage ceremony in a fashionable church said the words, "With all my worldly goods I thee endow," a wit sitting behind my friend whispered, "There goes Charlie's satchel." [Laughter.] The young Benedict was not a graduate of Union, although in favor of union. Marriage is a very serious business indeed, and gives rise to many weighty considerations. "Be sure to marry a woman with good common-sense," was the advice given me by my mentor, and I just hand it down to you. Common sense is the most uncommon and most valuable quality in man or woman. But before you have occasion to provide yourself with a helpmate, there comes the subject upon which I am to address you—"Wealth"—not wealth in millions, but simply revenue sufficient for modest, independent living. This opens up the entire subject of wealth in a greater or less degree. Let me give a few rules founded upon experience as to competence and wealth, and how to win them:

First—Concentrate your mind and effort upon one pursuit. It does not matter much what that pursuit is, so that it be useful and honorable, and be the first authority in that. Of course you have heard the advice, "Not to put all your eggs in one basket." It is long since I first told young men to reject that advice and pursue just the contrary course. "Put all your eggs in one basket and then watch that basket." More men fail to win competence and wealth from disregard of this advice, and from scattering their shot, than from any other cause. Whenever you see a man who is director in twenty different companies, and interested in various pursuits, put him down as one sure to become a Jack-of-all-trades and master of none. This is the age of specialization. I have known many men fail— but very few owing to their own business—generally because they have had investments in avocations which they did not understand.

There is a second rule: You must not be content with simply performing the part assigned you; you must do something beyond that, and watch your employer's interest at every point, no matter whether it is in your special province or not, and do not hesitate to apprise him promptly of anything that you see in any part of his business which does not commend itself to your august approval. You have heard, "Obey orders if you break owners." Do not let the graduate of Old Union be so stupid. Break them any time if you are clear that breaking orders will save owners, and then go boldly to your employer and point out to him how foolish he has been in giving such an order. Believe me, the young man who does not know the business of his special department much better than his employer can possibly do has not the elements of the future millionaire in him. You remember the story of Lincoln and his Secretary of War, Stanton. The President issued an order and sent it to his Secretary, who tore it up, saying that he was a foolish man who would issue such an order at this time, which was very likely, for Lincoln's heart was liable to run away with his head at times when stern measures were necessary. The officer returned and in great rage told the President how he had been insulted; but the truly great one was very difficult indeed to insult. The President said, "Stanton said I was foolish, did he? Well, I must go over and see him, Colonel, for Stanton generally knows what he is talking about." [Laughter.] And so will the wise employer act when any of you play Stanton.

There is another point: Never try to make too good a bargain either for yourself or for your employer. Be always fair, avoiding anything like sharp practice. It is a poor bargain when both parties to it are not benefited, and therefore happy at having made it. Every unjust advantage taken in business sooner or later proves a serious disadvantage. Men who become great millionaires, co-operating as they must with others, must secure and hold the implicit confidence of their associates and bear a reputation as being in all things fair, liberal, and considerate; their word must be better than their bond, and their desire to do the fair and liberal thing better than either word or bond.

Never speculate. The man who gambles in stocks in Wall Street is not more culpable than he who gambles at Monte Carlo; but he has much less sense, because the chances between winning and losing are not as equally divided in New York as at the regular gambling establishment. The life of a speculator, of course, is the life of a gamester; and this is fatal to the development of the reasoning and judging faculties in man. It is a life of intense excitement, fatal to thought and to study. There are but few instances of men who have won fortunes upon the exchange. They are up to-day and down to-morrow, and usually break down in middle life, shattered wrecks. Those of you who may become New York physicians will soon become acquainted with the lamentable results of stock gambling. I pray you, avoid speculation if you would prosper not only in wealth, but in health, happiness, and honor. Besides this, a moral consideration should prevent you. The man who wins the money of others renders no service to his fellows in exchange. All we get should be in return for some service rendered.

It is indispensable that the future competence-maker or millionaire should begin to save a portion of his earnings early, no matter how small these earnings may be. It is a great mistake, gentlemen, to think that good habits and ability go unrecognized in this age. The millionaire employer is constantly keeping his eye open just for these qualities in young men. It is not capital that he desires, but ability, character, and good, thrifty habits. Begin to lay by a portion of your earnings every month, and keep up that habit, and I should like to insure you at a very low rate your future millionaireship.

You always hear that drinking liquor is the dangerous rock in the path of the young. This is true; perhaps the most serious temptation to which a young man is exposed. I never like to preach to young men, knowing that they have sense enough not to like to be preached at; besides, they have a very wholesome contempt for the man who is always telling them to be goody-goody and who is not so awfully goody-goody himself. Because I have practised since my youth what I now recommend to you upon the liquor question you will, I hope, patiently hear me. The rule for young men, especially for a graduate of Union College, is that it is too low, too common, for him to enter a bar-room. He should not drink liquor between meals; and, indeed, when young and at college, it is better that he should not touch it at all. But I do not think that any harm can come from adhering to the rule never to go beyond drinking a glass of wine at dinner.

I know that the medical profession is generally of opinion that after you are forty this is not harmless, but beneficial. Therefore, gentlemen, postpone testing the truth of this until you are forty or thereabouts. I will give such nice young fellows leeway one way or the other of a few years: some who are not athletes may begin at thirty-five; others, if they so desire, wait until they are forty-five. Or it might be a good rule for those of you who intend to pursue a business career to resolve not to indulge until you become millionaires. [Laughter.] This will probably give you sufficient time to think the matter over and render your final decision, that of not only deliberate but mature judgment.

Believe me, my young friends, there is nothing that so completely spoils a young man's career as giving way, even once, to intemperance. I have seen this, in my own experience, over and over again. I know cases of several who occupied high positions, were entrusted with great responsibilities, their future promotion certain, and partnership within their easy reach. In one case I remember well, when the name was mentioned for this one, the partner said it was his duty to inform his associates—as indeed it was—that he knew this young man had upon a then recent occasion been in low company and had drowned the God-like reason as Cassius did, with like result. "Never more be officer of mine," was the decision of the firm, and the young man never knew why others were promoted and trusted and he restricted to ordinary duties. Avoid intemperance, if you would rise. Obedience to these things is requisite to win competence and wealth.

Now, what is wealth? How is it created and distributed? There are not far from us immense beds of coal which have lain for millions of years useless, and therefore valueless. Through some experiment, or perhaps accident, it was discovered that black stone would burn and give forth heat. Men sank shafts, erected machinery, mined and brought forth coal, and sold it to the community. It displaced the use of wood as a fuel, say at one-half the cost. Immediately every bed of coal became valuable because useful, or capable of being made so; and here a new article worth hundreds, yes, thousands of millions was added to the wealth of the community. A Scotch mechanic one day, as the story goes, gazing into the fire upon which water was boiling in a kettle, saw the steam raise the lid, as hundreds of thousands had seen before him; but none saw in that sight what he did—the steam engine, which does the work of the world at a cost so infinitely trifling compared with what the plans known before involved, that the wealth of the world has been increased one dares not estimate how much. The saving that the community makes is the root of wealth in any branch of material development. Now, a young man's labor or service to the community creates wealth just in proportion as his service is useful to the community, as it either saves or improves upon existing methods. Commodore Vanderbilt saw, I think, thirteen different short railway lines between New York and Buffalo, involving thirteen different managements, and a disjointed and tedious service. Albany, Schenectady, Utica, Syracuse, Auburn, Rochester, etc., were heads of some of these companies. He consolidated them all, making one direct line, over which your Empire State Express flies fifty-one miles an hour, the fastest time in the world; and a hundred passengers patronize the lines where one did in olden days. He rendered the community a special service, which, being followed by others, reduces the cost of bringing food from the prairies of the West to your doors to a trifling sum per ton. He produced, and is every day producing, untold wealth to the community by so doing, and the profit he reaped for himself was but as a drop in the bucket compared with that which he showered upon the State and the nation.

Now, in the olden days, before steam, electricity, or any other of the modern inventions which unitedly have changed the whole aspect of the world, everything was done upon a small scale. There was no room for great ideas to operate upon a large scale, and thus to produce great wealth to the inventor, discoverer, originator, or executive. New inventions gave this opportunity, and many large fortunes were made by individuals. But in our day we are rapidly passing, if we have not already passed, this stage of development, and few large fortunes can now be made in any part of the world, except from one cause, the rise in the value of real estate. Manufacturing, transportation both upon the land and upon the sea, banking, insurance, have all passed into the hands of corporations composed of hundreds and in many cases thousands of shareholders. The New York Central Railroad is owned by more than ten thousand shareholders, the Pennsylvania Railroad is owned by more people than the vast army which it employs, and nearly one-fourth of the number are the estates of women and children. It is so with the great manufacturing companies; so with the great steamship lines; it is so, as you know, with banks, insurance companies, and indeed with all branches of business. It is a great mistake for young men to say to themselves, " Oh! we cannot enter into business." If any of you have saved as much as $50 or $100, I do not know any branch of business into which you cannot plunge at once. You can get your certificate of stock and attend the meeting of stockholders, make your speeches and suggestions, quarrel with the president, and instruct the management of the affairs of the com-pany, and have all the rights and influence of an owner. You can buy shares in anything, from newspapers to tenement-houses; but capital is so poorly paid in these days that I advise you to exercise much circumspection before you invest. As I have said to workingmen and to ministers, college professors, artists, musicians, and physicians, and all the professional classes: Do not invest in any business concerns whatever; the risks of business are not for such as you. Buy a home for your-self first; and if you have any surplus, buy another lot or another house, or take a mortgage upon one, or upon a railway, and let it be a first mortgage, and be satisfied with moderate interest. Do you know, my dear young friends, that out of every hundred that attempt business upon their own account statistics are said to show that ninety-five sooner or later fail. I know that from my own experience. I can quote the lines of Hudibras and tell you, as far as one manu-facturing branch is concerned, that what he found to be true is still true to an eminent degree to-day: "Many are the perils that environ the man who meddles with cold iron."

The shareholders of iron and steel concerns to-day can certify that this is so, whether the iron or steel be hot or cold; and such is also the case in other branches of business.

The principal complaint against our industrial con-ditions of to-day is that they cause great wealth to flow into the hands of the few. Well, of the very few, indeed, is this true. It was formerly so, as I have ex-plained, immediately after the new inventions had changed the conditions of the world. To-day it is not true. Wealth is being more and more distributed among the many. The amount of the combined profits of labor and capital which goes to labor was never so great as to-day, the amount going to capital never so small. While the earnings of capital have fallen more than one-half, in many cases have been entirely ob-literated, statistics prove that the earnings of labor were never so high as they were previous to the recent unprecedented depression in business, while the cost of living, as you all know—or perhaps you college young men do not yet know this—the necessaries of life, have fallen in some cases nearly one-half. Great Britain has an income tax, and our country is to be subject to this imposition for a time. The British returns show that during the eleven years from 1876 to 1887 the number of men receiving from $750 to $2,500 per year, increased more than 21 per cent, while the number receiving from $5,000 to $25,000 actually decreased 2½ per cent.

You may be sure, gentlemen, that the question of the distribution of wealth is settling itself rapidly under present conditions, and settling itself in the right direction. The few rich are getting poorer, and the toiling masses are getting richer. Nevertheless, a few exceptional men may yet make fortunes, but these will be more moderate than in the past. This may not be quite as fortunate for the masses of the people as is now believed, because great accumulations of wealth in the hands of one enterprising man who still toils on are sometimes most productive of all the forms of wealth. Take the richest man the world ever saw, who died in New York some years ago. What was found in his case? That, with the exception of a small percentage used for daily expenses, his entire fortune and all its surplus earnings were invested in enterprises which developed the railway system of our country, which gives to the people the cheapest transportation known. Whether the millionaire wishes it or not, he cannot evade the law which, under present conditions, compels him to use his millions for the good of the people. All that he gets during the few years of his life is that he may live in a finer house, surround himself with finer furniture, and works of art which may be added: he could even have a grander library, more of the gods around him; but, as far as I have known millionaires, the library is the least used part of what he would probably consider "furniture" in all his mansion. He can eat richer food and drink richer wines, which only hurt him. But truly the modern millionaire is generally a man of very simple tastes and even miserly habits. He spends little upon himself, and is the toiling bee laying up the honey in the industrial hive, which all the inmates of that hive, the community in general, will certainly enjoy. Here is the true description of the millionaire, as given by Mr. Carter in his remarkable speech before the Bering Sea tribunal at Paris:

"Those who are most successful in the acquisition of property and who acquire it to such an enormous extent are the very men who are able to control it, to invest it, and to handle it in the way most useful to society. It is because they have those qualities that they are able to engross it to so large an extent. They really own, in any just sense of the word, only what they consume. The rest is all held for the benefit of the public. They are the custodians of it. They invest it; they see that it is put into this employment, that employment, another employment. All labor is employed by it and employed in the best manner, and it is thus made the most productive. These men who acquire these hundreds of millions are really groaning under a servitude to the rest of society, for that is practically their condition; and society really endures it because it is best for them that it should be so."

Here is another estimate by a no less remarkable man. Your friend, Mr. Dana, justly said at Cornell the other day:

·" That is one class of men that I refer to, the thinkers, the men of science, the inventors; and the other class is that of those whom God has endowed with a genius for saving, for getting rich, for bringing wealth together, for accumulating and concentrating money, men against whom it is now fashionable to declaim, and against whom legislation is sometimes directed. And yet is there any benefactor of humanity who is to be envied in his achievements, and in the memory and the monuments he has left behind him, more than Ezra Cornell? [Applause.] Or, to take another example that is here before our eyes, more than Henry W. Sage? These are men who knew how to get rich, because they had been endowed with that faculty; and when they got rich, they knew how to give it for great public enterprises, for uses that will remain living, immortal as long as man remains upon the earth. The men of genius and the men of money, those who prepare new agencies of life, and those who accumulate and save the money for great enterprises and great public works, these are the peculiar and the inestimable leaders of the world, as the twentieth century is opening upon us."

The bees of a hive do not destroy the honey-making bees, but the drones. It would be a great mistake for the community to shoot the millionaires, for they are the bees that make the most honey, and contribute most to the hive even after they have gorged themselves full. Here is a remarkable fact, that the masses of the people in any country are prosperous and comfortable just in proportion as there are millionaires. Take

Russia, with its population little better than serfs, and living at the point of starvation upon the meanest possible fare, such fare as none of our people could or would eat, and you do not find one millionaire in Russia, always excepting the Emperor and a few nobles who own the land, owing to their political system. It is the same, to a great extent, in Germany. There are only two millionaires known to me in the whole German Empire. In France, where the people are better off than in Germany, you cannot count one-half dozen millionaires in the whole country. In the old home of our race, in Britain, which is the richest country in all Europe—the richest country in the world save one, our own—there are more millionaires than in the whole of the rest of Europe, and its people are better off than in any other. You come to our own land: we have more millionaires than in all the rest of the world put together, although we have not one to every ten that is reputed so. I have seen a list of supposed millionaires prepared by a well-known lawyer of Brooklyn, which made me laugh, as it has made many others. I saw men rated there as millionaires who could not pay their debts. Many should have had a cipher cut from their $1,000,000. Some time ago I sat next Mr. Evarts at dinner, and the conversation touched upon the idea that men should distribute their wealth during their lives for the public good. One gentleman said that was correct, giving many reasons, one of which was that, of course, they could not take it with them at death.

"Well," said Mr. Evarts, "I do not know about that. My experience as a New York lawyer is that, somehow or other, they do succeed in taking at least four-fifths of it." Their reputed wealth was never found at death.

A leading divine in England participated in a discussion in *The Nineteenth Century* review, which took place between several well-known men upon my article in regard to the distribution of wealth during one's life. The reverend gentleman said that in an ideal Christian community a millionaire would be an impossibility, to which I took the liberty of saying in reply that it was a far guess ahead just what would exist in an ideal community; but one thing was certain, that at least no preacher would be required. [Great laughter.] The millionaire and the preacher, therefore, if he were correct, would take their exit together. What a delightful sight to see the Rev. Price Hughes and myself, or our successors, walking about arm in arm, looking for a new occupation, some light work, with heavy pay, which is generally desired by people in our position. Whatever the ideal conditions may develop, it seems to me Mr. Carter and Mr. Dana are right. Under our present conditions the millionaire who toils on is the cheapest article which the community secures at the price it pays for him, namely, his shelter, clothing, and food.

The inventions of to-day lead to concentrating industrial and commercial affairs into huge concerns. You cannot work the Bessemer process successfully without employing thousands of men upon one spot. You could not make the armor for ships without first expending seven millions of dollars, as the Bethlehem Company has spent. You cannot make a yard of cotton goods in competition with the world without having an immense factory and thousands of men and women aiding in the process. The great electric establishment here in your town succeeds because it has spent millions, and is prepared to do its work upon a great scale. Under such conditions it is impossible but that wealth will flow into the hands of a few men in prosperous times beyond their needs. But out of fifty great for-

unes which Mr. Blaine had a list made of he found
only one man who was reputed to have made a large
fortune in manufacturing. These are made from real
estate more than from all other causes combined; next
follows transportation, banking. The whole manufacturing world furnished but one millionaire.

But assuming that surplus wealth flows into the hands
of a few men, what is their duty? How is the
struggle for dollars to be lifted from the sordid atmosphere surrounding business and made a noble career?
Now, wealth has hitherto been distributed in three ways:
The first and chief one is by willing it at death to the
family. Now, beyond bequeathing to those dependent upon one the revenue needful for modest and independent living, is such a use of wealth either right or
wise? I ask you to think over the result, as a rule, of
millions given over to young men and women, the sons
and daughters of the millionaire. You will find that,
as a rule, it is not good for the daughters; and this is
seen in the character and conduct of the men who
marry them. As for the sons, you have their condition
as described in the extract which I read you from *The
Sun.* Nothing is truer than this, that as a rule the
"almighty dollar" bequeathed to sons or daughters by
millions proves an almighty curse. It is not the good
of the child which the millionaire parent considers
when he makes these bequests, it is his own vanity; it
is not affection for the child, it is self-glorification for
the parent which is at the root of this injurious dis-
position of wealth. There is only one thing to be said
for this mode, it furnishes one of the most efficacious
means of rapid distribution of wealth ever known.

There is a second use of wealth, less common than
the first, which is not so injurious to the community,
but which should bring no credit to the testator.

Money is left by millionaires to public institutions
when they must relax their grasp upon it.   There is no
grace, and can be no blessing, in giving what cannot
be withheld.   It is no gift, because it is not cheerfully
given, but only granted at the stern summons of death.
The miscarriage of these bequests; the litigation connected with them, and the manner in which they are
frittered away seem to prove that the Fates do not regard them with a kindly eye.   We are never without a
lesson that the only mode of producing lasting good by
giving large sums of money is for the millionaire to
give as close attention to its distribution during his
life as he did to its acquisition.   We have to-day the
noted case of five or six millions of dollars left by a
great lawyer to found a public library in New York,
an institution needed so greatly that the failure of this
bequest is a misfortune.   It is years since he died; the
will is pronounced invalid through a flaw, although
there is no doubt of the intention of the donor.   It is
sad commentary upon the folly of men holding the
millions which they cannot use until they are unable to
put them to the end they desire.   Peter Cooper, Pratt
of Baltimore, and Pratt of Brooklyn, and others are the
type of men who should be taken by you as your model;
they distributed their surplus during life.

The third use, and the only noble use of surplus
wealth, is this: That it be regarded as a sacred trust, to
be administered by its possessor, into whose hands it
flows, for the highest good of the people.   Man does
not live by bread alone, and five or ten cents a day
more revenue scattered over thousands would produce
little or no good.   Accumulated into a great fund and
expended as Mr. Cooper expended it, for the Cooper
Institute, establishes something that will last for generations.   It will educate the brain, the spiritual part of

man. It furnishes a ladder upon which the aspiring poor may climb; and there is no use whatever, gentlemen, trying to help people who do not help themselves. You cannot push any one up a ladder unless he be willing to climb a little himself. When you stop boosting, he falls, to his injury. Therefore, I have often said, and I now repeat, that the day is coming, and already we see its dawn, in which the man who dies possessed of millions of available wealth which was free and in his hands ready to be distributed will die disgraced. Of course I do not mean that the man in business may not be stricken down with his capital in the business, which cannot be withdrawn, for capital is the tool with which he works his wonders and produces more wealth. I refer to the man who dies possessed of millions of securities which are held simply for the interest they produce, that he may add to his hoard of miserable dollars. By administering surplus wealth during life great wealth may become a blessing to the community, and the occupation of the business man accumulating wealth may be elevated so as to rank with any profession. In this way he may take rank even with the physician, one of the highest of our professions, because he too, in a sense, will be a physician, looking after and trying not to cure, but to prevent, the ills of humanity. To those of you who are compelled or who desire to follow a business life and to accumulate wealth, I commend this ideal as the only one worthy of young men privileged to call themselves graduates of Union College. The epitaph which every rich man should wish himself justly entitled to is that seen upon the monument to Pitt:

He lived without ostentation,
And he died poor.

Such is the man whom the future is to honor, while he who dies in old age retired from business, possessed of millions of available wealth, is to die unwept, un-honored, and unsung.

I think I may justly divide you, my friends, into four classes:

First, those who must work for a living, and set before them as their aim the acquisition of a modest competence—of course, with a modest but picturesque cottage in the country and one as a companion "who maketh sunshine in a shady place" and is the good angel of his life. The motto of this class, No. 1, might be given as "Give me neither poverty nor riches." "From the anxieties of poverty as from the responsi-bilities of wealth, good Lord, deliver us."

Class No. 2, comprising those among you who are determined to acquire wealth, whose aim in life is to belong to that much-talked-of and grandly abused class, the millionaire, those who start to labor for the greatest good of the greatest number, but the greatest number always number one, the motto of this class being short and to the point: "Put money in thy purse."

Now, the third class comes along. The god they worship is neither wealth nor happiness. They are inflamed with "noble ambition;" the desire of fame is the controlling element of their lives. Now, while this is not so ignoble as the desire for material wealth, it must be said that it betrays more vanity. The shrine of fame has many worshippers. The element of vanity is seen in its fiercest phase among those who come before the public. It is well known, for instance, that musicians, actors, and even painters—all the artistic class—are peculiarly prone to excessive personal vanity. This has often been wondered at; but the reason proba-bly is that the musician and the actor, and even the painter, may be transcendent in his special line without being even highly educated, without having an all-around brain. Some peculiarities, some one element in his character, may give him prominence or fame, so that his love of art, or of use through art, is entirely drowned by a narrow, selfish, personal vanity. But we find this liability in a lesser degree all through the professions, the politician, the lawyer, and, with reverence be it spoken, sometimes the minister; less, I think, in the physician than in any of the professions, probably because he, more than in any other profession, is called to deal with the sad realities of life face to face. He of all men sees the vanity of vanities. An illustration of this class is well drawn in Hotspur's address:

> By heavens, methinks it were an easy leap,
> To pluck bright honor from the pale-faced moon;
> Or dive into the bottom of the deep,
> Where fathom-line could never touch the ground,
> And pluck up drowned honor by the locks;
> So he that doth redeem her thence might wear
> Without corrival all her dignities.

Mark, young gentlemen, he cares not for use; he cares not for state; he cares only for himself, and, as a vain peacock, struts across the stage.

Now, gentlemen, it does not seem to me that the love of wealth is the controlling desire of so many as the love of fame; and this is matter for sincere congratulation, and proves that under the irresistible laws of evolution the race is slowly moving onward and upward. Take the whole range of the artistic world, which gives sweetness and light to life, which refines and adorns, and surely the great composer, painter, pianist, lawyer, judge, statesman, all those in public life, care less for millions than for professional reputation in their respective fields of labor.. What cared

Washington, Franklin, Lincoln, or Grant and Sherman
for wealth? Nothing! What cared Harrison or Cleveland, two poor men, not unworthy successors? What
care the Judges of our Supreme Court, or even the leading counsel that plead before them? The great
preachers, physicians, great teachers, are not concerned
about the acquisition of wealth. The treasure they
seek is in the reputation acquired through their service
to others, and this is certainly a great step from the
millionaire class, who struggle to old age, and through
old age to the verge of the grave, with no ambition,
apparently, except to add to their pile of miserable
dollars.

But there is a fourth class, higher than all the preceding, who worship neither at the shrine of wealth nor
fame, but at the noblest of all shrines, the shrine of
service—service to the race. Self-abnegation is its
watchword. Members of this inner and higher circle
seek not popular applause, are concerned not with
being popular, but with being right. They say with
Confucius: "It concerneth me not that I have not high
office; what concerns me is to make myself worthy of
office." It is not cast down by poverty, neither unduly
elated by prosperity. The man belonging to this class
simply seeks to do his duty day by day in such manner
as may enable him to honor himself, fearing nothing
but his own self-reproach. I have known men and
women not prominently before the public, for this
class courts not prominence, but who in their lives
proved themselves to have reached this ideal stage.
Now, I will give you for this class the fitting illustration
from the words of a Scotch poet who died altogether
too young:

> I will go forth 'mong men, not mailed in scorn,
> But in the armor of a pure intent.

Great duties are before me, and great songs;
And whether crowned or crownless when I fall,
It matters not, so as God's work is done.
I've learned to prize the quiet lightning deed,
Not the applauding thunder at its heels
Which men call fame.

Then, gentlemen, standing upon the threshold of life, you have the good, better, best presented to you—the three stages of development, the natural, spiritual, and celestial, they may fitly be called. One has success in material things for its aim—not without benefit this for the race as a whole, because it lifts the individual from the animal and demands the exercise of many valuable qualities: sobriety, industry, and self-discipline. The second rises still higher: the reward sought for being things more of the spirit—not gross and material, but invisible; and not of the flesh, but of the brain, the spiritual part of man; and this brings into play innumerable virtues which make good and useful men.

The third or celestial class stands upon an entirely different footing from the others in this, that selfish considerations are subordinated in the select brotherhood of the best, the service to be done for others being the first consideration. The reward of either wealth or fame is unsought, for these have learned and know full well that virtue is its own and the only exceeding great reward; and this once enjoyed, all other rewards are not worth seeking. And so wealth and even fame are dethroned; and there stands enthroned the highest standard of all—your own approval flowing from a faithful discharge of duty as you see it, fearing no consequences, seeking no reward.

Such are my views, gentlemen, upon wealth and fame, and upon life and its duties. It does not matter much what branch of effort your tastes or judgment draw you to, the one great point is that you should be drawn to some one branch. Then perform your whole duty in it and a little more—the "little more" being vastly important. We have the words of a great poet for it, that the man who does the best he can, can whiles do more. Maintain your self-respect as the most precious jewel of all and the only true way to win the respect of others, and then remember what Emerson says, for what he says here is true: "No young man can be cheated out of an honorable career in life unless he cheat himself."

I am exceedingly obliged to you for the patience with which you have listened to me. If you are all half as successful and as happy as I wish, you will have no reason to complain. Good-by.

HENRY WHITE CANNON.

Henry White Cannon, President of the Chase National Bank of New York, was born at Delhi, N. Y., in 1850, and is of Puritan descent. He early showed an inclination for finance, and at twenty he was teller of the First National Bank in his native town, Delhi. In 1870 he accepted a position with the Second National Bank of St. Paul, Minn., and a year later, at twenty-one, he organized the Lumberman's National Bank of Stillwater, Minn., and here began that independent business career that has placed him in the first ranks of American financiers.

He demonstrated that he possessed the qualities essential to successful banking. Two years after the organization of the bank at Stillwater came the memorable panic of 1873, which caused the suspension of currency payments generally throughout the Northwest. Mr. Cannon brought his bank through this crisis successfully, paying every demand made.

While a resident of the Northwest he purchased and exchanged large amounts of government bonds for the National banks of that section and personally organized and carried to a successful completion a number of successful business enterprises incident to the needs of a rapidly growing community.

In May, 1884, at the earnest solicitation of the Congressional delegation of his adopted State, and by the principal bankers of New York and Chicago, Henry W. Cannon was appointed by President Arthur Comptroller of the Currency, to succeed Hon. John Jay Knox, who was one of the most able men that ever filled the position. The appointment was not made on political grounds, although Mr. Cannon was an earnest and active member of the Republican party, and his selection to succeed Comptroller Knox was a high tribute to his mental and moral worth and for a man of his years something extraordinary. But we must take into consideration Mr. Cannon's whole life, which from the time of his leaving school in his native town, had been one of preparation for just such a position as he was now called upon to-fill. A master of banking in all its complex details, and a close student for years of all the best works on political economy, banking and commercial law, he was therefore well fitted to undertake to administer the duties pertaining to the office of Comptroller of the Currency.

The financial crisis of 1884 began the same month that Mr. Cannon entered upon the duties of his office as Comptroller. It was general and extended throughout the country, exposing weakness in many unexpected places ; defalcations in large numbers were found and more receivers were appointed during that year than any other in the history of the Comptroller's office ; these receivers were all appointed by Mr. Cannon, and extraordinary labors were thrown upon the Comptroller's office. A number of extra bank examiners were employed and, in many instances, banks that otherwise might have suspended and gone into the hands of receivers were undoubtedly saved by Mr. Cannon's, timely action and practical knowledge of banking.

During this panic a resolution was introduced into the United States Senate requesting Comptroller Cannon to appear before the finance committeee and report upon the condition of the banks in New York City, where it was alleged that, as the Clearing House had discontinued making weekly reports, the banks were in a precarious condition and that extraordinary measures should be used. The following senators were members of that committee : Morrill, Sherman, Bayard, Beck, Aldrich, and others. Comptroller Cannon made report to this committee, showing that he was fully informed as to the condition of affairs in New York, and advised that no unnecessary publicity be given to their condition ; and he fully convinced the committee that the banks were daily increasing their cash reserves and that it was not necessary to resort to legislation or extraordinary measures. Mr. Cannon's action in this matter was undoubtedly of great service to the banks and the country. His relations as Comptroller to the chairman and members of the Clearing House committee were close and cordial.

The corporate existence of 971 national banks, representing a capital of over $270,000,000, expired during Mr. Cannon's term of office.

The act of July 12th, 1882, under which permission was given to national banks to extend their charters, had been in operation but a short time when Mr. Cannon became Comptroller, and inasmuch as the charter of more than 800 banks expired during the year ending November 1st, 1885, it became necessary to pay especial attention to this work. A new code of procedure was arranged. It was necessary in all instances where a charter was given that a careful examination of the affairs of each bank should be made, and as the law provided that the new charter can be given only when the Comptroller is satisfied with the condition of the bank to be extended, the personal and difficult duties arising from this work were very great and required arduous labor.

Comptroller Cannon's reports for 1884 and 1885 were highly esteemed. In both reports a number of suggestions and recommendations were made, which were worthy of note. The report of 1885 contained, among other things, a careful study of the banknote issues of other countries, and also the following important recommendation to Congress in relation to silver legislation: "It is best for the interests of the United States to issue a circulation based on silver, (the Comptroller) believes that the circulation should be issued upon coin and bullion which contains a sufficient number of grains of silver to have an intrinsic value, . . . and (the Comptroller) is of the opinion that under certain restrictions and regulations it would be far more correct in principle to issue silver certificates based on a deposit of silver bullion, to be valued in exact proportion of silver to gold, than to continue the issue of certificates under the present law." The suggestion embodied in the recommendation, which was also contained in the report for 1884, has since become a law.

During Comptroller Cannon's term of office a complete change in the political complexion of the Government took place. The election of Grover Cleveland to the Presidency caused many changes to be made, but the office of Comptroller being non-partisan, and Mr. Cannon's views on finance being in accord with those of President Cleveland, as they were with President Arthur's, he was urged to remain during his full term of office, viz., six years. He enjoyed the full confidence and esteem of the Secretaries of the Treasury with whom he served, and he was frequently called in consultation in regard to some of the most important measures connected with the administration of the national finances. Judge Folger was Secretary when Comptroller Cannon was first appointed. Hugh McCullough followed for an interim, and afterward Daniel Manning. As there seemed very little prospect of legislation, either in reference to banks or silver, Comptroller Cannon preferred to return to active business life, rather than to remain in Government service, so early in 1886 he resigned and transferred his residence to New York City February

1st, and accepted the vice-presidency of the National Bank of the Republic in New York City, the president being Hon. John Jay Knox, his predecessor in the office of Comptroller of the Currency. November 1st, 1886, he resigned from the vice-presidency of this bank to accept the position of president of the Chase National Bank of New York, where his mature thought and ripe judgment have produced results that are phenomenal, and Henry W. Cannon as a member of the Clearing House executive committee and president of the Chase National Bank is a power that will be felt for good throughout the country. On the death of Aqueduct Commissioner Howe, Mayor Grant, of New York, appointed Mr. Cannon to the vacant commissionership as a mark of appreciation, in the name of his townsmen, of Mr. Cannon's integrity, business judgment, industrious care of trusts under-taken, and his legitimate popularity in the metropolis generally. We need hardly say that this token of estimation met with general approval. There is unusual complaint nowadays on the score of the kind of men that receive municipal recognition and preferment, but this a redeeming instance and we trust we shall hear more of them. His advice is frequently sought by the officers of other banks and by Treasury officials, and in every instance it has proved discreet and wise. In January, 1891, he was appointed by President Harrison, a member of the Assay Commission.

Title, guarantee, railroad, and mercantile companies have called upon him to serve in their boards of direction. In social life Mr. Cannon is an active participant, being a member of the Union League, Century Club, Sons of the Revolution, Metropolitan Club, New England Society, Royal Statistical Society of London, and many other social and art clubs, and is a member of the Kane Masonic Lodge.

Mr. Cannon frequently addresses financial and commercial bodies upon finance and kindred topics, and is a frequent contributor on financial subjects to newspapers and banking and other journals. His standing as an authority on financial questions is well illustrated by his appointment by President Harrison, in August, 1892, as one of the five members from the United States to the International Monetary Conference which convened at Brussels from November 23d to December 17th, 1892. Mr. Cannon assisted very largely in carrying on the negotiations with foreign governments preliminary to the calling of the conference, and it was natural, therefore, that he should be a member of it. In all the deliberations of the conference Mr. Cannon took a most active interest, and was especially prominent in his capacity as the American member on the sub-committee appointed to consider and amend the famous compromise plan submitted to the conference by Mr. Alfred de Rothschild.

As financier and successful business man as well as a close student of political economy Mr. Cannon's advice is frequently sought and he possesses in a marked degree the faculty of giving due consideration to the feasible as well as the ideal.

BANKING AND CURRENCY.

By Hon. Henry W. Cannon.

Mr. President and Gentlemen:—In the progress of civilization various trades and employments have become distinct in themselves. Just when and where the business of banking originated we do not know, although we find that banking was practised essentially as it is now in Rome about three hundred years B.C. In early times dealers in property and commodities were compelled to resort to barter and exchange of one piece of property for another and one commodity for another; but with advancing civilization gold, silver, and copper were utilized as money, and gradually bills of exchange, promissory notes, and other instruments of credit were invented and came into general use. The business of banking is dealing in credit, but a credit system, such as now in general use by banks and bankers, was not possible until within a comparatively recent period. Credit and currency supply the means for the economic exchange of property.

MacLeod, in his " Theory and Practice of Banking" states that the word " currency" is a " Yankeeism" and that its use in a broad sense originated in this country. He defines currency as follows:

1. Coin Money—Gold, silver, and copper.

2. Paper Currency, *i.e.*, promissory notes and bills of exchange, with all their varieties.

3. Simple debts of all sorts, such as credits, bankers'

books, call deposits, book debts of traders, and private debts of individuals.

Nearly all of the transactions in banking have to do with one or another of the three kinds of currency defined by MacLeod. In other words, the banker deals in that which represents a transfer of property or commodity. He does not buy or sell property, but handles that which represents purchases and sales. The profession of banking is carried on by private bankers, or by joint stock banks having shareholders who contribute capital for the business; the Bank of England, Bank of France, and the Imperial Bank of Germany being examples of the largest institutions of this character in the world, and the National and State banks in this country are in the same category. Usually banking institutions chartered by the general government have the privilege of issuing, under proper restrictions and regulations, bank-notes which circulate among the people as money in addition to the authority conferred by law which permits them to receive deposits, make loans, and conduct what is known as a general banking business. Banks chartered under the laws of the several States of the Union formerly issued bank-notes, but at the time of the passage of the National Bank Act a tax of 10 per cent was imposed by the National Government, which was prohibitory, and at the present time there are no State bank-notes in circulation.

In addition to private bankers and incorporated joint stock banks, we have in the United States loan and trust companies, which are authorized to act as trustees for corporations, individuals, and of estates, and which also act as guardians, receivers, registrars, and financial agents for cities, railways, and corporations, and who receive deposits upon which they pay interest and which they reloan for profit. The trust companies do not usually transact a general banking business, although there are some exceptions to this rule. Institutions called "savings banks" are chartered under the laws of the different States of this country, in order to inculcate and encourage habits of thrift and economy among people of small means. Those organized under the laws of this State (and certain other States in the Union) simply receive money for investment in securities designated by the statutes for the benefit of depositors, and any profits arising after payment of reasonable interest is laid aside as a guarantee fund. In some of the European countries savings banks are under the direct supervision of the general government, and in some instances are connected with the postal service of the country in order to be directly accessible to the working-people. In some of the States of the Union banks receiving deposits of savings use them, to a certain extent, for commercial business, but institutions of this character should not be regarded, strictly speaking, as savings banks.

A general banking business is conducted in the same manner by private bankers and joint stock banks. I do not now refer to the issue and circulation of bank-notes, which will be considered later. A general banking business consists in discounting and negotiating promissory notes, drafts, bills of exchange, and other evidences of debt; in receiving deposits, buying and selling exchange, coin, and bullion, and in loaning money on personal and other securities. The receiving of deposits covers the receipt of money, checks, bills of exchange, as well as other items of credit received from depositors. All such items are mingled with those of the bank itself, and the general fund so derived, including the capital of the bank, is used in discounting and negotiating promissory notes, etc. The bank

23

undertakes to return to the depositor his money and the proceeds of all items of credit together with such compensation for use of same as may be agreed upon.

The individual or corporation dealing with a bank or banker may be a depositor or a borrower, or may act in a dual capacity as a depositor and borrower.

In early times men of known wealth, integrity, and ability in small communities (and in large communities as well) were entrusted with the money of their neighbors and acquaintances as private bankers, and a large business is still transacted by private bankers in this and other countries; but the great bulk of the banking business, at the present time is conducted by chartered institutions whose shares are owned by individuals, and as chartered banks are subject to certain restrictions and examinations under National or State authority the depositor or dealer is not compelled to rely so completely upon the wealth and standing of the manager of the institution as when dealing with a private banker, although of course it is absolutely necessary that the management of all banks should be above suspicion as regards integrity and ability. A dealer with a bank who deposits coined money or paper currency does so because it is a convenience—a measure of safety—and he has the benefit of paying for property or commodities by checks, which relieves him of risk in handling or transporting money, and a bank account is an advantage in many ways. The dealer who not only deposits money, but arranges for credit against promissory notes or bills of exchange, or in any other manner, has the advantage of anticipating the settlement of a transfer of property or commodity by the use of the credit against which he is permitted to draw checks and money if needed. In fact, his credit on the books of the bank is the same as so much money in hand.

The profits arising from the conduct of a banking business are small in comparison to the aggregate of business done as measured by the unit of value in the country where it is conducted—*i.e.*, considering the aggregate volume of business in dollars, the profit of the banks and bankers in this country is small as compared with returns from many other trades and employments. This being the case, it is obviously necessary for the manager of a bank to conduct its business in a conservative and prudent manner, and all loans and advances must be made upon undoubted security and to persons of unquestioned wealth and integrity. The profits of a banker arise principally from the interest received for the use of credit or, as is generally stated, for the use of money advanced. A bank not only uses its own capital in making. advances but also such portion of the amount of money standing to the credit of its dealers as is deemed prudent. It is of course necessary for the bank or banker to have at all times a sufficient amount of coin or paper currency to meet the demands of depositors and dealers; for, while the bulk of the business of banking is conducted by means of checks and bills of exchange, a certain proportion of deposits is liable to be withdrawn in actual money at any time. The percentage of coin and paper currency necessary to be kept on hand by banks and bankers varies in different countries and communities. In many of the banks in Europe, what is termed the "till cash" is comparatively small in proportion to the business done. In the United States, what we call the reserve of National and State banks has been a subject of legislation, and our statutes provide that bankers shall keep a certain amount of cash on hand in proportion to their deposits, the amount required to be kept on hand in this country being larger in proportion to liabilities than the amounts usually carried by banks abroad.

As we have observed, the dealers or customers of a bank not only deposit coined money, paper currency, etc., but they are able to obtain credit against which they issue checks, as well as against cash deposits, and these checks, in turn, are deposited by others to whom they are given, and checks and bills of exchange drawn against banks and bankers furnish a circulating medium which greatly increases and facilitates trade and commerce. Checks are being constantly issued in every village, town, and city where a banking business is carried on, and their use is so general in every community that I am sure you are already well acquainted with many of their functions.

The banking business has reached such a state of perfection that the bulk of all checks drawn by dealers and banks are paid through what is known as the "Clearing House." Banks in this country, as well as in Europe, by a simple arrangement and regular exchange and offset of checks among themselves by this system, so arrange their affairs that only balances or differences between checks in the hands of one bank and those in the hands of another are actually paid in money. The Clearing House Association of the city of New York, for instance, is composed of sixty-four banks, and for convenience in making payment by check on the part of the Government, the Assistant Treasurer at New York is also a member. All of the banks that are members of the association send a representative to its offices with all of the checks held by each bank upon all of the other banks, and make their exchanges of checks in this manner, instead of being compelled to send them by hand to each separate institution. This arrangement enables an expansion of

credit which would otherwise be impossible, and econo-
mizes the use of coin and paper money to an enormous
extent. The aggregate amount of exchanges of checks
which have been paid by being passed through the sixty-
one clearing house associations of the United States
for the year ending December 31st, 1892, amounted
to sixty-two billion, six hundred and eighty-four million, three hundred and forty-eight thousand and three
hundred and seventy-nine dollars, and the total amount
paid through the Clearing House Association of New
York City during the year 1892 was thirty-six billion,
six hundred and sixty-two million, four hundred and
sixty-nine thousand and two hundred and one dollars.
These enormous sums indicate, to some extent, the
wonderful credit system in use in modern banking,
which invention has rendered invaluable service to the
advancement of trade and commerce throughout the
world. It is exceedingly difficult to explain, in a short
lecture, how important this business of dealing in
credit is to society. Credit is that intangible something which man creates and which he can destroy. It
enables trade and commerce to penetrate to the utter-
most parts of the earth. It permits the merchant to
multiply his transactions; it gives the manufacturer
means to employ almost unlimited labor; it arranges
for the mining of the precious metals; it enables the
nations to carry on war and assists them in the maintenance of peace. The bulk of the business of the
world is done by the use of credit, and the additional
facilities given to it by the great clearing house associations of the world, by the safe and proper conduct
of the great banks, add to the intelligence, wealth, comfort, and happiness of the human race.

It may not be inappropriate to consider briefly some
of the qualifications necessary to success in banking.

A student intending to become a banker should study political economy and should become familiar with the resources of the country, State, city, or town in which he conducts his business. He must be acquainted with the general conditions of trade and commerce in his neighborhood. He should study carefully the history of banking, and inform himself regarding those disturbances to credit which are often referred to as panics, and which periodically, during the present century, have interfered with the regular conduct of business and disturbed and destroyed credit. The student should be well versed in the National Bank Act, the law of the several States under which banking is conducted, and would do well to familiarize himself with commercial law. The banker must be able to analyze balance sheets of corporations and individuals, and be competent to determine from statements taken from the books of merchants, manufacturers, etc., whether or not their business is properly conducted and whether they are entitled to credit. He should have a general and technical knowledge of accounts, and a comprehensive knowledge of all forms of promissory notes and bills of exchange in all their varieties. He should be acquainted with coined money and paper currency, and familiar generally with business usages. In addition to integrity and general ability, a bank officer must be accurate, prompt, painstaking, and must be able to economize time and concentrate his mind upon the duties of the moment. A bank officer occupies a most responsible position. He is to all intents and purposes a trustee, having in charge other people's money. Their credit and the business prospects of an entire community frequently rest upon the sagacity and business capacity of bankers.

While it is not possible to recite the history of banking in the United States at this time, I will refer briefly to some of the first chartered banking institutions of this country and to the origin and growth of the National banking system, together with certain facts connected with National bank-notes and paper currency issued by the General Government.

The first bank organized in the United States had its origin in a meeting of the citizens of Philadelphia, the intention being to collect a fund by subscription to assist the Government in supplying the army with the common necessaries of life.

In 1781 Robert Morris, then holding the office of Superintendent of Finance under Congress, arranged to grant it a charter as the Bank of North America, and afterward it was granted a perpetual charter by the legislature of Pennyslvania, and became a State banking institution.

On December 13th, 1890, Alexander Hamilton, then Secretary of the Treasury, proposed the organization of the first Bank of the United States. The charter of this bank expired by limitation in 1811 and Congress declined to permit an extension.

On April 10th, 1816, the second Bank of the United States was chartered, and in 1832 President Jackson vetoed the bill for the re-chartering of the bank, and in 1833 the public deposits were withdrawn from it and the bank was compelled to discontinue business.

The legislature of Massachusetts was the next, after Pennsylvania, to grant bank charters, and five banks were organized in that State between 1772 and 1800.

The Bank of New York was organized in this State in 1791. The first bank organized in Ohio was chartered in 1803, and the first bank established under the territorial government of Illinois was in 1813.

Early in the present century, in nearly all of the States, bank charters were granted and joint stock

banks, under State authority, were favorite organizations for conducting the banking business, and, as heretofore stated, joint stock banks chartered by the various
States are still doing their share of the business of this
country, but since the passage of the National Bank
Act, which imposed a tax of 10 per cent on State bank-
notes, they do not emit a circulating medium. After
the failure of the second Bank of the United States, no
banks were chartered by the General Government until
the passage of the National Bank Act, which was approved by the President on February 25th, 1863. The
National banking system was not advocated or commenced in the interest of any political party, and during the thirty years of its existence it has been free
from political control or sectional influence, and since
1875 it has substantially been a free bank act—*i.e.*, any
group of reputable citizens desiring to organize a
National bank in any part of the United States, under
the provisions and restrictions of the Act, can obtain a
charter through the Comptroller of the Currency upon
paying in the proper amount of capital and fulfilling
the requirements of the statutes.

There are in existence at the present time 3,798
National banks with a capital of \$683,748,120, and
although the number of banks operating under general
laws or special charters of the various States is somewhat greater than the National banks (there being in
existence at the present time 3,963 State institutions
engaged in the banking business), the superiority of
the National system is, in many respects, unquestioned,
although banks organized under the statutes of many
of the States stand deservedly high in the estimation of
our people. It is generally conceded that the excellence of the National banking system is largely due to
its being conducted under the direction and supervision

of the General Government, and even if the privilege of issuing bank-notes should be hereafter denied to them, National banks will undoubtedly continue to exist and be organized as banks of deposit and discount.

The continued growth of the system demonstrates that they are no longer organized for the purpose of issuing circulating notes; but in order to obtain the credit of institutions organized under the laws of the General Government National banks are compelled, under the bank act, to report to the Comptroller of the Currency five times each year (for some day antedating the call) respecting the condition of their affairs, and to submit, in addition to balance sheet, full schedules describing carefully their assets and giving memoranda of all large advances and the security therefor. The principal items in the reports are published in the local papers, and the National banks are examined by an accountant appointed by the Comptroller of the Currency, at least once annually, and full memoranda as to the condition of the bank and statements concerning its affairs are forwarded to Washington and there kept on file. The Comptroller of the Currency is authorized, under the law, to enforce the various statutes, and a most careful supervision is exercised over all institutions. The system has furnished for many years a most excellent paper currency, secured by deposit of Government bonds with the Treasurer of the United States, and bank-notes reissued under such careful provision of law that the general public scarcely realize that they are simply promises to pay and not actual money.

National bank-notes are redeemable in legal-tender notes, which in turn are redeemable in coin. Bank-notes which circulate among the people as money should be issued under such stringent rules and regulations as to make it impossible for the holder to sustain loss. For obvious reasons, coin cannot be used as a basis for bank-note circulation. No profit would be made by a bank putting out circulation against coin, and this method would not provide additional currency as coin can at any time be used as money. Next to coin and bullion the debt of a sound government is considered the best basis for circulation, as government bonds can be readily converted and the bank-notes redeemed from their proceeds. The fundamental principle underlying bank-notes is their redemption when desired, and as National bank-notes are guaranteed by the Government itself, and are redeemable at the Treasury Department at Washington from funds provided by the banks, the Government having authority to sell the bonds deposited unless the redemption fund is constantly kept good, our National bank-notes have always been beyond question and have circulated as freely as if emitted by the Government itself, and no loss has occurred to any holder. The redemption of the debt of the United States, and the gradual reduction of interest thereon, have for some years reduced and restricted the issuance of circulation by National banks. Furthermore, under existing statutes banks are permitted to issue circulation only to the extent of 90 cents on a dollar of bonds deposited, and are compelled to pay a tax of one per cent per annum on circulation outstanding. Inasmuch as the least the Government can do is to redeem its securities at par, there would be no risk in permitting National banks to issue circulation to the par value of their bonds, and the present tax on circulation is excessive and frequently restricts new issues to a considerable extent.

It is necessary during certain periods of each year that large amounts of currency from various money centres should be distributed throughout the country in order to make advances on maturing crops and for other purposes. At other certain seasons the return flow of currency to the centres makes it possible for our business to be properly and safely conducted with a less volume of currency outstanding. For this and other reasons it is believed that bank-notes should form a large part of the circulation of our currency, on the theory that notes can be issued when needed and redeemed when they have performed their function. The direct issues of paper money by the Government are immediately paid out after their redemption and therefore do not furnish a flexible currency for the use of the people.

Our enormous agricultural, manufacturing, and commercial interests employ the great majority of our people, and during the past we have needed an annually increasing amount of money to properly transact our business and conduct their enterprises; and as the Government itself has now discontinued the coinage of silver and issue of paper money, it is believed by many that some provision should be made for bank-note issues to be used by our people as occasion may require.

Recently some discussion has arisen as to whether or not the prohibitory tax of 10 per cent imposed on State bank notes should not be repealed in order that bank-notes may again be issued by banks organized under the laws of the various States. In my opinion such a course would not be wise under existing conditions. It is true that the redemption of the debt of the United States, and the gradual reduction of interest thereon, and the tax imposed, have reduced and restricted the issuance of circulation by National banks. But from present indications, while the interest on the public debt is not liable to materially increase, the redemption and payment of the bonds now outstanding will be postponed and, very likely, the revenues of the Government may be somewhat curtailed, and it may be necessary for the United States to make a further issue of securities. At all events the bonds now in existence amount to a very considerable sum and would serve as a basis for National bank circulation for some time to come; and if banks were permitted to issue circulation to the par of their bonds, and the tax is somewhat reduced, our country would continue to be provided with a large amount of flexible currency in the shape of bank-notes, which would probably be sufficient in volume, in addition to the direct issues by the Government now outstanding, to meet our requirements for some time in future. And, in my opinion, bank-notes based upon Government bonds, issued under one general law, under the supervision of the National Government, furnish a much better circulating medium than any bank-notes which might be issued under the laws of the various States, no matter how well the latter might be secured. Under existing circumstances National bank-notes circulate as freely as if emitted by the Government itself, and they are interchangeable at par at all times with coin and with paper issued directly by the Government. And I doubt whether bank-notes, issued under State charters, could be freely circulated at par with the paper currency now issued by the Government and with National bank-notes. Furthermore, an issue of State bank-notes would undoubtedly lead to differences of value in bills of domestic exchange throughout the country, and the mercantile community would experience trouble and expense in making collections and remitting funds from point to point. Under existing conditions the cost of what is termed exchange—*i.e.*, compensation for making payments at distant points— is almost entirely eliminated in the United States, and many business men of the present day do not fully appreciate the difficulties experienced in making collections and doing business between distant points during the time when State bank-notes were freely used.

The issuing of currency by the Government has been criticised on the theory that it is a dangerous prerogative and that no legislation can provide for a Government issue of money which will be flexible enough for business requirements. It is well known that the issue of paper currency was begun by our Government soon after the commencement of our Civil War. In 1862–63 Congress authorized an issue of $450,000,000 of legal-tender notes, which substantially amounted to a forced loan upon the people. These notes were used by the Government to carry on the war, and over $449,000,000 of them were outstanding on the third day of February, 1864. They were gradually retired until May 31st, 1878, when there remained outstanding of the original issue $346,681,016, and this is the amount of the original legal-tender notes now outstanding, the validity of their use as money having in the mean time been sustained by a decision of the United States Supreme Court. The Government has, for the convenience of the people, provided for the issue of other paper currency. We have in circulation gold certificates, silver certificates, and Treasury notes. Gold certificates represent gold coin deposited with the Treasurer of the United States, which is held in trust for the holder of the certificate. They are substantially a warehouse receipt for gold coin, which is not in any way considered an asset of the Government, and is available at all times for redemption of certificates represented by it. Similar certificates are issued for silver dollars, coined under the act of 1878, the dollars being held for the redemption of certificates in precisely the same manner as gold coin. Under existing statutes the United States is conducting its business on a gold basis. The unit or standard of value in this country is the gold dollar 25.8 grains in weight and possessing a fineness of nine-tenths; but we have in use in the United States a large amount of legal-tender silver money, consisting of dollars 412.5 grains in weight and nine-tenths fine. Our people are not inconvenienced by the bulkiness of silver coin, as these dollars are in use principally through silver certificates heretofore mentioned. It is estimated by the Director of the Mint that we have in use in this country, including the coin and bullion held by the Treasury, upward of six hundred million dollars in gold. We have coined under the act of 1878 four hundred and twenty millions of silver dollars which form a part of our currency system, and are either in use as coin or by their representatives. We have also issued upward of 153 million dollars of Treasury notes, based on silver under the act of 1890. The 573 million dollars of circulation based on silver, and the 346 million dollars of legal-tender notes heretofore mentioned, which are in use by our people, are all maintained on a gold basis and interchangeable at par, in spite of the fact that the gold value of silver during the past twenty years has fallen enormously. The question as to whether or not the United States should continue to use large amounts of silver currency has been discussed in Congress for the past fifteen years, and the matter became so serious in the opinion of many persons high in authority that the President of the United States called a special session of Congress for August 7th last, which has now resulted in the repeal of the Silver Purchase Act, and as the subject is still of vital interest, its consideration naturally becomes a part of this address.

It is not my intention to rehearse the history of the fall in the gold value of silver during the past twenty years further than to say that, starting with the demonetization of silver by Germany, growing out of the legislation of 1871–73, the mints of Europe have been closed, one after another, against silver coinage until at this time not a silver coin of full debt-paying power is struck on the Continent of Europe. For nearly a century prior to 1875 the relative value of silver to gold in purchasing power in the commerce of the world remained practically constant at about fifteen and one half to one. During this period the mints of most of the countries of Europe were open to the free mintage of silver coin of full debt-paying power. Since 1873, in the brief period of twenty years and with the mints of Europe closed to the coinage of silver, its commercial value, as measured by gold, has depreciated over forty-five per cent in spite of the efforts of the United States, acting in monetary isolation among the great commercial nations, to use silver as a money metal. The action of the Latin Union in 1876 in discontinuing silver coinage broke the link between gold and silver, which had apparently kept the price of the former, as measured by the latter, constant at about the legal ratio, and when this link was broken the silver market was opened to the influences of all the factors which go to affect the price of a commodity. The Government of the United States, with its natural and accumulated wealth, with its large stock of gold and with its rich mines of gold and silver, has used every effort to increase the use of silver throughout the world, but of late years has found no responsive voice in Europe to its appeal for its enlarged use as money. And as the principal nations of Europe apparently distrust silver as currency and have made gold their sole legal-tender money, the United States, believing it impossible to alone fix and maintain a ratio between gold and silver for all the world, has gone out of the market as purchaser of silver for currency purposes and closed its mints to silver coinage, and hereafter proposes to use the white metal for subsidiary coinage only, and it is impossible to predict what will be the future of silver as a money metal. It seems clear that unless some agreement can be had with the other principal nations gold monometallism will prevail, and while there may be a difference of opinion among our people on this question, I believe that the action which has recently been taken by our Government was the only wise course to pursue under the circumstances.

During the last quarter of a century careful and persistent researches have been made as to the functions of metallic money, and international conferences and monetary commissions composed of the most learned and distinguished men in monetary science throughout the world have met and discussed statistics of trade and the precious metals. Unquestionably the intelligent, painstaking, and exhaustive inquiries which have been made by the various conferences and commissions, and by well-known monetary authorities and experts, have been of great service in increasing the knowledge of the people of the world as to the use of metallic money and as to the relations of gold and silver. Unfortunately, however, the labors of conferences and the researches of individuals have not been successful in accomplishing any practical results so far as the use of gold and silver as money on a common international basis is concerned; and as the principal nations insist upon a single gold standard, the United States cannot afford to inject into its currency system a sufficient amount of silver money to hazard in any way its gold standard, or to have any question about the payment of all, or any part, of our international balances in gold when desired.

There is no nation in the world whose people are so favored as ours. Our country, which extends from the Atlantic to the Pacific ocean, from the Gulf of Mexico to the frozen sea, has a population of over sixty-five millions of intelligent and industrious citizens, who live under one form of general government, who speak a common language and have a common unit and standard of value, and a banking and currency system so perfect that all of our money is interchangeable at par and can be transmitted from ocean to ocean by telegraph at only a nominal charge. When we compare the complex monetary systems of Europe with our own, we cannot fail to be convinced that we are the most enlightened, progressive, and prosperous people in our banking and currency matters as well as in all other pursuits. •

24

FRANCIS V. GREENE.

Francis V. Greene was born in Providence, R. I., June 27,
1850. He was educated at the United States Military Academy at
West Point, graduating first in a class of fifty-eight members, in
June, 1870. His first service was in the Artillery, but in 1872 he
was transferred to the Corps of Engineers. During the next four
years he was employed as assistant astronomer and surveyor
with the joint commission for the survey and demarcation of the
boundary line between the United States and British possessions
from the Lake of the Woods to the Rocky Mountains. In 1876 he
was assigned to special duty in the office of the Secretary of War
in Washington, and in June, 1877, was sent abroad by the Government to witness and report upon the military operations during
the war between Russia and Turkey, being assigned for this purpose as military attaché to the United States Legation at St.
Petersburg. He accompanied the army in the field, and was
present at all the principal battles of the war, reaching Constanti-
nople with the advance guard in February, 1878. He returned to
St. Petersburg in July, 1878, and after collecting data for his
report returned to the United States in January, 1879. His report,
entitled "The Russian Army and its Campaigns in Turkey,
1877-78," was published in two volumes in April, 1879, and was
reprinted in England, and extracts from it translated in Germany,
France, and Russia. In 1879 he was assigned to duty as assistant to the Engineer Commissioner in Washington, D. C., and for
the next six years had immediate charge of engineering work
upon the streets, roads, and bridges in Washington and the District of Columbia. In July, 1885, he was assigned to duty as
Instructor of Practical Military Engineering at West Point. In
January, 1886, he resigned from the army and became vice-
president and subsequently president of the Barber Asphalt
Paving Company, which latter position he now holds. This company is the largest paving company in the world, and has made
a specialty of asphalt pavements during the last sixteen years.
It has branch offices in all the principal cities of the United States,

and has laid pavements to the extent of more than eight million square yards, or about five hundred miles in length, in more than forty different cities in the United States.

He entered the National Guard as major and engineer of the First Brigade, State of New York, in November, 1889, and in February, 1892, was elected colonel of the 71st Regiment, which position he now holds. This regiment is quartered at the new armory at Park Avenue and Thirty-fourth Street.

In addition to the history of the Russian campaign above noted, he is the author of "Army Life in Russia," "The Mississippi" (campaigns of the Civil War), and of a biography of Nathanael Greene ("Great Commanders" series). He has also contributed to magazines from time to time numerous articles upon military and historical subjects.

ROADS.

By Francis V. Greene.

Mr. President, Ladies and Gentlemen:—My predecessors in this course of lectures have not only been men of distinction compared with whom I am unknown, but they have also spoken to you on very distinguished subjects. You have heard about diplomacy from the Ambassador to Great Britain; about journalism from the foremost editor of the day; about wealth from one of the most successful accumulators of that desirable article, and you have heard from others especially qualified to speak about other subjects which appeal to the imagination. Compared with these, the subject of roads is essentially commonplace, a part of the every-day routine of the struggle for existence, and yet it is true that roads and civilization go hand in hand, each mutually dependent on the other, and each in turn cause and effect of the other. The transition from the nomadic, pastoral, semi-barbarous manner of life to a commercial, trading, militant organized civilization is marked by the construction of roads. Considering roads in the broadest sense as means of communication and transport on land, and thus including railroads, common roads, and city streets, it is true now, as it has been for 3,000 years, that the degree of civilization to which any people have obtained is accurately measured and indicated by the condition of their roads. The history of Rome, of India, and Peru amply attest the accuracy of this statement. But roads belong to the material side of civilization; they form part of the broad and solid foundation upon which the structure is reared, and of which literature, philosophy, science, and the arts are the domes and pinnacles.

Of this essentially prosaic subject I am to speak to-day in the effort to show you on the one hand what relation roads bear to civilization and the prosperity and comfort of mankind, and on the other hand how they should be constructed and maintained.

At the outset you will naturally ask how it is, if roads are so intimately connected with civilization, that the United States, which claim to be among the most civilized nations in the world, should confessedly have roads so bad that they are justly described as intolerable. But the answer is not far to seek. The United States have the largest and best roads in the world. But they are in the form of railroads. And the construction of these railroads has absorbed so much energy and capital that there has not until now been time to construct good common roads, nor has the necessity for them been evident.

It is well to glance briefly at the origin and development of this magnificent system of railroads. When the Colonies, from which the United States have grown, were first settled, they occupied a narrow strip along the Atlantic seacoast, and such settlements as were made in the interior were made on the banks of navigable rivers. Such commerce as they had, not only with Europe, but among themselves, was carried on by means of vessels. This condition continued down to the Revolution, and for nearly a generation after it. When during the first third of this century the population began to spread westward, the necessity for good roads became manifest, and during the time of Monroe, Clay, and Calhoun the question of internal improvements was one of the burning questions of national politics; those who believed in a liberal construction of the constitution being favorable to the construction of roads by the general Government, and those who insisted on a strict construction of the constitution denying the power of the general Government to spend money for any such purpose. It was finally decided that the general Government should undertake the construction of a national road, which, following up the Valley of the Potomac, should cross the Alleghanies, descend to the Ohio at Wheeling, and then go on to St. Louis. This work was begun in 1806, but it was carried on very slowly, and before much of it had been finished steam railroads were introduced, and it was seen at once that they would be immensely superior to the old form of road. The construction of the national road was therefore abandoned and private capital undertook the construction of steam railroads; and for sixty years this has continued, until now the United States have nearly 180,000 miles of line, and more than 50,000 miles more of second track and sidings. In this work the best talent both in a mechanical and administrative capacity has been employed for the last two generations. The result is that, while the United States have but one-twentieth of the population of the world, they have more than one-half of its railroads; they have but one-fifth of the population of Europe, but they have one and a half times as many railroads. These railroads are in a large measure the source of its rapid growth in wealth, for they have penetrated wherever the population has penetrated, and often in advance of it, thus affording facilities for communication and for commerce such as are possessed by no other country in the world. The capital invested in them is counted by the thousands of millions of dollars and their employees by the hundreds of thousands. The task has been so prodigious that the amount of either capital or thought that could be devoted to the construction of other forms of communication has been comparatively small.

It is evident, however, that there must be a limit to the building of railroads, and it would seem as if that limit had been practically reached in certain parts of the country. It is impossible to have a railroad leading to every farm, although this condition is closely approximated in New Jersey, where it is said that there is no point in the State which is more than seven miles from a railroad. In the older and more settled portions of the country the railroads are so numerous and the rates are so low that they yield but a small return on the capital invested, and the construction of new railroads has ceased to be an attractive field for investment. The rates of freight have been steadily reduced year by year until they are now barely one-fourth of what they were thirty years ago. Still the transportation problem cannot be considered as satisfactorily solved if it costs as much to carry a ton of wheat or potatoes to the railway station as it does to carry it 400 miles over the railroad. So that with the practical completion of the railway system in a large section of the country an agitation has sprung up in favor of the improvement of the common roads. These are needed for a double purpose: first, the purposes of commerce to serve as feeders to and distributors from the railroads; second, for the purpose of health and pleasure, for the use of bicycles and pleasure carriages. As already stated, the common roads have been comparatively neglected during the construction of the railroads. Still we have an enormous number of roads—for the most part, in bad order. In New York there are

8,110 miles of railroad and about 80,000 miles of common road; in Massachusetts 2,121 miles of railroad and 17,145 of common road; in New Jersey 2,176 miles of railroad and about 18,000 miles of common road. Statistics for all the States are not available, but if the ratio were the same in them as in the three States named the total length of roads in the United States would be about 1,800,000 miles. It is probably not so great as this. Gen. Roy Stone estimates it at something over 1,300,000 miles. These roads have grown up regardless of system or method, and for the most part have been built without reference to engineering prin, ciples. As the country was settled, rude tracks were laid out connecting neighboring villages, and these in turn were united to form highways between towns and villages. The method of constructing and maintaining them was by the "labor tax," in which each taxpayer was required to furnish a certain number of days' labor in the spring for the purpose of digging up the ditches and throwing their contents into the middle of the road. Their condition was so bad that about fifty years ago private capital was invoked for the purpose of improving the more important roads, and charters were given in many States for "turnpike companies," which were authorized to collect toll from every passing vehicle, animal, and man, and in return were required to keep the road in order. The system was never a success; the farmers considered the tax unjust, the roads were not kept in proper order, and many of the companies lost money. Some surrendered their charters and others were bought out by the State or county. The old system of the "labor tax" was then restored, or in lieu of it a money tax was levied. Until within the last few years this system was universally followed, each county taking care of its own roads, and by means of a road tax in the form of either labor or money. The State exercised no supervision, and skilled engineers, as a rule, were never employed. In Massachusetts the road expenditures, outside of cities, in 1893, were $1,156,944, or $66.30 per mile; in New Jersey, $778,470.82, or $43.24 per mile; in New York, about $2,500,000, or about $30 per mile. If the average expenditure in other States was only $18 per mile, the total for the entire country would be about $20,000,000. It is not too much to say that the greater part of this sum produced no useful result, and was wholly wasted.

The bad condition of the roads began to attract widespread attention something over ten years ago. Certain elementary principles were evident at a glance, to wit: the price of farm products is fixed at the great cities or centres of consumption and distribution, and is wholly beyond the farmer's control, and the cost of transportation is a principal factor in determining his profit, or the possibility of any profit. On the railroads this has been reduced until it varies, according to bulk, from one cent to four mills per ton per mile. But the average roads are so bad that a two-horse team and wagon, the value of which is $3 per day, cannot haul a ton of produce more than ten miles and return in a day. The cost of road transportation is therefore 30 cents per ton per mile, or about forty times as great as the rate on the railroad. The average distance from the farm to the nearest railway station is at least ten miles, so that it costs as much to get the goods to or from the railroad station as to carry them 400 miles on the cars. It only needs to state these elementary facts to show what an enormous drain bad roads make on our resources. It is evident that an improvement in these conditions is imperative, and the remedy is equally evident, for it has been proved not only by mechanical experiment but by actual test that the same force which draws one ton on a muddy earth road will draw four tons on a hard macadam road. On the improved roads in New Jersey loads of four to five tons are habitually drawn by a two-horse team. This effects a saving of fully three-fourths of the cost of hauling to the station, and reduces the cost of road transportation from thirty cents to seven and one-half cents per ton per mile. What this saving amounts to may be imagined when it is known that the New York Central Railroad alone carries nearly 20,000,000 tons of way freight in a year. If this is hauled only two miles by road to or from the station, and a saving of twenty-two and one-half cents per ton per mile could be effected, it would mean a total saving of nearly $9,000,000. These figures may seem exaggerated, but they will no longer appear so when we realize the saving actually accomplished by the reduction in railroad rates in the last twenty-five years. For instance, in 1869 the average freight rate on the New York Central Railroad was two and four-tenths cents per ton mile; in 1893 it was seven mills. This saving, on the business of 1893, is upward of $64,000,-000. This is the result which has been accomplished by the application to the railroad problem of the highest available talent. During these same twenty-five years little or no attention has been given to the road problem. The roads are as bad now as they were in 1869, and the cost of transportation over them is as great now as it was then. In the next twenty-five years the results accomplished on the common roads are likely to be as remarkable as those achieved on the railroads in the last twenty-five years.

So much for the dollars and cents side of the road-improvement question. But there is another and hardly less important side, and that is the use of the roads for health and pleasure; and this appeals not so much to the farmer as to the inhabitants of cities. At the ·beginning of this century three per cent of the population lived in cities of 8,000 inhabitants or upwards, and there were six such cities; in 1890 there were 448 such cities, and about thirty per c ent of the entire population lived in them. In New York about sixty per cent of the population lives in cities and in Massachusetts 69 per cent. In proportion as the urban population grows, and possibly in still greater proportion, the number increases of those who desire to escape to the country for pleasure during a part of the year. And nearly all country pleasures, sports, and amusements are dependent in a greater or less degree on the condition of the roads. The driving element, not only in the more expensive form of coaching, but also in the plain American buggy and "carry-all," is constantly increasing. But the most extraordinary increase, among those who find pleasure on the road, is in the number of cyclists, or wheelmen—and lately wheelwomen. Colonel Pope, who is one of the pioneers in the manufacture of this machine and at the same time a most ardent and effective advocate of good roads, estimates the number of bicycles made last year (1894) at 350,000, and the number that will be in use this season at 1,000,000. Every one of these wheelmen is a preacher, in season and out of season, of the gospel of good roads; and they are not scattered and disunited like the farmers, but they live in cities, are thoroughly organized, have their clubs and leagues, support a monthly magazine with a circulation of 100,000 copies, devoted to good roads and called by that name, have a chief consul at their head, make their wishes known with no uncertain sound in legislative halls, and at the polls are disposed to consider all political issues secondary in importance to that of road improvement. Their influence in the agitation for good roads has been of the highest value, and it is quite probable that they will be more potent in framing road legislation than any other class. A machine which enables a man to travel with pleasure, without discomfort, and practically without expense, forty miles in a day, is evidently one which "has come to stay," and the numbers of wheelmen are likely to reach extraordinary proportions in the next few years. And, as already stated, every one of them is a preacher of road improvement.

The agitation for good roads thus rests on two distinct bases, business, or economy in transportation, and pleasure. It has been in progress with ever-increasing volume for more than ten years. During that time, as General Stone has shown, "sixteen States have passed new road laws, more or less radical in their nature, and one has amended its constitution to permit the adoption of such laws. Many hundreds of miles of good roads have already been built, in localities widely separated, under varying conditions and through various methods of administration, finance, and construction." It has also been proposed to have roads built by the Federal Government, but this idea has met with little encouragement. Out of it, however, has grown a law, passed by Congress in 1893, providing for a bureau in the Department of Agriculture to collect information in regard to road improvement in the different States, and to disseminate this by means of publications. The bureau consists simply of a Special Agent, Gen. Roy Stone, in charge, and his clerks; but the information which it has obtained and published is of great value. His inquiries have been confined to, first, the legislation passed or proposed in the different States; second, the methods and cost of construction in different localities; third, the existence of suitable road materials in different parts of the country, and the rates at which railroads are willing to transport them. The bureau has now published ten bulletins in pamphlet form, like those issued by the Census Bureau, and they contain information of great value which is not elsewhere accessible.

The general trend of the legislation enacted in the sixteen States before referred to is to provide that the road tax shall be paid in money and not in labor, to authorize the county supervisors, under certain conditions to assume entire charge of the roads, and to issue county bonds for their improvement. But to this rule there have been important exceptions. In Pennsylvania an act is pending which requires the State to pay $1,000,000 per annum, this sum to be divided among the counties in proportion to the road tax paid in each. In Massachusetts a State Highway Commission has been appointed, which has already collected a mass of important statistics, a knowledge of which is necessary to a proper study of the problem. This commission is authorized, under certain conditions, to assume control of any particular highway, designate it as a State road, and improve and maintain it at the expense of the State, subject to appropriations made by the Legislature. In New York two measures have been proposed and have passed one branch of the Legislature, but failed to become laws. One contemplated the construction of State highways connecting the adjacent county seats, to be paid for by the State at an estimated cost of $10,000,000. The other provided for the construction or improvement of roads under the supervision of State and county officials, one-third of the cost to be paid by the State, one-third by the county, and one-third to be assessed upon the adjacent property. But the State in which the most novel legislation has actually been enacted and in which the most important practical results have been obtained is New Jersey; and it is worth while to examine these laws and the effect of them somewhat in detail. The first law, passed in 1888 and enlarged in 1891, abolished the road overseers, gave the township committee full control over the roads in the township, authorized them to levy taxes and borrow money for road improvement, and required all road taxes to be paid in money. The second law, passed in 1889 and amended in 1891, authorized the county freeholders, on a vote of a majority of the voters in the county, to assume exclusive control of any road in the county, to levy taxes and borrow money for its improvement, and to assess one-third of the cost on the cities or townships in the county and the remaining two-thirds on the county at large. The act further provided for letting the work by contract on definite plans and specifications, and under the supervision of a competent engineer. Under these laws Essex County, "though only twelve miles square, has built more than 200 miles of fine telford and macadam roads; . . . Union County has borrowed $455,000 at four per cent on five-twenty bonds and covered the county with a complete system of telford and macadam roads; . . . and Passaic County, adjoining Essex and Union, has built during the past four years about sixty-five miles of macadam roads." Moreover, and most important, "with the interest of the bonds added to the annual tax levy, the rate of taxation is lower than before the building of the roads," and the value of the property along the roads has increased from thirty to fifty per cent.

These quotations are from the annual report of Edward Burroughs, State Commissioner of Public Roads.

The third and most radical of the laws is what is known as the "State Aid Law," passed in 1891. It provides that on petition of the owners of two-thirds of the lands bordering on any public road not less than one mile in length, praying that the road may be improved and agreeing to pay one-tenth of the cost, the County Freeholders shall improve the road, and one-tenth of the cost shall be paid by the abutting property, one-third by the State, and the balance (56⅔ per cent) by the county. The State is limited to an expenditure of $75,000 in any one year for its share of such improvements, and the county to one-half of one per cent of its assessed valuation. Under this law ten miles of road were built in 1892, twenty-five miles in 1893, over sixty miles in 1894, and still a larger amount is projected for 1895, the applications being in excess of the limit named in the law. At first the cost was about $6,000 per mile; but by reducing the width of the metalled part of the road, and by a large reduction in the price of material, the cost has been reduced to $3,000 per mile. At this rate the law makes possible an expenditure of $225,000 a year, which will build seventy-five miles of road.

These laws appear to afford a satisfactory solution of the problem. They provide the machinery for improving the roads in any one of three methods, at the expense of the township, at the expense of the county, or a division of the expense in certain proportions between the State, the county, and the abutting property; and the decision as to the methods is determined by the votes of those most interested. These laws have produced more definite results than those in all the remaining fifteen States combined, and they have made the roads in New Jersey famous throughout the land. They are popular with all classes of the people in that State, and they are worthy of careful consideration by the legislators of other States. In States like New York and Massachusetts, where two-thirds of the population and three-fourths of the assessed valuation of property is in the cities, the provision for State aid enables and requires the cities to pay a share of the cost, and this is manifestly proper, since they share largely in the benefits.

The cost to the farmer, who derives the greatest benefit, is reduced to a bagatelle; General Stone states that in New Jersey the annual road tax is about ten cents per acre and the assessment about four cents additional. In spite of this small cost, it is a remarkable fact that the road laws in New York, providing for improvement at the cost of the State, under which three-fourths of the expense would fall upon the cities, have been defeated by the representatives of the farmers. Possibly when the matter is more fully understood the result will be different.

And now in regard to the construction of roads. All historical accounts of roads begin with the famous Roman roads. Wherever the Roman armies penetrated, in Africa, in Thrace, in Spain, in Gaul and even in Britain, they spent a considerable part of their time in building solid roads, and many of them are to be seen to this day. In France hundreds of miles of them serve as the foundations of the existing roads of that country. The Roman roads were about three feet thick and consisted of four layers: first, a layer of large stones laid dry; second, a layer of rubble masonry or coarse concrete; third, a layer of fine concrete; fourth, a layer of dressed stone or paving-blocks. These roads were solid and durable, and their lines were well laid

25

out, but in no other respect were they good. They
were at least three times too thick, involving a useless
expenditure of labor and material, which is the most
unpardonable fault in engineering constructions. And
they were intolerably rough, especially as the Romans
had no springs on their vehicles. During the Middle
Ages the roads were everywhere neglected. The art of
road-building was first revived in France in the seventeenth century, and in the eighteenth century it made
great progress under a celebrated engineer named
Trésaguet, who anticipated by two generations the
method of Telford. An enormous amount of road-
building or rebuilding was done under Napoleon during the Consulate and the Empire, and the admirable
system of French roads, which are generally considered
the finest in the world, was then substantially completed. For the last eighty years the efforts of the
French engineers of the Ponts et Chaussées have been
devoted to the maintenance of existing roads rather
than the construction of new ones. To this subject of
maintenance the best engineers in France have devoted their thought and study; they have written numbers of text-books and memoirs on the subject, and they
have brought the art to the highest point of perfection.
In England the roads remained in a horrible condition
until the early part of this century, when they were
nearly all rebuilt by Telford and Macadam. Telford
was an educated engineer and architect, who in addition to roads built houses, docks, canals, and famous
bridges like that over the Menai Straits. He was engaged in reconstructing the roads of Scotland, England, and Wales, at various times from 1803 to his
death in 1834. Macadam was a comparatively uneducated roadmaster, and nothing else. He was appointed
superintendent of the roads in the Bristol district in

1816, and between that date and his death in 1836 he rebuilt over 20,000 miles of roads in various parts of Great Britain.

I do not deem it necessary to go into details in regard to the roads of Telford and Macadam, for the reason that equally good roads have recently been built in America, of which I shall speak later on. Both built their roads of broken stone and drained them thoroughly. Telford used a foundation of larger stones placed in position like a rough stone pavement, and he used fine material to bind the surface. MacAdam discarded the foundation or "pitching," rejected the use of binding material, and insisted on having the road compacted and its smooth surface formed by the action of the vehicles after the road was opened to traffic—a painful and tedious process.

The subject of the construction of roads is a very large one. It has occupied the attention of engineers for several generations, and a great number of books have been written in regard to it. There is also a great variety in the forms of construction, depending upon the traffic to be carried, the nature of the country over which the road is to pass, the road materials available, and the amount of money which can be used for construction. It is impossible in a brief discussion like this to go into the matter at all in detail, and I do not think I can do better than to describe the construction of some roads recently built in America under what may be called average conditions. I have already spoken of the roads which have been built under the recent road legislation in New Jersey. Those of Union County are particularly good, and I will briefly describe their construction.

Union County lies about twenty-five miles southwest of New York, contains about one hundred square miles,

and its population in 1890 was 72,467. Its main roads are
thirty-five miles in length. Before their improvement
was undertaken in 1890 most of them were mere mud-
tracks. On the passage of the legislation enabling
the county to borrow money on its bonds for their improvement, a competent engineer, Mr. F. A. Dunham,
was appointed to take charge of the work. He immediately made a survey of all the roads for the purpose of determining the gradients and the data necessary for preparing proper plans and specifications·
When these were completed the work was advertised
and let by contract to the lowest responsible bidder.
The prices for grading were **from** twenty-three to
forty cents per cubic yard; for telford pavement from
eighty cents to one dollar and twelve cents per square
yard. There was also a certain amount of work to be
done in the way of drainage, culverts, bridges, etc.
The width of the roads varied, according to the locality
and the traffic, but the average width was forty-four
feet, with a crown or rise in the centre of twelve inches.
Of this width, ten feet had a telford foundation, fourteen feet had macadam metal, and two wings, ten feet
width, on each side were of earth. The road was first
graded to its approximate form and then the space of
ten feet in the middle was excavated to a depth of
twelve inches. This was then thoroughly rolled in
order to compact the earth on which the stone portion
of the road was to be built. Next the telford was laid.
This consisted of irregular pieces of trap-rock about
eight by twelve inches on the under side, four by six
inches on the upper side, and eight inches in height.
These were placed by hand as closely together as possible, and the spaces in the surface were filled in with
spalls and smaller pieces of stone, which were wedged
into the openings as tightly as possible. A small

amount of fine trap screenings was then spread over the telford for binding, and it was then thoroughly rolled. The macadam was placed over this in two layers, each of which was two inches thick, the first layer consisting of stone broken to two inches in size, and the second of stone broken to one and a half inches in size. Each layer was finished with a small amount of fine binding material and then thoroughly rolled with a ten-ton roller, the surface being kept constantly wet by a sprinkling-cart while the rolling was in progress. After the stone road in the middle was completed the earth roads on the side were rolled, and the road was finished.

These roads have given great satisfaction to all the residents in the county; they have been in use for several years with very slight repairs and are still in excellent condition. They can be maintained so, with proper care and at small cost, for a long period. When the upper courses of macadam stone are worn out it will be necessary to resurface them with fresh layers of broken stone, and the road will then be in good condition for another term of years.

The cost of these roads was a little more than $8,700 per mile, and they may be taken as a type of the most expensive roads that it is necessary to construct anywhere outside of the boundaries of cities and towns.

In the southern part of New Jersey the roads have been constructed on a much smaller scale, the width of the road being about twenty feet and the metal portion only eight feet; the telford foundation has been omitted, and the thickness of the macadam reduced to eight inches. The cost of these roads has been about $3,000 per mile.

In New York some excellent roads have been built in the vicinity of Canandaigua, where the town bought a stone-crusher and steam roller. They built "macadam roads consisting of a crushed-stone roadbed about eight feet wide and nearly a foot deep in the centre of a turnpike some twenty-five to thirty feet in width, sloping enough to shed the surface water, but not too steep to drive on any part of it, at an expense of $400 to $700 per mile, the smaller sum in cases where the stone had been contributed and drawn into piles by the neighboring farmers without expense to the town." The very low cost of these roads is due to the small cost of the stone; part of it was furnished free by the neighboring farmers, and all of it was obtained at a very low cost, not exceeding twenty to thirty-two cents per cubic yard.

While it is not possible to construct important highroads in the vicinities of large cities at any such price as this, yet it is possible to duplicate this work on ordinary country roads wherever the farmers are willing to co-operate. The plant necessary for the purpose consists of a portable stone-crusher and steam engine costing about $4,000, and a steam roller costing about $2,500, or a total expenditure of $6,500. These should be owned by the county, and can be moved to any part of it where the road building or repairing is in progress. The broken stone can in the great majority of cases, especially in the Middle and Eastern States, be obtained from the fields. The stone is an injury in the fields and a benefit on the roads; and all that is necessary is to collect it in the fields, haul it to the road, and deposit it in piles there. A large part of it is already broken to the proper size, at least for the lower course, and the rest of it can be run through the crusher at an expense of about twenty cents per cubic yard. The crusher can move along the road every night or twice per week, thus reducing the haul of the stone to and from the crusher to a minimum.

Long experience has shown that the only form of durable road is one made with crushed stone. There has been a difference of opinion among engineers as to the necessity for the telford foundation, but the generally accepted opinion now is that the telford should be used, and is worth more than it costs on roads of heavy traffic. On roads of light traffic, like those of Canandaigua, it can be omitted. The size of the stone can vary in the different courses, if anything is to be gained by it, the larger stone, say up to three or four inches in size, being placed in the lower third, stone of about two and a half inches in the middle third, and stone of one and a half inches in the upper third. A small amount of stone dust or screening is necessary for a finishing coat. On the other hand, if any great expense would be incurred by separating the stone into different sizes, this can be omitted and the entire road made with stone not exceeding two inches in size. The minimum thickness should be eight inches, and it should be laid in two layers, each of which should be thoroughly rolled by the heavy steam roller. Of the different kinds of stone the most durable is the trap-rock or basalt, such as is found in the Palisades of the Hudson; the next most durable is granite and gneiss, then "flints" or quartz, then limestone, and finally sandstone. There is great difference in the hardness of different varieties of limestone, and the softer varieties as well as the sandstones are almost worthless for road purposes. Shaley and laminated stones should not be used, and stone containing a large amount of mica is also very undesirable. Oyster-shells have been used in the construction of roads, but for the surface coat they are not suitable, as they quickly grind to powder. They can, however, be used to advantage in the lower courses. Gravel is also used, and it makes a road intermediate in durability between stone and earth. There is, however, a wide range in the quality of different gravels. Some of them contain pure quartz pebbles and sand, with a small amount of clay, all mixed in such proportions and of such size as to form a compact and very durable road when properly rolled down. There are some very remarkable beds of gravel of this character near Vicksburg and at other points in the lower Mississippi Valley. Other gravels consist of soft clay pebbles and a large proportion of clay, and roads made with these are very deficient in durability.

It is the practice on the Continent of Europe to carry the macadam from gutter to gutter; and, in fact, a great number of the highroads of France and Belgium are paved their entire width with heavy granite blocks. Such roads are durable, but otherwise undesirable. The practice is, however, universal in America, and it is a good one, to confine the stone or metalled portion of the road to a width varying from eight to sixteen feet in the centre, and to have wings or earth roads on each side from eight to fifteen feet each in width. This arrangement not only reduces the first cost, but it furnishes earth roads which are travelled by nearly every one in the summer on account of giving a softer material for the horses' feet. The wings are used not only for pleasure traffic, but in dry weather for hauling heavy loads. This use is beneficial to the earth wings, as it compacts and consolidates them, and thus affords a slope for the water to run off, and in addition it saves by so much the wear on the stone portion in the middle.

One of the most useful results accomplished by the Road Bureau in the Department of Agriculture is the collection of data in regard to road materials throughout the entire country. General Stone has carried on a correspondence with every important railroad in the country on this subject, and he has obtained answers from them which indicate not only a willingness but an active desire on the part of all the railroads to co-operate to the fullest extent in the improvement of the common roads. It is evidently to their interest to do so, because the common roads not only act as feeders to their own system, but in addition the bad roads cost them an enormous and unnecessary expense. Every one who travels over a railroad must marvel at the enormous numbers of empty freight cars which he sees standing idle as he enters and leaves each town. These cars are counted by the hundreds of thousands, and every one of them represents from three to five hundred dollars of capital, which lies idle during the greater part of the year. The principal reason for their lying idle is the bad condition of the roads. It is only during certain months that the farmers can haul their produce to the railway station, and then there is an enormous demand for cars, and all the cars for a short period are brought into use hauling a load one way and going back empty. After the rush is over the cars again lie idle for months. Now, if the roads were in such condition that the farmers could deliver their produce regularly throughout the year, probably one-third of the rolling-stock could be dispensed with, and the trains in a majority of cases would haul loads both ways instead of coming back empty. The information obtained by General Stone makes it possible not only to determine at just what points in each State suitable road material can be obtained, but it shows that the railroads are willing to transport this material at surprisingly low figures; some of them are willing to transport it free of cost, others at half usual rates, others at actual cost as nearly as it can be determined.

As the result of all his inquiries General Stone estimates that the average cost of moving broken stone by railroad would be about two mills per ton per mile; or, in other words, a cubic yard of broken stone, weighing 2,800 pounds, could be carried 100 miles for twenty-eight cents, or for the cost of moving it about one mile on an average road by wagon. There is hardly any State, even in the prairies of the West, where a stone quarry cannot be found within 200 miles by rail of any particular road to be improved, and the cost of fifty-six cents per cubic yard for transportation is by no means prohibitive. It would seem, therefore, as if broken stone suitable for road purposes could be brought within the financial resources of nearly every county in every State.

In some portions of the country there are tracts of sand, and no stone is available. Fairly good roads can be made in such cases by mixing clay with the sand, if clay is available, and then rolling it. Some interesting cases are cited in Wisconsin, where roads have been made by uniting shavings with sand.

In the prairie districts of Illinois and elsewhere fairly good roads have been made in the following manner: "The road is made by ploughing two furrows sixteen inches wide and about twelve inches deep under what are to be the wheel-tracks, turning the earth inward, and two more for ditches, also turned inward, which results in a slight raising of the roadbed, then filling the inner furrows with field stones or coarse gravel and finishing with a light coating of fine gravel."

Where the road runs through wet soils or springy places it must be thoroughly drained, or all work upon it will be thrown away. These drains can be made by excavating a trench about fifteen inches wide and one to two feet deep in the centre under the metalled portion of the road and placing at the bottom of this a tile drain or a rough-stone box drain; the trough is then filled with stones from two to five inches in size. Where the road crosses a water-course or other low point provision must be made for allowing these drains to discharge through the sides of the road.

Street pavements are only a special form of roads. They differ from ordinary roads in that they are designed to carry extra heavy traffic, and they are surrounded by houses containing a large population, so that questions of comfort, sanitation, and noise are considered, which can safely be disregarded in the case of roads through an open country. As in the case of common roads, so with street pavements, comparatively little attention was paid to the subject in this country until within the last fifteen or twenty years; and while the situation has partially changed and competent engineers have begun to study the problem, yet it is still true that the question of transportation within city limits has never received any such careful thought as has been devoted to every detail of the railroad problem. There is every reason to believe that if the streets were properly and smoothly paved a reduction in the cost of transportation within cities could be effected only inferior in magnitude to that which has been effected by the reduction of rates on the railroads, of which I have already spoken.

The materials in common use at the present time for street pavements are stone blocks, asphalt, brick, wood, and macadam. Macadam is being rapidly excluded from use in city streets on account of its many objections. On any but the lightest traffic it is the most costly form of pavement that can be used in cities. In London and Paris macadam is being taken up and replaced by other materials as rapidly as possible on account of the expense of maintaining it, which was in excess of sixty cents per square yard per annum where the traffic is at all heavy. For a street forty feet wide this is the equivalent of over $13,000 per annum per mile. Even where the traffic is not heavy the street is alternately mud or dust according to the amount of water placed upon it either in the form of rain or street-sprinkling, and it is practically impossible to keep it properly cleansed. The wood pavement as laid in this country has everywhere proved a failure. It has sometimes been laid in the form of rectangular blocks, sometimes treated with a process for preventing decay, and sometimes untreated. In other cases it has been used in the form of round blocks obtained by sawing off the trunks of the small straight pine found in the States along the upper lakes. In this form it is very cheap, being frequently laid for less than one dollar per square yard. But in all its forms it is lacking in durability, its life being about five years under ordinary traffic. In London and Paris the wood pavement has been laid in the form of blocks on a concrete foundation. The foundation is durable and the surface is pleasant to drive over, being smooth and noiseless when first laid; but it is not durable, and the cost of the foundation added to the cost of constant renewals of the wearing surface makes it very expensive. In general terms, it may be said that any material of vegetable origin, subject to rapid decay, is unsuitable for a street pavement, both on the ground of lack of durability and on the ground of health.

The modern pavements, therefore, are of stone blocks, asphalt, or brick. Whichever is adopted should be laid on a concrete foundation, which is a permanent, durable structure, the wearing surface being a veneer, which can be renewed from time to time as it is worn out by traffic. Stone block-pavements are generally adopted on steep grades and on streets which are subjected to heavy traffic. Trap-rock, granite, and sandstone are the kinds of stone used for making paving-blocks, but the latter are so deficient in durability that they are but little used, and the trap-rock is extremely slip-pery. The principal stone pavements, therefore, are of granite, and the chief supply of them comes from the quarries of Maine, Massachusetts, and Rhode Island. The cost of granite-block pavements with a concrete foundation is from $3.00 to $4.50 per square yard, de-pending upon the varying cost of labor and materials in different localities, and even in different parts of the same city. These pavements are durable and com-paratively smooth during the first three or four years after they are laid; then if there is any traffic the edges are broken down and the surface becomes similar to that of cobble-stones, and in this condition they will sustain traffic for twenty or thirty years. They are, however, rough and uncomfortable to drive over, and are very objectionable on the score of noise.

The asphalt pavements are of two kinds. One is a natural bituminous limestone found in France, Han-over, Sicily, and other parts of Europe, and consisting of about ninety per cent of limestone in an impalpable form, and ten per cent of bitumen. The material is crushed and ground to powder and then heated to a temperature of about 300°, taken to the street, spread and raked on a concrete foundation, and compressed by tamping or rolling. The thickness of the asphalt coating is from two to two and a half inches. This form of pavement was introduced into Paris about forty years ago, and it has since been laid in Berlin, London, and several other European cities. It has not

reached a very great development because of its extreme slipperiness. It has been occasionally tried at
different times during the last twenty-five years in
America, but no large amount of it has been laid on
account of its slipperiness, and a very considerable
portion of that laid has been taken up and replaced
by other materials. The other kind of asphalt pavement is an artificial sandstone, consisting of about
ninety per cent sharp silicious sand and ten per cent
of bitumen, which acts as a cement to bind the particles of sand together. The chief source of supply for
this bitumen is a remarkable asphalt lake on the Island
of Trinidad, about one hundred acres in extent, and
containing an apparently inexhaustible supply of the
best quality of asphalt. This asphalt and the sand are
separately heated to about 300°; a small amount of
limestone is added, and the materials are then incorporated in a mechanical mixer, producing a uniform
and homogeneous mixture of sand, limestone, and asphalt. This is then hauled to the street, spread, raked,
and rolled in the same manner as previously described.
The gritty nature of this surface, owing to its sand
constituent, renders it free from the objection on the
score of slipperiness, and this form of pavement has
obtained a wide development in America during the
last twenty years, over 1,000 miles of it having been
laid in upward of 90 cities in the United States and
Canada. It costs from \$2.50 to \$3.50 per square yard,
according to the varying prices of labor and materials
and the different thickness of foundation and surface,
which can be varied to suit the traffic of any particular
street. It is usually laid under a guarantee of five
years, during which it is kept in order free of expense; and after that time it can be maintained for
an indefinite period in good order at an expense not

exceeding ten cents per yard per annum on streets of ordinary traffic. It is readily and easily repaired by simply heating the surface and adding fresh material; and, under a proper system of maintenance, in which any defect is repaired the instant it appears, the surface is always in good order. The pavement is smooth, almost noiseless, durable, and, if properly cleaned and occasionally washed, can be kept cleaner than any other form of pavement.

The brick pavement has attained a rapid development in the last few years in different parts of America. It has been long used in Holland, but its use on any considerable scale in America dates only from the last ten years. Its durability depends entirely upon the kind of clay which is used and the care with which it is burned. Some clays are incapable of producing a good paving-brick, and in several Western cities the brick pavements laid with improper clays have gone to pieces in a few months. The burning should be stopped short of complete vitrifaction; otherwise the surface would be so glassy that horses could not stand upon it. On the other hand, if the burning is not carried far enough, the bricks soon break up under traffic. The best clays for making paving bricks are found along the Ohio River, in the vicinity of Wheeling, and in certain parts of Illinois. When made of proper clay and burned just to the right degree, bricks make an excellent pavement, for small cities. No special plant or facilities are required for laying them, and they are very cheap in price. Including concrete foundation, their cost varies from $1.50 to $2.50 per square yard, according to the locality and the distance which the bricks have to be transported.

And now one word in conclusion—and it should always be the last word—in regard to roads of all kinds;

that is, the necessity for prompt and systematic repairs. Therein is the secret of the success of the French roads, and ît is the observance of this principle on railroads which makes possible high speed, comfort, and low rates. In America this principle has been wholly disregarded on the common roads, and but slightly observed on city streets. Any road, railroad, or pavement is subject to incessant pounding and rubbing. This is what it is built for. Now, this pounding and rubbing must inevitably produce wear, not only on the road itself, but on the vehicle and animals which pass over it. That road is the best which produces the smallest amount of aggregate wear or damage to the road and vehicle combined; and the greatest source of economy both for the road and the vehicle is the prompt repair of any defect the moment it appears.

Sincerely Yours,
Thomas L. James

THOMAS LEMUEL JAMES.

THOMAS LEMUEL JAMES was born in Utica, N. Y., March 29th,
1831. His grandparents on both sides emigrated to the United
States from Wales in 1800. After studying in the common
schools and the Utica academy, he learned the printer's trade in
the office of the Utica *Liberty Press*, and in 1851 bought the
Madison County Journal, a whig newspaper, published at
Hamilton, N. Y. In 1856, when the Republican party made its
first canvass, his paper was united with the *Democratic Re-
flector* under the name of the *Democratic Republican.* He
continued in journalism for ten years, meanwhile also serving as
collector of canal tolls at Hamilton in 1854-55. In 1861 he was
appointed an inspector of customs in New York city, and three
years later was promoted to be weigher. In 1870 he was appointed deputy collector and placed in charge of the warehouse
division and the bonded warehouses of the port. The records
of the division were in confusion, and the general work from one
to three years behind, but in one month Mr. James reported the
exact condition of the division, and within six months he had
brought the business up to date. The prevailing laxity had given
way to the utmost efficiency. He was appointed by General
Arthur, who had become collector, a member of the civil service
board of the collector's and surveyor's offices, was made its chairman, and was among the earliest and most steadfast of public
officials in advocating and applying the reform of the civil service
by establishing the system of appointments upon the basis of
examination and merit. On March 17th, 1873, Mr. James was
appointed postmaster of New York by President Grant. He was
reappointed four years later by President Hayes. His service
is recognized as marking a new era in postal administration. The
two aims which he kept steadily in view were, first, to bring the
office and its working force up to the highest state of efficiency;
and second, to improve and increase the postal facilities wherever
practicable. The deliveries were multiplied, fast mails were recommended and obtained, the foreign mails were expedited and the

security of the mails was increased by careful devices. After the removal of General Arthur from the collectorship, the President tendered the appointment to Mr. James, but he declined it on the ground that, having been General Arthur's deputy, he could not consent to supersede him. In 1880, when David M. Key resigned the Postmaster-Generalship, President Hayes offered this place in his cabinet to Mr. James, who, on consultation with his friends, declined it. The same year the Republicans named him for mayor of New York, but he declined the nomination.

When President Garfield announced his cabinet, March 5th, 1881, Mr. James was included as Postmaster-General, and two days later entered on the duties of the office. The assassination of the President and the accession of Vice-President Arthur caused a complete recast of the cabinet, and Mr. James retired January 2d, 1882. Though he thus served only ten months, his administration was not too brief to be distinguished by important and lasting reforms. When he began he found an annual deficit of $2,000,000, which had varied in amount every year from 1865, and, with one or two exceptions, from 1851. His policy of retrenchment and reform was immediately begun. The reductions that he made in the Star service amounted to $1,713,541 and those in the steamboat service to over $300,000, thus effecting an aggregate saving of over $2,000,000. In co-operation with the department of justice, Mr. James instituted a thorough investigation into the abuses and frauds in his department, the result of which was the famous Star Route trials. In his annual report to Congress he announced that, with these reforms and with retrenchments in other directions which he indicated, a reduction of letter postage from three to two cents would be possible, and it followed soon afterward.

While Postmaster-General, Mr. James negotiated a money-order convention with all the Australian colonies, and with the island of Jamaica.

Retiring from the Post Office Department on January 4th, 1882, he became president of the Lincoln National Bank and the Lincoln Safe-Deposit Company of New York. The degree of A.M. was conferred on him in 1863 by Hamilton College, and that of LL.D. by Madison University in 1883, and by St. John's College in 1884.

THE POSTAL SERVICE OF THE UNITED STATES.

By Gen. Thomas L. James.

In the Post Office exhibit at the Centennial Exposition at Philadelphia was a double picture showing the postal service at the begining of the century and as it is to-day. On one side was a postman—perhaps Franklin — on horseback, jogging over a corduroy road, "through the forest primeval," making a mile or two an hour; and on the other a representation of the fast mail train, the "catcher" taking a pouch from the "crane" as it passes at the rate of fifty miles an hour! Standing in the foreground is the pretty daughter of the village postmaster with the mail pouch just thrown from the car in her hand, a group of rustics, with ill-concealed admiration in their eyes, watching her as the swiftly passing train goes on its journey. This picture is not, perhaps, a work of art, but it is an "object lesson," giving at a glance the progress that our country has made in a hundred years.

Of all the executive departments of the Government, the Post Office is the one nearest the masses and the one with which they are most familiar. In fact, it is the popular department, and its value is understood by the entire people. In addition to its work of collecting, transporting, and delivering legitimate mail matter—letters, newspapers, and magazines—it is the greatest express company on the continent, since it has

an office at almost every cross-road, even carrying merchandise (considering the distance) cheaper than its
rivals. Its registry system affords a means of forward-
ing valuable packages with almost absolute security at
a slight additional cost above the rate of postage. It
is the most popular banking institution on this side of
the Atlantic. The transactions of its money order
system, not only with our country, but with every
nation in the civilized world, reach well-nigh fabulous
sums. Its drafts are easily obtained, and are the best,
cheapest, and safest commercial paper in the world; its
notes are gilt-edged, and its obligations have never
gone to protest. With the creation of the postal sav-
ings-bank system this great department, in its organization, will be perfect.

The "post" is, probably, the oldest institution in the
world. It runs back beyond the memory of man and
almost beyond the record of history. Its antiquity is
shown by many references in the Scriptures: in Biblical times letters were dispatched by special messengers or by travellers. The Hebrew and the Persian
kings sent their letters "by post, on horseback, riding
the swiftest steeds that were used in the king's service."

We read, too, in Chronicles: "So the posts went with
the letters, and the kings and his princes, throughout all
Israel." The letters were usually closed, as is shown by
the fact that "sealing clay" is mentioned in the Book
of Job. Letter-carriers, in the persons of messengers,
were known as early as the first century. Jewish patri-
archs availed themselves of them to send messages
from Palestine to the remotest seats of learning in
Babylon. The ordinances of the High Tribunal (San-
hedrin) were dispatched, for instance, to fix the dates of
the holiday through these messengers. The letter-car-

rier was called "*dawar*," which means really "pedler," because of his going from house to house.

The word "letter," from the Latin *litera*, carries us back to the time when writing-tablets were smeared or covered with wax; while the word "mail" meant originally a spot or spotted surface, being applied to a net with its spotting or mesh of holes, and was afterward used in describing the chain armor worn by the knights of old; thence it passed to the iron bag, which at first covered and conveyed the letters.   The office of " Master of Postes" was instituted by Henry VIII., which gives us the origin of the term "postmaster."   I shall not undertake to say who was the world's first postmaster, but I have been told that when a Union College student was requested by his professor to name him he promptly replied that it must have been Cadmus, since he read that Cadmus brought letters to Greece.

The Assyrian and Persian monarchs established stations at a day's journey apart, where they kept relays of saddled horses all ready for the courier, so that he could carry with great speed the orders of his monarch. The Roman Empire, however, was probably the first to organize a postal service.   The word "post" originated from the custom of Roman couriers being stationed at posts at certain distances apart, where they waited the dispatches that were to be carried forward.

Coming closer home—to the American continent— when the Spanish conquerors reached Peru they found that the Peruvian monarchs had a well-established system to forward the dispatches of the government.   All along their postal routes small buildings were erected at a distance of less than five miles apart, in each of which a number of couriers were stationed.   These men were dressed in a peculiar livery, carefully trained to the work, and selected for their speed and fidelity. As the distance each courier had to cover was small, and as there was ample time to rest at the stations, they ran over the ground with great swiftness, and messages were carried through the whole extent of the long routes at the rate of 150 miles a day.

When France and England in the thirteenth and fourteenth centuries established systems of mounted posts, it is scarcely probable that they knew they were simply imitating a system that had been employed by the Persians and Romans. But their systems were almost exactly the same, and all alike were solely for the transmission of Government dispatches. What a vast difference between that age and the present time! *Then*, governments were the only ones that had a right to use the postal service. *Now*, the Government's mail is almost lost sight of in the immense correspondence of the people.

The development of the postal service is so nearly alike in all countries that it is unnecessary to treat separately of its ancient history. First, there was the establishment, by the Government, of post routes for the transmission of official dispatches. Then the system was thrown open to the uses of the public. Then, private individuals, seeing the profit of the business, started rival systems—to be swallowed up eventually in the monopolization of all postal business by the Government.

A curious anecdote will illustrate the religious progress of the age, and, possibly, point a moral in the history of religious persecution. Macaulay tells us that the first man to establish a private post route in London was William Dockwray. No sooner had he commenced this laudable enterprise than Titus Oates, who was flourishing about these times, published broadcast the statement that the new method of delivering letters was simply a Jesuitical conspiracy in disguise; and averred that, if the mail bags were searched, they would not be found to contain staid comunications in reference to business and social matters, but letters full of incendiary Jacobin doctrines, of the worst and most treasonable description.   Mark the contrast between those times and our own! Emerson, in speaking of the common honesty and faith which prevails in the world, once used the post office as an illustration: "To think," said he, "that a bit of paper, containing our most secret thoughts, and protected only by a seal, should travel safely from one end of the world to the other without any one through whose hands it had passed having meddled with it!"   This reference of Emerson to a letter as "a bit of paper containing our most secret thoughts," recalls what one of his contemporaries, the poet Longfellow, has written.   In one of his lyrics, Longfellow sings of

> "Kind messages, that fly from land to land,
>   Kind *letters* that betray the heart's deep history,
>   In which we feel the pressure of the hand,
>   One touch of fire, and all the rest is mystery."

Printing is popularly known as "the art preservative of all the arts."   It is distinctively that, but it must not be forgotten that another of the great preservative forces is the postal service. By common consent, the letters of famous people constitute one of the most charming and instructive departments of literature.   It is true that but for the printing-press these wise and witty letters would not endure for all time.   It is equally true that if, in the first instance, the post had failed to deliver them, if they had been lost from the mails to which they were confidently entrusted, they never would have reached the press. One of the most notable publications of last year was the letters of James Russell Lowell. These letters covered a period of over half a century, and for wit, humor, incisive criticism, keen observation of men and things are hardly to be surpassed. But the fact that our library shelves are enriched by these expressions of Lowell's many-sided genius is due, in no small measure, to the fidelity and efficiency of the postal service, especially the American post office. I have not time further to dwell upon this consideration. But we have only to think of the letters of Charles Lamb, of Sydney Smith, of Walter Scott, of Charles Dickens, of William M. Thackeray, and, more recently, of that great, that well-beloved religious leader, Phillips Brooks, to realize how much poorer the reading public would be if these effusions had gone astray and become hopelessly lost in the dead-letter office.

One day a letter reached *The Tribune* office, whose envelope was inscribed " H. G."—only that, and nothing more. The postmark showed that it had been mailed from a small place on the frontier of Kansas. The postmaster of the place may have been a humorist, or may have labored under the impression that the initial letters " H. G." were patented, and that nobody but Horace Greeley had a right to use them. At all events, he placed the letter in a mail bag bound east, and in due time it reached Mr. Greeley. They say that when Horace opened it, he found enclosed simply a two-dollar bill, but not a scrap of writing, and that, as soon as he noticed the postmark, he remarked to one of his business associates, who had brought him the letter, " You want to credit Jake Simmons of Kansas two dollars for a subscription renewal. This letter's just like Jake. Jake is one of the most epigrammatic fellows I ever met."

The stranger visiting the New York Post Office and looking from a side gallery into the main room of the building, crowded with busy clerks who toss letters about in a seemingly aimless manner as if they were so many pieces of waste cardboard, will probably take a practical view of the situation: his surprise will not be that a letter arrives safely and promptly at its destination, but that in the midst of what seems "confusion worse confounded," it arrives at all.   Many men are so constituted by nature that they cannot appreciate, much less understand, the really simple principles upon which such vast enterprises are carried on,—or rather, I should say, "the principle," for there is but one, and that is founded on the idea that "Order is Heaven's first law." The practical value of this homely phrase is nowhere better illustrated than in the work of the post office of the Great Metropolis.

Until the proclamation of Charles I., issued in 1635, there was, literally, no post office in Great Britain as we now understand it.   Merchants engaged in foreign trade had their letters left at some central office, generally at a coffee-house or taverns whence they were conveyed by crown messengers to their destination.

In 1692, Thomas Neal received letters-patent in England to take charge of the whole postal business of the Colonies; but his patent terminated in 1712, when the ministry of Great Britain took possession of the Post Office Department of North America, under an Act of Parliament passed in 1710.

The first post office in America was established at New York, in 1672, 224 years ago.   In 1710, the Post-master-General of Great Britain designated New York city as the chief letter office of the country.   The rates of postage for all letters and packages from New York to any place within sixty miles thereof, and thence back to New York, were fixed as follows:— Single sheet, fourpence; double, eightpence; treble, one shilling; an ounce, one shilling and fourpence.

But the postal service, even in those early days of our country's history, did not begin to meet the demands of the people until that able, many-sided man, Benjamin Franklin, was made postmaster at Philadelphia; and, afterward, Postmaster-General of the Colonies. He held that position for a number of years, and was a model public official. He crushed a newspaper monopoly of that day, compelling the post-riders to carry all newspapers offered, instead of carrying only those issued by the postmasters, as had been the custom theretofore. He advertised the list of letters remaining in the post office, and introduced what was then called "fast mails." Instead of a mail between Philadelphia and New York once a week in summer and twice a month in winter, he started a mail from each of the two cities twice a week in summer and once a week in winter. He improved the postal-roads, compelled the post-riders to quicken their pace, and, on the whole, introduced so much "business principle" into the management of the department that a commission, headed by a Mr. Findley, was sent over from England to inquire into his doings and examine his accounts. The Colonial post office had, until this time, never been a source of revenue to Great Britain, and Dr. Franklin was to have for himself and his associate 600 pounds a year if they could make that sum out of the profits of the office. Franklin says that during the first four years the business was managed by him the office became upwards of 900 pounds in debt, in consequence of the improvements he had instituted, but afterward the service began to be profitable. After the visit of Special Agent Findley, it was found that the American postal revenues yielded three times as much to the British Crown as the post office of Ireland. The special agent reported that Franklin was perfectly upright and honest in his accounts; but added that he was in direct opposition, politically, to the policy of King George; and, on this report reaching the British Ministry, Franklin was summarily dismissed.

One of the first acts of the Continental Congress was to appoint a Postmaster-General for the United Colonies, at a salary of $1,000. Franklin was chosen to this office, being allowed a secretary at a salary of $340, with power to appoint such deputies as he saw fit. This Congress established a line of "posts" from Falmouth in New England to Savannah, Georgia, with many cross post-roads. The pay for deputies was 20 per cent on all sums under $1,000, and 10 per cent on all sums above $1,000 a year.

During the revolutionary struggle postal matters were, of course, lost sight of for the time being. Franklin departed for France in 1776, his place being taken by Ebenezer Hazard, who had been deputy post-master in New York city. It is stated that the earnings of the New York post office from 1775 to 1776 were only $550. The entire revenue of the Post Office Department was something less than $5,000. The postmaster was not able to employ an assistant, and states, in a memorial, that he was obliged to leave the city of New York to keep near the headquarters of the army, "who are almost the only persons for whom letters now come by post;" he adds, that owing to the frequent removals of the army, he was subjected to extraordinary expense and fatigue, "having paid an exorbitant price for every necessary of life, and been obliged for want of a horse, which could not be procured, to follow the army from place to place on foot." This is the first instance on record of a travelling post office in the United States; and this postmaster, a year or two afterward, was Postmaster-General of the United Colonies.

Directly after the inauguration of General Washington in April, 1789, the organization of the Post Office Department followed, and Samuel Osgood, of Massachusetts, was appointed Postmaster-General. The Act of Congress creating the department recites that the Postmaster-General "shall not keep any office separate from the one in which the mails arriving in New York are opened and distributed, that he may by his presence prevent irregularities and rectify mistakes which may occur." This was certainly a wise provision; but it occurs to me that the time of the present head of the department would be more than fully occupied in correcting errors and rectifying mistakes in the New York post office alone, 103,354 having occurred in a single year. Not a large number, however, when it is considered that over 900,000,000 pieces of mail matter were handled. General Osgood had but one clerk, and there were but 75 post offices and 1,875 miles of post-routes in the United States; the cost of mail transportation being $22,081, the total revenue $37,935, the total expenditures $32,140, leaving a surplus of $5,795. At the close of the fiscal year ending December 1st, 1892, the total number of offices was 67,567; the number of miles traversed in the transportation of domestic mails exceeded 363,000,000; the cost of transporting the mails being $42,000,000. The gross revenue for the same period was nearly $61,000,000; the total expenditures were $66,000,000, leaving a deficit of over $5,000,000. The Post Office Department, however, is gradually becoming self-sustaining.

It has been officially stated that the whole history of the mail service of the country divides itself into two periods of fifty years each, the first period stretching from 1784 to 1834, which was the "era of the stage-coach," and the second period from 1834 to 1884, when the railroads had become the great medium for the transportation of mails. The difficulties of the stage-coach conveyances are graphically described by Dickens in his "American Notes," in which he details his experience in travelling between Columbus and Sandusky, Ohio, in the old mail coach. He says: "The great portion of the way was over what is called the 'corduroy' road, which is made by throwing trunks of trees into a marsh and leaving them to settle there. The very slightest of the jolts with which the ponderous carriage fell from log to log was enough, it seemed, to have dislocated all the bones in the human body. It would be impossible to experience a similar set of sensations, in any other circumstances, unless, perhaps, in attempting to go up to the top of Saint Paul's in an omnibus."

In 1802 the United States Government ran its own line of stages between New York and Philadelphia. This continued three years, and the profits amounted to $12,000. In the early contracts, no mention was made of any other kind of service on post-roads except stages, sulkies, four-horse post coaches, horseback, packet, and steamboats; though an act of Congress, constituting every railroad in the United States a post-road, was approved in 1838. Postmaster-General Barry, in his annual report to the President, in 1834, makes mention of the use of the railways for the purpose of mail transportation, and says, "If the transportation can be secured upon the railroads which are now being constructed, in some instances already finished, it would be of great utility to the public;" and adds that the distance between Washington and New York does not exceed 240 miles, and that the mails may be delivered at all times to a certainty, allowing ample time for stopping at important places, in sixteen hours. Postmaster-General Amos Kendall, in his report, curiously suggested that "if the wheels of the car, in which the mails are conveyed, can be constructed so that they can be used alike upon the railroad and the streets of cities, the department will furnish an entire car containing the mails, to be delivered at one depot and received at the other." It is almost needless to add that the company declined to entertain any such proposition, stating that it would virtually subject their operations to the control of the Post Office Department.

How little the railway authorities respected the carrying of the mails is attested by the fact that the route agents between New York and Philadelphia complained to the department that "nearly every night dead bodies are placed in that portion of the car assigned to the carrying of mails between Philadelphia and New York, and the mail bags are packed around the coffins." A vigorous letter was written by the Postmaster-General to the president of the railroad, which resulted in the issuance of an order by him forbidding such an unwholesome and unnatural intermingling of correspondence and cadavers.

The present efficient Railway Mail Service of this country was commenced under the administration of Montgomery Blair, by Mr. George B. Armstrong, then connected with the post office at Chicago.

An example of how great has been the progress of the country in postal affairs was told me the other day by Mr. Brinckerhoff, a neighbor of mine, who said that about thirty years ago he came from San Francisco to Sacramento by steamboat, and delivered the first package of letters to the post-rider of the Pony Express, who was waiting at the latter place to receive it, and who instantly mounted on his steed and started on his journey across the continent.

Remember, that before 1854 the postage rate on a single letter, carried thirty miles, was 6¼ cents; over and under eighty, 10 cents; over 80 and under 150, 12½ cents; over 150 and under 400, 18¾ cents; and over 400, 25 cents. If a letter weighed over an ounce, the rates were multiplied by four. Previous to the reduction of rates, the postage on many letters sent from the seaboard cities as far west as Indiana was a dollar or more. When, in 1854, the rates were reduced, birds of evil omen, as usual, were found to resist the change, and predict that the measure would bankrupt the country.

One of the greatest achievements by the United States Postal Service, during the stage-coach period, was the successful establishment of the overland mail between the Mississippi River and San Francisco by tri-weekly stage-coaches, when three-fourths of the country lying between the Mississippi River and the Pacific Ocean was not only a desert, but was infested, at certain points along the route, by savage and warlike tribes of Indians. Congress passed a law authorizing the establishment of a mail service, to consist of three trips a week by four-horse post-coaches, between a point to be designated on the Mississipi River and San Francisco, and limiting the time to twenty-one days. The Chamber of Commerce of St. Louis, imbued with the idea of securing St. Louis as the terminus in the Mississippi Valley, in opposition to Memphis (which had every appearance of being chosen by the then postal authorities), selected a committee to find a contractor of energy, spirit, and character, able to undertake the work, and to secure his influence in bidding for St. Louis. They came to the State of New York, and secured one of the best, strongest, and most able contractors for mail service in the history of the Post Office Department, in the person of John Butterfield of Utica.

It was surmised that the intention had been to make the route from Memphis to San Francisco in order that the whole service might be in Southern territory, and that it might be used as a coadjutor, in the intended movement for secession, to unite California with the Southern States in the rebellion; and that a bid from St. Louis to San Francisco would not be recognized if a bid from Memphis to San Francisco were submitted. The result of a conference on this subject led to a bid being made for a double terminus at the East, one at St. Louis, the other at Memphis. This bid was accepted. To ascertain how this service could be carried on, and to arrange the preliminaries for its successful working, fell to the lot of an alumnus of this college. He did not stand then (over a third of a century ago) before the public by any knowledge of his work, in so high a position as a great master of logistics as his subsequent career in the service of his country proved him to be. To him was given the task of preparing the organization of this service. Ambulances, with a party of men and implements for cooking, were started from a point at the then extreme Western terminus of the railway, about 150 miles west of St. Louis. The expedition went overland by way of Fort Smith, through El Paso, Tucson, Arizona, Los Angeles, to San Francisco, the route known as " The Southern Route," and now traversed by the Southern Pacific Railway. Odometers were attached to the wheels of the stages to measure the distances travelled every day; diaries and records of each day's work, the streams crossed, and the distances made every hour, were kept, and full re-ports made.   These reports were brought back, and the work of laying out the time-schedule, the route, and all arrangements were placed in his hands.   A sheet of paper, about two feet in width and the length of this college chapel,—between 50 and 60 feet,—was laid down on a mathematical scale, with the days and hours represented by the vertical lines, and the points, dis-tances, and stations in horizontal lines, giving twenty-one days as the period of time between the two cities. From this study and calculation the time-tables were made, printed, and distributed to the employees.   The service commenced and continued uninterruptedly, ex-cept, occasionally, from raids by the savages.   At the expiration of the first three months, the postmaster at St. Louis, in his report to the Post Office Department, stated that the arrival of the mail from San Francisco overland by stage had been more regular than the ar-rival of the mails from New York.   The service con-tinued until secession broke out, when it was destroyed and broken up by hostilities on the part of those in re-bellion against the Government.   It stands to-day as the grandest record of postal mail service by stage communication in distance, regularity, and character ever known in the postal history of any country.

The contractor who performed this great work, and who by so doing stamped his name across the conti-nent, was the father of the distinguished general who founded this course of lectures and at whose request I am here to-day.   I trust I may be pardoned for saying that, while General Butterfield won undying fame in the army of the Potomac, with Meade at Gettysburg, with Hooker above the clouds at Lookout Mountain, and has written his name indelibly with his sword on the annals of our time, still, I apprehend, the name of

27

" Butterfield" will be equally well known in the history of the republic by this great triumph of John Butterfield, who by his dauntless courage, skill, and persistency, proved that " Peace hath her victories more renowned than war," and that

> "Beneath the rule of men entirely great,
> The Pen is mightier than the Sword."

The Railway Mail Service, one of the most important and well-regulated branches of the Postal department, strictly speaking, did not originate in this country. That is to say, the idea of having a separate compartment fitted out in a rude way with conveniences necessary for the distribution of the local way-mail, and which was afterward adopted, had been for some time in use in Canada, where, in turn, the idea had been borrowed from the mother-country.

There have been several claimants for the honor of starting the present railway mail system in the United States. Some have given credit to Col. G. B. Armstrong, who, in 1864, was assistant postmaster at Chicago. But the reports that were made to the Post-Office Department before this time show that the travelling post office was no new thing.

Mr. W. A. Davis, a clerk in the St. Joe, Mo., post office, in 1862, suggested the idea that letters should be sorted on the cars between Quincy and St. Joseph, thus saving much time, and allowing the overland mail to start more promptly. He was the first official to distribute through mails and the first to have a car specially prepared for this purpose, which was done in the case of the work just referred to.

Two years later, Colonel Armstrong, under the direction of the Hon. Montgomery Blair, arranged for this service, and afterward became the first General Railway

Superintendent, an office which he held until ill-health compelled him to resign in 1871. He was succeeded by Colonel Bangs, of Illinois, who was a progressive reformer, and full of original ideas for the improvement of the service. Colonel Armstrong built the framework of the system, while the genius and originality of Colonel Bangs clothed it with flesh and endowed it with the breath of life. In 1871 he found that the service was carried on in an aimless sort of way. He at once started to improve it, and introduced " business principles" into its management, the only principles, by the way, upon which any great enterprise, private or governmental, can be successfully carried on. He removed the sluggards and the incompetents, rewarded the industrious and the efficient, and, judged by his methods, he might be well called the father of Civil Service Reform. In 1874 he suggested that a fast and exclusive mail train should be established between New York and Chicago, the distance to be run in twenty-four hours, a feat which it is now conceded can be accomplished. This report was favorably received by Postmaster-General Jewell, who authorized Bangs to negotiate with the New York Central & Hudson River Railroad, and the Lake Shore, for a fast mail train, which should leave New York at four o'clock in the morning, arriving at Chicago in about twenty-four hours. But there was no appropriation to carry out this laudable scheme. Commodore Vanderbilt was not sanguine of its success, and his dealings with the Post-Office Department theretofore had not inspired confidence in the way in which that branch of the Government was managed. William H. Vanderbilt, the vice-president of the road, was, however, favorably disposed to the scheme. By an arrangement with Colonel Bangs, it was stipulated that Mr. Vanderbilt should build twenty cars, and that all mail matter originating at or coming to the New York post office which could reach its destination at the same time by this line should be sent by this train, the railway companies having the right to demand the weighing of the mail matter, all railroads being paid according to the weight. Mr. Vanderbilt constructed the finest and best-equipped mail train ever seen on the continent. The officers on the cars were picked men, and the service was a marvel of completeness and efficiency. He ran it for ten months, always on time; but he, too, realized the truth of the prophecy made by the sagacious old Commodore, who had told him that within a year he would know the Post Office better than he did at that time. The Government, by a gross breach of faith and against the indignant protest of Colonel Bangs, took the mails of three States from this road and gave them to another line. Soon after, the Government reduced the compensation of the trunk lines—already inadequate—for carrying the mails, and the result was that Mr. Vanderbilt and Thomas A. Scott, of the Pennsylvania road, who had also engaged in the service, declined to continue it any longer.

When this most important service of the Government started in 1864, the only clerk regularly appointed on the route from New York to Washington was the late Mr. H. G. Pearson, afterward postmaster at New York city and the ablest postal official that ever trod the continent. He drew the plan for the first postal car, and under his direction it was built. At the present time there are 6,400 employees engaged in this service. The time of transmission has been shortened between New York and Washington from thirteen hours in 1864 to five hours in 1893. Letters have been transmitted during the past summer between New York and Chicago in twenty hours, while the time across the continent has been reduced from twenty-five days in 1860 to four days and a few hours in 1893.

What will be the future of the Railway Mail Service in America you can determine as well as I. Judging from what has been accomplished in thirty years, he would be a very rash prophet who would predict what may not be done in this line in the future.

Among the earlier proposals for mail service we find, in 1835, that the horse was allowed the contract because he could make better time than the railroad, which sometimes stipulated, in taking the contract, that the schedule requiring eleven miles an hour should be removed. In 1835, complaint was made that the transportation of the mail between New York and Philadelphia took more than thirteen hours, a journey which is now regularly performed in two hours.

In considering this great subject of the Postal Service we should not forget that the little "postage stamp" is one of its most curious and interesting features. In a certain form it has been used for nearly four hundred years. In Paris, in 1663, slips were placed around letters for the purpose of passing them to their destination. These slips bore the inscription "postpaid" such and such a date. Stamped sheets of paper were also in use and took the place of the stamped envelope of a later day.

When "postage stamps" were first used in the United States they were of only two denominations: "five cents" and "ten cents." In 1851 they were replaced by "one," "three," and "twelve cent" stamps. In 1855 a "ten cent" stamp was issued; and soon after a complete series was made ranging in value from five cents to ninety cents.

Many persons in this audience have doubtless heard of the party who wants to collect a million cancelled stamps. I say "wants," for I suppose he is still in existence to torment the lives of postal officials and the general business public. That person, whether mythical or otherwise, has caused a vast deal of annoyance to postmasters, high and low, and newspaper editors, who were supposed to know all about him and the object of his peculiar scheme, which always had a benevolent basis. When once such an idea is started, every merchant or business man who has a large correspondence, is bored to death by pretty young women, industrious boys, and benevolent old ladies who are anxious to contribute their quota of stamps to the great million stamp enterprise.

They say this idea of collecting one million stamps originated in the ingenious brain of a German, who was a stamp collector himself, and who wanted to collect easily and without expense to himself a large number of cancelled stamps. He announced that for every million stamps sent to him an orphan would be cared for in the Syrian Home: afterward it was a mission in China, the Sisters of which agreed to save from the jaws of the crocodiles in the Yellow River at least one Chinese baby each year and Christianize it. Then came the old lady or gentleman who was to be cared for in a Home located in London, New York, or Cincinnati. The scheme, though fraudulent, certainly served to demonstrate the generous impulses of humanity; for, judging from the results, a vast number of persons must have engaged in the enterprise of stamp collecting. It is estimated that the ingenious swindler collected no less than one hundred million stamps in the United States alone.

I found the other day, in an English magazine, some new Post Office Rules, which the editor said were taken from an American newspaper;

"A pair of onions will go for two scents.

"It is unsafe to mail apple or fruit trees with the fruit on them.

"Alligators over ten feet in length are not allowed to be transmitted by mail.

"Ducks cannot be sent through the mail when alive. The quacking would disturb the slumbers of the clerks on the postal cars.

"It is earnestly requested that lovers writing to their girls will please confine their gushing rhapsodies to the inside of the envelope.

"Nitro-glycerin must be forwarded at the risk of the sender. If it should blow up in the postmaster's hand he cannot be held responsible.

"When watches are sent through the mail, if the sender will put a notice on the outside, the postmaster will wind and keep in running order.

"When letters are received bearing no direction, the persons for whom they are intended will please signify the fact to the postmaster that they may at once be forwarded.

"The placing of stamps upside down on letters is prohibited, several postmasters having been seriously injured while trying to stand on their heads to cancel stamps placed in this manner."

At the post office in Limerick:

Miss Pom Posity: "How long will this letter take to reach my frind in Italy?"

Irish Postal Clerk: "Faith, marm, I can't soy roight fur shure; but it ought to be afther raching him on Froiday nixt, onless he's out wid his orghan."

I would like to follow the history of the postal service since the formation of the government, to note its marvellous growth and its constant improvement, to review in detail the contest of fifty years ago between

that great man, Amos Kendall, and the Star Route ring
of that day; to show how, under his efficient administration, the department was, in two years, redeemed
from debt and made self-sustaining, the mail service
greatly improved, and a surplus of $700,000 accumu-
lated. To speak of Judge Holt's sturdy attempt to stem
the tide of extravagance and corruption during the
closing days of Buchanan's administration, when the
deficit reached the enormous sum of nearly $11,000,000;
of the establishment of the Money Order and Registry
systems, and the important reforms inaugurated by one
Montgomery Blair, the most efficient Postmaster-General of the century; of the efforts and success of John
A. J. Creswell, who abolished the franking privilege; of
Marshall Jewell's war and victory over the straw bid-
ders; of the reduction of postage under the administration of Frank Hatton; of the necessity of the enlarging
and cheapening of the Money Order system, the extension of the free delivery service, special and fast trains
and more of them for the railway post offices, and the
establishment of postal savings-banks; but I must forbear, for the time allotted me does not admit of even a
résumé of postal history from Colonial days until the
present.

But the figures I have already presented show that in
less than a century this department has grown most
wonderfully. The post office at Schenectady, N. Y.,
has a larger income to-day than the whole department
had then. The expenditure of the department last
year was greater than the total expense of the United
States Government at the time of the administration of
President Fillmore.

The constant tendency of the postal system has been
toward the extension of the privileges of the mails to
every branch of correspondence and every form of lit-

erary production. Its facilities first made possible the cheaper publication of newspapers, and, later on, of standard works of literature, by placing upon all periodical popular reading-matter the lowest rate of postage ever known in a civilized land; viz., one cent per pound throughout the United States. This low rate has practically developed the popular libraries, by which the best standard works of English literature have been published in ten-cent volumes and made accessible to the people of the most distant States and Territories; and has enabled the present generation to possess every important new publication in science as well as fiction. In no other country have the masses ever before enjoyed such inestimable advantages for the acquirement of desirable knowledge; and no money expended by the Government in any of its multiform agencies has ever conferred such enormous advantages. This extension of the reading of good books by the masses is in itself one of the marks of the progress of civilization and of the widening benefits of a government of the people and for the people. This impulse and direction must not be changed. There must be no step backward, and this law, now so clear and explicit, must not be repealed, as has been heretofore threatened, because it would cut off the privileges of popular literature. There must be no tax upon knowledge, and the vested interests not only of publishers, but of the people, must be regarded.

Without doubt, the most urgent need of the Postal Service is the total elimination of partisan considerations as affecting appointments and removals in its working force. There are no "public offices" which are so emphatically "public trusts" as those whose duties comprise that of handling the correspondence of the people; because upon the proper and skilful performance of these depend, to a far greater degree than in the case of any other function accomplished through government agency, the business and social welfare of the entire community. The effects of ignorance, carelessness, or dishonesty in any other branch of the public service, although to be deplored, are not to be compared with those which follow the existence of such evils in the Post Office. For what reason did the framers of the constitution reserve to the Federal Government the "establishment of post offices and post roads," with all that such a restriction implies. Why has Congress, from time to time, under the authority given by the same clause, guarded by several statutes against the infringements of the monopoly thus assumed? Can any reason be given, except that the custody, transportation, and delivery of the correspondence of the entire people involve a "public trust" too important to "the general welfare" to permit of its being placed in the hands of the States, liable to conflicting state restrictions, or left to the conduct of private or corporate enterprise? And, if, as must be admitted, this is the sole justification for the existence of this enormous government monopoly, can there be a more flagrant abuse of a "public trust" than the perversion of the vast machinery of this branch of the public service into an agency for furthering the ambitious ends of local or other partisans by allowing them to distribute its "patronage" as rewards for party services among those who, by reason of their inexperience, if for no other graver cause, are incompetent to replace the skilled workman, who must be rotated out in order to give them room? The Civil Service Law, applied to the larger offices only, has done much, where faithfully administered, to maintain efficiency; but it leaves a vast majority of the post offices of the country untouched and at the mercy of local partisans.   I am not to be understood, when advising reform in this direction to be among the present needs of the service, that the abuse which I have pointed out is specially prominent now; for I am not making a political speech.   The reform is not only a present necessity, but it was one in the past, and will be one in the future, until the force of public sentiment shall compel acquiescence in the reasonable demand that what was so eminently "meant for mankind" shall not be given up to party—that the very non-political business of letter-carrying which the Government has monopolized shall be conducted by it solely with a view to the prompt and expeditious carrying of letters, and not with the object of "carrying" Indiana, Alaska, or Buncombe County.

Another pressing need of the Postal Service seems to me to be a careful revision and codification of the statutes governing its operations—the simplification of the present intricate and unwieldy "Regulations" which now are (and for many years have been) a bewildering and oft-times contradictory jumble.   I doubt if one official can tell what comprises, respectively, the four classes of domestic mail matter, and what is the lawful rate of postage on each.   And yet this information should be within the familiar knowledge of every citizen who has occasion to use the post office (that is to say everybody), and would be, but for the kaleidoscope changes in the postal laws and regulations caused by acts of Congress and acts of Postmasters-Generals and their assistants.   I am far from being an Anglomaniac, but confess that I have always admired the stability which characterizes the methods of the British post offices, so far as they affect the essential requirements which the public are called upon to remember; and I think that this stability is due to the fact that, as a rule, Parliament in that country lets the details of postal business severely alone, entrusting them practically to the hands of a skilled expert,—for Post-masters-General may come and go, but the secretary of the General Post Office "goes on forever," and runs the department in the light of his own knowledge and experience, leaving the nominal head to give his entire attention to his duties as one of Her Majesty's political advisers.

The third and last need of the Post Office to which I shall refer is in the direction of economy; and by this I do not mean the cheese-paring system of reducing salaries and withholding needful outlay. True economy would be displayed by expenditures in large cities sufficient to secure the best possible service,—for first-class service at those points goes a long way in securing it everywhere If the post office at New York, Boston, Philadelphia, Chicago, or Brooklyn be short-handed, poorly equipped, compelled to pay niggardly salaries to its employees and resort to all sorts of make-shift experiments in vain efforts to get a quart into a pint measure, it is impossible that their correspondence to or from other points can be dispatched or delivered with the "certainty, celerity, and security" which should characterize those operations. It is true, I believe, that in ordinary private business a generous, judicious expenditure is sure to bring liberal returns; and I know from experience that the same rule applies equally well in post office business. I hope grace may be given to our legislators and others in authority to realize the wisdom of seeking first the efficiency of the service in the full assurance that, if not "all other things," at least a corresponding revenue will be added thereto, and the postal service of the United States become not only the cheapest, but the best in the world.

My task, which, unlike many tasks, has been one of pleasure, is nearly completed. I have tried to show that the progress of our Postal Service is parallel with the development of the country; and that, from a few sparse settlements on the Atlantic coast, it has followed the sun in his triumphant course across the continent. It is the pioneer of Christian civilization, each step in its mighty movement marking the march of the Republic toward a higher and nobler destiny—more than realizing the Arabian story of cities springing up by magic. With its advance, the wilderness has become the granary of the world and the home of an empire of freemen. At its command the Indian runner, the post-boy, the Pony Express, the Overland Mail coach, superseded each other in quick succession, followed by the thunder of the locomotive, as it speeds with its train of post offices on wheels over the iron highways which span the continent, until now less than five days separate New York from the "Golden Gate," a shorter time than was required a century ago to send a letter from New York to Boston. It is the champion of progress, closely allied to the mechanic's shop, the factory, the printing-press, the school, and the church. It cements together in a closer bond men and nations, and is one of the forces helping to bring about in every-day life the Fatherhood of God and the brotherhood of man.